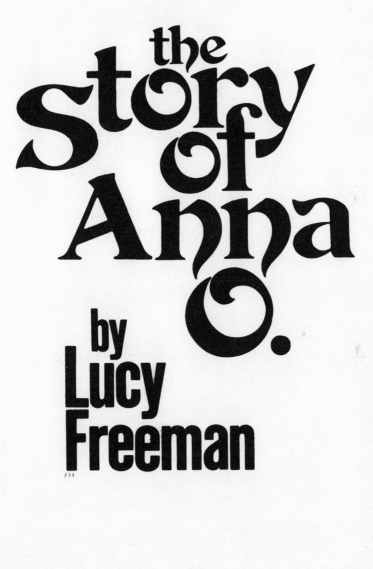

the
story
of
Anna
O.

by
Lucy
Freeman

WALKER AND COMPANY
New York

Contents

To Walter A. Stewart, M.D.

Teacher and friend

Introduction

Lucy Freeman is a remarkable woman, a professional writer who specializes in the psychiatric area and has spent thousands of hours immersing herself in her field of interest. Thirty-three other books have come from her pen, either alone or in collaboration.

In the present volume she does her many intelligent lay readers a favor, but she has performed an even greater service to psychiatrists, psychoanalysts, and medical historians. She has taken a famous patient and made that patient come alive, a human being, a distinguished personality whose brief medical history is all that we have known of her until now.

Anna O. was the cornerstone in the formation of Freud's discoveries and theories—yet he never saw her. He only heard about her in clinical detail from a colleague and friend who had treated and perhaps "cured" her.

Grasping the implication of Breuer's revolutionary discovery about the human mind, Freud persuaded Breuer to collaborate with him in the first book about psychoanalysis, *Studies on Hysteria*, containing Breuer's famous essay on Anna O. On the basis of discoveries inherent in that study, augmented by other experience and knowledge, Freud began to put together a hypothesis about how people get sick emotionally—and how they may get well.

Lucy Freeman has done a very clever but wholly rational thing. She first acquaints us with the patient who is to become immortal. We learn how the patient suffers. We meet her physician, the popular—indeed rather fashionable—but also very conscientious general practitioner to whom she was referred. We hear in detail of the treatment he gave her, how she responded, and how intrigued he became with her curious symptoms, their waxing and waning and waxing again. We go with him day after day to visit her sickbed; we witness the final, catastrophic, climactic visit that so frightened him; we learn just what led to his dropping the case.

In the second part of her book, the author deals with the former patient as a person, recording the distinguished and significant social contributions she made, conjuring up the petty everyday experiences that made up the fabric of her life.

Finally, in the third section, the patient, the person, her doctor, and her psychoanalyst by remote control are fused, as it were, in an explanation of a girl who became a woman who became a patient who became a philanthropist and social reformer. The revealing rays of the psychoanalytic searchlight are turned on each facet of her life and the logical correctness of the development becomes clear.

This is more than a fascinating biography. It is an exposition of the continuity of the threads that in the usual "case history" are seen only in tangles. It is a humanization of the famous patient reported by Josef Breuer and Sigmund Freud as Anna O.

Karl Menninger, M.D.
February, 1972

Acknowledgements

Though the first two sections of this book appear fictional in style, they are based on fact. The first is founded on Dr. Josef Breuer's case history of Anna O. in *Studies on Hysteria*. The second contains facts and anecdotes supplied either by Bertha Pappenheim through her writings or by those who knew her.

Bertha Pappenheim might have gone down· in history merely as a case study in hysteria had it not been for Dora Edinger. Dora Edinger wrote *Bertha Pappenheim: Her Life and Letters,* which was published in Frankfurt in 1963 by Ner-Tamid Verlag. Five years later an English translation of the biography entitled *Bertha Pappenheim: Freud's Anna O.* was brought out by Congregation Solel in Highland Park, Illinois, sponsored by the Chicago Institute for Psychoanalysis, who considered that such an important contribution to the world of psychoanalysis should be supported. The biography contained a number of Bertha Pappenheim's letters and other writings translated by Dr. Edinger.

Historian, biographer, and educator, Dr. Edinger worked with Mary Beard when she was editor of biographies of women for the *Encyclopedia Britannica.* She was also a librarian and adult educator in Evanston, Illinois. At present she is in charge of the library of the Society for the Advancement of Judaism in New York City.

Dr. Edinger has given me much information not included in her own biography of Bertha Pappenheim for which, either personally or by letter, she interviewed hundreds of Bertha Pappenheim's acquaintances, checked records, wrote many authorities, including Dr. Ernest Jones, and tried to locate all of Bertha Pappenheim's writings that were not lost or destroyed.

In addition to the factual help Dr. Edinger gave me on this book, she also offered great moral support. She was always thorough, always patient, always indefatigable and always available. Eminent historian that she is, she was careful to check all new material obtained in interviews, warning, at times, about conflicting stories, or advising, "Better not use, dear," when a detail, such as a reported romance in Bertha Pappenheim's early life, could not be confirmed.

Dr. Edinger supplied the photographs on the front and back jacket. The front photo was taken in 1890 in Frankfurt, the back photo, an untouched passport photograph, around 1915. Dr. Edinger also contributed a volume of Bertha Pappenheim's "Prayers" translated into English by Dr. Estelle Forchheimer and printed privately with funds donated by the late Max Warburg, Bertha Pappenheim's second cousin.

The photograph used as frontispiece was loaned by Mrs. Eugene Kamberg of Kew Gardens, New York, who, like Bertha Pappenheim and Dora Edinger was a member of the board of the Home for Wayward Girls and illegitimate Children in Isenberg. In 1954 the West German government used this photograph on a commemorative stamp in their Helpers of Humanity Series.

A number of women who were colleagues of Bertha Pappenheim managed to escape the Hitler holocaust and emigrated to the United States where they carried on welfare work, inspired by her example. Mrs. Kamberg is president of Help and Reconstruction, Inc., which sponsors a nursery school and kindergarten for children in Washington Heights, New York, and sends two hundred children yearly to summer camps.

Mrs. Jenny Wolf of Chicago, another member of the board of the Home, gave willingly of her time and memory in recalling her fourteen-year friendship with Bertha Pappenheim and her work with unwed mothers and illegitimate children. She brought with her to the United States a desk and secretary from Bertha Pappenheim's little house, several of the hand-made bead necklaces, and notes Bertha Pappenheim took the day the two women sat listening to Hitler's first harangue on the radio. After Mrs. Wolf arrived in Chicago in 1938, with five other women she started Self-Help

Inc. of Chicago, which established a home for the aged on the city's south side in 1951 and built a second such home on the north side of the city in 1963.

Mrs. Leo Goldschmidt, the former Alice Bock, married Bertha Pappenheim's first cousin and now lives in New York City. She owns two of the silver goblets from the famous collection of Siegmund Pappenheim, Bertha Pappenheim's father. The goblets were sent to Mrs. Goldschmidt by Wilheim Pappenheim, Bertha Pappenheim's brother, after she, her late husband and two daughters, emigrated to America. Wilheim Pappenheim wrote Mrs. Goldschmidt from Vienna that he thought she might like to place the silver goblets on the altar when her daughters were married. Their correspondence continued until his death in 1937. She still has in her possession an old address book which lists his name and telephone number: "Gardisonsgasse 7. Vienna 9. A 20517 (Private)."

My thanks go not only to these women but also to Mrs. Adolph Pappenheim of Riverdale, New York, whose late husband was one of the five sons of Wolf Pappenheim II, first cousin to Bertha Pappenheim; and to Wolf Pappenheim II's great grandson, Dr. Wolfgang Pappenheim of New York City, a graduate of the Institute of the British Psychoanalytical Society and a member of the International Psychoanalytic Association. The Breuer family is also represented in the United States by a psychoanalyst, Dr. Ernst Hammerschlag, Breuer's nephew by marriage, who gave me an interesting word-picture of his famous uncle. I would also like to acknowledge the help given me by a number of Breuer's other relatives who live in this country but prefer to remain anonymous.

Special thanks go to other psychoanalysts who encouraged me in the writing of this book: Dr. George H. Pollock, director of the Institute for Psychoanalysis in Chicago, who has written articles on the relationship between Bertha Pappenheim, Breuer and Freud; Dr. Walter A. Stewart, of the faculty of the New York Psychoanalytic Institute, whom I consulted for an interpretation of Anna O.'s symptoms based on the available knowledge of her life, and Dr. Richard Karpe, psychoanalyst, of Hartford, Connecticut, who has done research on the life of Anna O. My thanks also to Dr.

Kurt Eissler, founder of the Sigmund Freud archives, and Dr. Henri Ellenberger, psychiatrist, of the Department of Criminology of the University of Montreal, Canada, who is engaged in research on the years following Bertha Pappenheim's treatment by Breuer.

Arnold Jacob Wolf, Rabbi of Congregation Solel, Highland Park, Illinois, and Louis I. Heller, Administrator of Congregation Solel, were also of invaluable help.

One of those who knew Bertha Pappenheim the longest, Helene Kramer, lives at the Home of the Daughters of Jacob in the Bronx, New York, but because of ill health could not be interviewed. However, Dr. Edinger had interviewed her at length several years ago, obtaining many important facts about Bertha Pappenheim's life.

Thanks also go to Arnold Heller, who lived in Frankfurt and described that city to me, and whose aunt, the late Rika Heller, was director of a home for children in nearby Hofheim Taunus, and to John Wykert, author, who was born in Vienna and brought that city to life for me geographically.

I am grateful too to Phyllis Rubinton, librarian of the New York Psychoanalytic Institute, who helped locate articles in psychoanalytic journals on Anna O. and Bertha Pappenheim. I wish also to thank Glenn Miller, librarian at the Institute for Psychoanalysis in Chicago.

Last but far from least, my deepest thanks go to Ghislaine Boulanger, senior editor at Walker and Company. From the first, she had deep faith in this book, one I have wanted to write for many years. As its editor, she helped explore its essence and shape its form. She showed how a feeling of drama might be brought to Breuer's case history of Anna O. as well as to the life of Bertha Pappenheim, while not deviating from the facts. It was an exciting, as well as enjoyable, experience to work with her and learn from her.

Lucy Freeman
New York, New York
February, 1972

PART I

The Patient

"... her life became known to me to an extent to which one person's life is seldom known to another."

Josef Breuer
Vienna, 1895

1

The Jargon

The slight young man, his reddish-blond hair covered by a hat to protect against the December chill, walked into the spacious old apartment house on *Liechtensteinstrasse.* Behind him in the street waited the rented coach drawn by two horses; a lone horse would not have been suitable for one of Vienna's most sought-after physicians.

He climbed two flights of stairs to the top floor. Facing the apartment door, he raised the oval brass knocker.

A maid opened the door, took his hat, overcoat and gloves. She led him to a parlor filled with costly antiques. A black Biedermeier cabinet glistening with silver and gold goblets stood in one corner, reaching almost to the ceiling. Portraits of stern-faced ancestors scowled from the walls.

Rising from a tapestried sofa, a thin, dark-haired woman with a rather sad face, walked over to him. She held out her hand.

"Thank you for coming, Dr. Breuer," she said. "I've been very worried about my daughter's cough."

Breuer, who lived not far away, in the heart of Vienna at Brandstätte 8, had hurried there when he received this mother's message. He knew she, as everyone, lived in terror of tuberculosis. His own brother had been a victim fifteen years before at the age of twenty. The Viennese, dancing to Strauss waltzes, enjoying opera and theater, devouring Sachertorte behind the etched-glass doors of coffee houses, did so in sur-

3

face gaiety, haunted by the specter of a disease that had struck down so many it was feared far more than any enemy army that might storm the city—as many an enemy had.

"When did your daughter first start to cough?" Breuer asked.

"About two weeks ago, the past week, ever since December 7th, she has refused to get out of bed. I called in neurologists because her right arm and both legs seem completely paralyzed. But the neurologists couldn't find any physical cause. She can move the fingers of her left hand a little, but not enough to eat. Her governess has to feed her, though all she will eat is oranges. She has trouble turning her head. Her neck seems paralyzed too."

The mother hesitated, then went on, "She also complains of headaches on the left side of her forehead. And her eyes blur so she can't see to read or write. The eye doctor said she has a squint caused by the paralysis of a muscle. She's always tired but never falls asleep until dawn."

"May I see her?" Breuer asked.

"Of course."

She led him down a wide, brown carpeted hall. Stopping at a closed door, she opened it slowly, as though fearing to confront the occupant. He followed her into a luxuriously furnished, feminine bedroom. Heavy green taffeta drapes framed the windows, intricately woven laces covered the bureau, the tables and the backs of chairs.

A portly governess sat beside the bed, where a young woman lay under a white satin coverlet, motionless as a corpse.

She did not turn her head to look at the visitor but seemed sunk in deep despair. Her long dark hair was tied at the nape of her neck with a ribbon to keep it from tumbling over her delicate features.

Suddenly she coughed and the sound was like a shot in that silent room. The governess glanced nervously at the mother.

Breuer walked closer to the bed. He saw that the young woman's eyes were blue and slightly glazed. She seemed oblivious of everyone in the room, off in a world of her own, a world far removed from the Vienna of this Christmas week of 1880.

He bent over her, said softly, "Can you hear me?"

The blue eyes turned to stare at him but the lips did not move.

He thought he recognized a case of hysteria, which he had come across in a number of women. The word "hysteria" was derived from the Greek *hystera,* meaning uterus or womb. A woman might suddenly find her legs or arms paralyzed, or be seized by dizzy spells or headaches, or lose vision or hearing, all without any apparent physical cause. Such symptoms had puzzled the physicians of Europe for centuries. They did not know the cause or how to treat a hysterical patient and usually were unsympathetic, blaming the woman for pretending to be sick.

Breuer, one of the most famous doctors in Austria, was continuing his family's medical tradition. His grandfather had been the village surgeon at Mattersdorf. When Breuer was only twenty-six, he had won a scientific reputation for his research. He discovered the automatic control of breathing by the vagus nerve, thereafter called the Hering-Breuer reflex, named in honor of him and Ewald Hering, the professor who had started him on the research. At thirty-two, Breuer studied the labyrinthine passages of the inner ear and discovered that the semicircular canals control equilibrium—his second contribution to permanent scientific knowledge. He conducted the latter research while in private practice, which he entered at twenty-nine. He had quickly earned the reputation of a "doctor's doctor," among his patients was Dr. Ernest Brucke, director of the Institute of Physiology at the University of Vienna founded in 1365, the oldest German university in existence. Breuer's fame also came from his diagnostic skill, a rare talent in the days before the X-ray and other modern medical tests. He was known too as the doctor with the golden touch because he often healed where other physicians failed.

Breuer had become interested in hysteria and its treatment by hypnosis. A few physicians were daring to follow in the footsteps of Mesmer, who had been forced to flee Vienna when the medical profession charged him with charlatanism for advocating the use of hypnosis as a cure for hysteria.

But now, a century later, an enterprising Viennese doctor might visit a woman diagnosed as hysteric, hypnotize her, then "suggest" while she was in the hypnotic trance that when she woke she would no longer suffer from her physical symptom. Sometimes this worked temporarily, particularly if the physician was a man of charm whom the woman wished to please. But as soon as he stopped seeing her, the symptom would return.

Believing this young woman might be suffering from hysteria, Breuer asked the mother, "Is anything worrying your daughter?"

A look of pain crossed the mother's face. "She's been very upset about her father. He's in the next room." She turned her head to the wall at her left. "The doctors say he has an abcess on his left lung that won't heal. Since the fall, when he became ill at our country home, they lance his back and drain the fluid from his lung every time it fills up."

Breuer realized this meant her husband was probably dying of tuberculosis that had infected his left lung. The puncturing of the lung and removal of the fluid as it accumulated in the pleural cavity enabled him to breathe, kept him alive a while longer.

"At first my daughter and I took turns nursing him," said the mother. "I stayed with him during the day and she watched at night."

"For how long?" Breuer asked.

"Five months. Then, a few weeks ago, she started to act very strangely. She would stop talking in the middle of a sentence as if forgetting what she meant to say. She would repeat her last words and stop again before she finished the sentence. She lost her appetite. She couldn't sleep. So I hired a night nurse for her father. Even so, she got worse day by day. I called in a number of specialists. They examined her but couldn't find anything wrong. They suggested I consult you. They said if anyone could help it would be you."

The young patient coughed again, her only communication with those in the room. It was a nervous cough, thought Breuer, not the cough of a diseased lung.

"I'd like to try hypnosis on your daughter," he said. "We have no guarantee it will help her. But there seems little else to do since any organic cause has been ruled out by the specialists."

"Please try anything you wish, Dr. Breuer." The mother's

voice held gratitude.

"May I be alone with her?"

"Of course." The mother signalled the governess to accompany her out of the room.

Breuer walked to the large window, drew the wooden shutters together to shut out the light. Then he pulled a chair close to the bed. He placed on her forehead his long, sensitive fingers, the fingers that had performed precise, controlled, painstaking research in the physiology laboratory.

Softly he said, "Close your eyes. Breathe deeply. Feel peaceful. You are falling asleep . . . asleep . . . asleep."

The young woman's eyelids flickered as if she were trying to fight his suggestion, then slowly they closed over the blue eyes. Her breathing became deeper, regular. She had fallen swiftly into the hypnotic trance, a very suggestible patient.

Breuer asked gently, "Is something troubling you?"

She shook her head from side to side, a denial. It *is* hysteria, he thought in triumph, she can move her neck muscles, she relaxed under hypnosis.

"Are you sure?" His soft voice.

A jumble of words, the first since he entered the room, spilled out of her lips. They sounded like "ush-kid-rup-bach-not." He could not understand them. They might as well have been Sanskrit.

"Can you speak more slowly?" He hoped thus to catch some of what she was saying.

Again a stream of unintelligible jargon.

He did not try to make sense of the words. He let her mutter on. At least she was trying to speak, where before she had been mute.

2

The Words

The following day Breuer again drove through the cold city to the apartment house where a father lay critically ill in one room, a daughter paralyzed in another.

Again he dismissed mother and governess from the patient's room, closed the wooden shutters, sat by the bed, and hypnotized the young woman.

And again she spoke only gibberish. He listened carefully. Then he asked, "Could you talk more slowly?"

She made an effort. He could now catch a few words. They sounded like, "Jamais—acht—nobody—bella—mio—please—liebchen—nuit."

He realized she was speaking in four languages—English, German, French, and Italian.

Suddenly she stopped. She coughed nervously. "Please keep talking." He urged, his voice low, warm.

He did not know why, but he was loath to do as other physicians, to "suggest" to the hypnotized young woman that she "give up" her paralysis, her blurred vision, her cough. He was more interested in what this young woman was saying. Why was she using a mixture of languages? What was she trying to tell him? Were her thoughts somehow related to her illness? He sensed that, while under hypnosis, a part of her mind went on thinking, a part no scientist had ever explored, perhaps a part equally as important as the one which controlled her thoughts while awake. He was interested in "control." Had he not achieved recognition for his research into what "controlled" the body's breathing, and the body's balance? Now it was a question, an equally provocative one, of the "control" of mental balance. Why could she not "control" her disorganized thoughts?

After half an hour of trying to make sense of words in four languages, he woke her from the trance, saying, as his hand lightly touched her soft forehead, "Now you will wake. You will open your eyes. You are awake."

Her lids fluttered, opened. But the blue eyes still stared out into the room as though they saw nothing, nobody.

When he walked down the hall, her mother, waiting for him in the parlor, asked anxiously, "Is she any better?"

"It's too soon to tell," he said; then, curious, he asked, "How many languages does your daughter speak?"

"German, English, French, and Italian," said the mother.

"How is your husband today?" Breuer asked.

"Not well." Her face, ordinarily sad, now expressed deep anguish. "The doctors don't hold out much hope. I don't dare tell my daughter."

"You are wise," he said. "She seems unhappy enough."

"Do you think you can help her, Dr. Breuer?" The mother's voice held a pathetic plea.

"I'll do my best." The warm, expressive eyes, which at times could be tender and at other times thoughtful, almost detached, conveyed to her the feeling he had only one concern in the world—to ease her daughter's pain.

"I'll be back tomorrow," he said, to reassure her.

"How long will you . . . keep trying?" Her lips trembled.

"As long as I must."

The gentle voice was firm. He had time, he was only thirty-eight, and his patient had time, too, she was only twenty-one.

3

The Sentence

He kept visiting the young woman day after day, determined to ease her suffering. Sometimes she spoke only jargon, sometimes even under hypnosis she remained mute, sometimes words in four languages flowed endlessly.

One day he did not darken the room during the hypnosis, but handed her pencil and paper and asked her to write with her left hand what she was thinking. She might make sense if she wrote rather than spoke, he thought. But the words she scrawled were unintelligible too. So he resumed asking her to talk each time she became silent, urging her on, jargon or no.

"Say anything you feel like saying. Anything at all," he suggested.

One evening, for he was now visiting her after supper because of his busy schedule during the day, when she entered the hypnotic trance, he asked, "What were you thinking about today?" expecting the usual incoherent answer.

Suddenly she said, in perfect English, as though confiding to a friend, "I really don't like her. I don't like her at all."

"Who?" Breuer tried to keep his voice steady, the elation out of it.

"That overstuffed governess who skulks around this room like the witch in Hansel and Gretel, as if she's waiting to toss me in the oven and bake and eat me." There was anger in her voice.

She fell silent.

"Please go on," he urged.

But she would talk no more. He thought she might be ashamed of speaking so frankly about feelings she had been taught to conceal, for she seemed the perfect lady, as did her mother.

He woke her from the trance. He asked, "Do you remember what you told me a few minutes ago?"

For the first time, she looked at him as though she were aware of him. Her eyes fluttered from the reddish-blond hair, to the expressive grey eyes, to the sensitive mouth.

"No." It was a whisper. But it was the first word she had spoken to him while conscious.

"Do you know who I am?" he asked.

Another whisper. "Yes . . . . The doctor."

"Do you know who you are?"

A slight smile, her first, curved her lips. "Yes."

He felt in his bones, for it was a physical as well as an intellectual sensation, the same excitement that surged within when he discovered something new, a feeling of exultation at having achieved what no man had before.

For some reason, he did not know why, his young patient for the moment had escaped her world of inner terror, led out of it by his healing hand.

4

The Two Worlds

A few visits later Breuer was greeted at the front door of the apartment by the young patient's mother. A smile softened the sad face.

"You *are* helping my daughter, Dr. Breuer," she said. "Today she talked to me. In anger, but she talked. She accused me of stealing and hiding a book she wanted to read. And she threw a pillow at her governess who was trying to straighten up the room, saying she didn't want one thing moved."

"Threw a pillow?" Breuer was amazed his young patient could manage such an act with her partially paralyzed left arm.

"It didn't go very far, but she threw it. And she tore a button off her dressing gown."

At least she no longer lies in mute despair, Breuer thought, she feels well enough for a show of anger.

"Is she sleeping better?" he asked.

"She still can't fall asleep before dawn, then she sleeps fitfully for a few hours, just as she does in the late afternoon. At sunset she falls into a deep sleep which lasts about an hour. When she wakes, she is usually very irritable. She tosses around until you arrive."

A thought occurred to Breuer, and he asked, "Did she sleep in the mornings and afternoons during the five months she nursed her father?"

"Yes. She went to sleep in the morning after she finished

her night of nursing, woke for lunch, then slept later in the afternoon."

"That routine seems to have carried over into her illness," Breuer said. It was as though part of her still lived in the time when she had taken care of her father at night.

That evening, under hypnosis, his young patient once again spoke only jargon. But he caught the word "sister," a word she uttered several times. On his way out of the apartment he asked her mother, "Does she have a sister?"

The mother's eyes dimmed with tears. "She *had* a sister. For eight years. My first child, another daughter, was born when I was nineteen. She died at the age of eighteen."

"You had two children then?"

"Four," she said.

"And the others?"

The mother bit her lips. "There was another girl. My second baby. She was born when my first daughter was four but lived only two years."

"And the fourth?"

"Our son." Her eyes flashed with pride. "He is the youngest. He was born a year after my third daughter, the one you are helping."

"Where does he live?" Breuer asked.

"Here. You haven't seen him because he studies very hard at law school and comes home late at night. He isn't very tolerant of his sister's illness. He thinks she is putting us through a lot of unnecessary dramatics when life is difficult enough."

"She can't help it," Breuer said.

"I know," said the mother. "And I know how earnestly you're trying to help her. You're giving her so much time. Other doctors would have spent one or two hours with her and then never returned."

"She's making progress," he said.

"And I am very grateful." Again there were tears in her eyes.

"I know how hard it is for you." He sympathized with this woman, whose home had practically become a hospital.

A few evenings later he arrived earlier than usual, to find his young patient coming out of a deep sleep. As she drifted for a moment in the shadowy realm between the sleeping and waking worlds, he heard her murmur "tormenting."

Then again: "Tormenting."

She kept her eyes tightly shut as though trying not to see what tormented her.

When she was fully awake, he hypnotized her. Repeating her word, he asked softly, "What torments you?" He spoke in English, the language she had used, as a scholar he knew English well.

She mumbled a few disjointed phrases: "Don't know—over there—some big—crawling—crawling—"

"What is 'over there'?" he asked.

She lapsed into jargon again and made no sense the rest of his visit.

The next evening, after he nodded dismissal at the hated governess, turned the lamp low, pulled the chair to the side of the bed, and hypnotized his patient, he repeated the question, "What torments you?"

"There is a darkness in my head," she said, and would say no more. Just the nervous cough.

The following evening as he entered the room, she was sitting up in bed, clad in a royal blue silk dressing gown which made her eyes appear even bluer. She looked at him wistfully, as if she had been waiting for him.

At his first words, "Sleep . . . sleep," her eyes closed quickly, almost eagerly, and her breathing became slow, regular, the paced breaths of the hypnotic trance.

"Is there anything you want to tell me?" he asked.

In a voice filled with sudden fear she said, "It's the snakes! They were here again."

"Where?"

She pointed to a far corner of the room. "They crawled out of there." She shuddered. "And then they slithered across the room and disappeared over here." She pointed to a near corner.

She went on, her voice rising, "It was horrible! I was scared to death. I screamed for help. But that monster of a governess wouldn't do a thing. She sat in her chair like a zombie and ordered me not to be so stupid. She said there were no snakes in the room. But there were! I saw them. I tell you, I saw them!"

She started to sob, tears streamed down her cheeks. "Help me! Help me!" she pleaded. "Please destroy the snakes so they won't come back."

Breuer took out his handkerchief and wiped away her tears, as her paralysis made it impossible for her to do so.

"How often do you see the snakes?" he asked.

"I never know when they're coming." Her lips trembled.

"How many are there?"

"Sometimes just one. Sometimes two or three. Big, black snakes!" Her face twisted in disgust.

Breuer knew this to be a hallucination, yet he also realized that the images in her mind were frighteningly real to her, terrorizing her as completely as though live black snakes had been let loose to crawl across the floor of her bedroom.

After he woke her from the trance, he asked, "Do you remember telling me you saw snakes today in this room?"

A look of shame flooded her face. "I know I was mistaken, just like the governess said. There probably were no snakes. Maybe I mistook strands of my hair for snakes." A pause. "Or my brown hair ribbons."

Breuer realized she was living in two worlds. In one, she was coherent, able to express her feelings, even angry and fearful ones. In the other, she was possessed by hallucinations and images so terrifying she could not think or speak logically, her powers of perception and thought broken down so that she spoke only nonsense.

5

The Fairy Tales

The weeks were passing swiftly and one evening as he entered the room, his young patient, now articulate and coherent much of the time, said, "I couldn't think very clearly today, Dr. Breuer. My mind seemed all mixed up. And I felt as if the walls of the room would topple over on me."

After he had placed her in the trance, he asked, "What were you thinking today?"

"I was very angry because my mother insisted I eat even though I wasn't hungry. She *ordered* me to eat, so I threw a pillow at her."

She fell silent. He waited for her to speak further.

She said, "Today I made up a story about a poor orphan .girl who had no family and who wandered into a strange house in search of somebody to love. She found that the father was suffering from an incurable disease and expected to die. His wife had given him up as hopeless. But the little orphan, refusing to believe the man was doomed, sat by his bed day and night, taking care of his every need, and slowly he came back to life. He was so grateful that he adopted her and she found somebody to love."

Breuer suddenly realized she was telling this story in German, her mother tongue. Up to now she had spoken only English when she was coherent.

He noticed something else different. When she finished the story and he woke her from the hypnotic trance, she seemed unusually calm and cheerful. Her eyes had lost most of their hazy stare and the squint had vanished.

She said to him, "I feel gehaglich."

This was a word she made up, which sounded, Breuer thought, like the German "behaglich", meaning comfortable.

"Do you recall telling a story while you were under hypnosis?" he asked.

"I might have," she said. "I often make up fairy tales. I call it my private theater. When I did household chores, it made the work less drudgery."

The next evening, and many of the following ones, under hypnosis she created sad but, he thought, charming little stories which reminded him of Hans Christian Andersen's *A Picture-Book Without Pictures,* first published in 1847 when he was a little boy of five. He could read the stories himself, for his father, a Talmudic scholar, had taught him to read at four. The book was a collection of thirty brief episodes, each representing an evening's observation of the moon for a month. The episodes were filled with references to death, grief and mourning, as were his young patient's stories whose theme centered on a girl anxiously sitting by the bed of a sick man.

Some evenings she was unable to tell a story but remained silent, or talked nonsensically. The following day he would hear from her mother or governess that she had been exceptionally irritable and upset by trifles, quite unlike her manner on the day after she had spun her little sagas. When he hypnotized her, she would then tell him *two* stories, as though to make up for the one omitted the evening before.

There were times when, under hypnosis, she would again speak of snakes in the room and tremble in terror. One evening she described a new hallucination.

"I see death's heads," she said. "Skulls. Fleshless bones, grinning at me."

Occasionally she had this hallucination during the day. One night as he entered the apartment, her mother stopped him to say, "My daughter has such extreme moods. One minute she is very cheerful. The next, her world falls apart."

"Such as?"

"Today she accused her governess of lying when she said she couldn't see grinning skulls. My daughter insisted skulls had entered her room, and she kept ordering them to go away. The governess tried to calm her down. My daughter again threw a pillow at her."

"There will be such moments," he said.

He noticed that on the days she had hallucinated, she seemed very upset in the evening, and some of her symptoms would return. She might squint again. Or it might be more difficult for her to turn her head as her neck muscles had once again become rigid. But after hypnosis, when she had told him what had happened during the day, she felt in better spirits.

One evening in mid-March as he entered the apartment, her mother was waiting for him, a grateful smile on her face. "My daughter was able to get out of bed this morning," she said. "The governess helped her walk down the hall so she could see her father for a few moments. She was very happy. She misses him so much."

"Did he enjoy seeing her?" Breuer asked.

"He kissed her and begged her to come tomorrow. There's been a real change in her, Dr. Breuer, thanks to you."

"Does she sleep better?"

"She still doesn't fall asleep until dawn. But now she keeps busy at night. She writes letters—as well as she can with her left hand—requesting donations for the Temple, something she has done for years. Or she sketches scenes of Vienna. She's very artistic."

He noticed that his young patient, like her mother, now smiled once in a while. It was a sad smile, though occasionally there was something seductive about it, like a flirtatious little girl trying to win over her father so he will not be angry if she misbehaves. He thought her very attractive, with her patrician face and delicate features. He sensed a certain charm, a hidden vitality, that even her illness could not disguise. He admired her imaginative, creative mind, her intelligence and her intuition. He also felt in her an energetic and tenacious will, as though she had always had her own way and intended to go on having it, no matter how strong the opposition. Her parents had spoiled her in one way, deprived her in another, he thought, so that when she had to face the inevitable griefs of life, such as a dying father, she broke down psychically.

He wondered if she had ever been in love and thought of her mother who, at the same age, had been married three years. But his young patient never spoke of any man she had loved or a wish to marry. He thought possibly she might never have kissed a man, since this was an Orthodox Jewish family, by tradition very moral. Her daydreams, which emerged under hypnosis as fanciful tales, seemed the only way she could speak of love and hate, and her hallucinations brought out her terror and fear.

Now that she was expressing her feelings to him—perhaps the first time in her life that she had expressed them to anyone —she was losing the need to chain her limbs to the bed.

On the first day of April, she walked across the room by herself, willing and able to stand alone. He had been visiting her for more than three months, and it was as though she were slowly coming alive under his very eyes.

He felt the sense of victory that belongs to the healer, victory achieved not through fighting but through wisdom and— waiting.

6

The Great Trauma

Silver birches in the woods around Vienna were tipped with green and daffodils bloomed in the *Prater,* the large, beautiful park edging the Danube.

The winter evening's chill had given way to spring's caressing warmth as Breuer, after climbing the familiar stairs, knocked on the door of his young patient's home. It was four days after she had walked across the room without help.

A second later, as though she had been waiting for him directly behind the door, the maid opened it. Her usually pale face was reddened, she looked as if she had been crying for hours.

"Oh, Dr. Breuer!" she gasped.

"What has happened?" His first thought was that his young patient had suffered a relapse.

"Her father's dead, sir! He died during the night."

The apartment was unusually still as he walked down the hall. Approaching his patient's room, he noticed her door was closed. In recent months it had always stood open, inviting him in.

Loud voices sounded from inside her room. He knocked at the door. The governess flung it open. Her face flushed, she said worriedly, "Dr. Breuer—please hurry. We can't control her."

He saw his young patient on the bed, angrily trying to thrust herself out of it, her mother holding her back.

Breuer walked over to the mother, said, "I'm very sorry about your husband. My deepest sympathy."

Then, to the daughter: "Shall we start our visit?" He nodded at the mother, telling her with his eyes she could leave her daughter in his care.

His young patient fell back exhausted on the sheets. After they were alone, and she was in the trance, he asked, "How do you feel?"

She lay mute.

He tried to reassure her. "Your father had the best medical care in Vienna. Everything possible was done to save him."

Still not a word. Not even the nervous cough.

He was aware how devastated she must feel at her father's death. It was the most severe psychic trauma she could experience. She had been touched by death twice before; she had heard talk of the sister who died two years before her own birth, and when she was eight the sister who was ten years older had died. But neither of these deaths could touch her as deeply as that of her father, who had obviously adored her as much as she did him.

Breuer himself was no stranger to death. He had lost his mother when he was between three and four years old. She had died giving birth to his younger brother Adolf. Her mother had moved into their home to bring up the two motherless boys, for his father never remarried. Breuer's grandmother, his substitute mother, died when he was in his adolescence, and then Adolf had died of tuberculosis at twenty. The last death in the family had been that of his father, nine years before.

He understood his young patient's grief all too well, and when she would not talk to him that evening or the next, he was not surprised. He was ready to wait until she was prepared to emerge from the frozen state into which she had retreated to hide from feelings too overwhelming to face head on.

The third day after her father's death, as Breuer walked into her room, she looked as if most of the life had drained from her slim body. Her vision was dim, she squinted at him for a long time, as though to make sure it was he. Finally she said in a faint voice, "Hello, Dr. Breuer."

Then, as if that effort took all her energy, she sank back

into her broodings, barring all intruders to her inner world.

He hypnotized her at once, then said, "How do you feel?"

"I can't recognize anyone but you." Her voice was weak even under hypnosis. "Everyone—except you—looks like a wax figure. Other people have no connection to me. When they come into my room, I feel upset. I don't want to see anyone but you."

"Don't you even recognize your mother?"

"Yes, if I do recognizing-work."

"What is that?" He was puzzled.

"I say to myself, when someone walks in, 'This person's nose is very long and straight, her hair is dark, so it must be my mother.' Or, 'This person's nose is rather wide, his hair is red, so it must be my brother.' It is work to discover such details because I can hardly focus my eyes."

She was now speaking English, which meant that her governess, who spoke only German, could not understand her. This made it difficult for his patient because her right leg was again paralyzed, though not as markedly as before. Unable to get out of bed, she was dependent on the governess.

The next day her mother met him at the door and said anxiously, "My daughter refuses to eat. She hasn't had any food in three days."

"Send a tray to her room," he suggested. "I'll try to persuade her to take something."

She lay silent on the bed, though a faint expression of welcome in the blue eyes showed she was glad he was there. When the tray arrived, he took it from the maid, sat by the side of the bed, and without a word, fed her, spoonful by spoonful. She did not protest.

Then he hypnotized her. And now she spoke. She said, "Sometimes I don't know what happens to me. I have two selves. A real one. And an evil one which forces me to behave badly."

"You didn't behave badly," he said. "You were in shock because of your father's death."

"He is dead, isn't he?" Her voice was sad.

"Yes. And you must accept his death. His suffering has ended."

From then on, she seemed to recover slowly. She allowed

the governess to feed her, she talked freely under hypnosis, she started to walk by herself once more.

Breuer had to leave Vienna on April 15th to visit a former patient who had suddenly fallen ill in Berlin. He did not wish the young woman in her stricken state to be without medical help, so he asked a colleague to take over until his return. On the day before his departure, he invited the colleague to her home to introduce him.

As they walked down the hall to her room Breuer said, "I want to mention her peculiarities so you will know how to handle her. She is a brilliant, sensitive young woman in spite of occasional incoherence and hallucinating. She reads French and Italian, translating them into English as she reads, with a fluency and literacy that would do justice to a professor. When she writes, with her unparalyzed left hand, she uses Roman printed letters, copied from her edition of Shakespeare."

He went on, "She may, under hypnosis, go into an *absence*," the French word for a trance-like state in which there is lack of contact but no delusions. "Or suddenly, in the middle of a sentence she may utter words that make no sense. You have to be prepared for a contradiction—you may find a girl with her mind completely clear or you may find an irresponsible patient pursued by hallucinations."

"What kind of hallucinations?" asked the colleague.

"She may imagine snakes in the room. Or see death's heads."

They entered his young patient's room to find her sitting in a chair, wearing a flowered green and white silk dress. She said, "Good evening, Dr. Breuer." She ignored the strange man, acting as though he were not in the room.

Breuer introduced his colleague, explaining, "He will take care of you while I am away."

"I'm very glad to meet you," the colleague said, putting out his hand.

She seemed oblivious to his words and the proffered hand.

Breuer, trying to show her intelligence and versatility, took a volume of Carlyle from the bookcase near her bed. He asked her to read a passage aloud, to show how she could translate French into English swiftly and accurately.

She said, with a laugh, "This is like an examination," and read the passage, but to Breuer alone, still ignoring the colleague.

Then she stood up to return the volume to its proper place in the bookcase. She walked past the colleague, who was puffing on a cigar, as though he were invisible. Placing the book back on the shelf, she turned and walked past him again on the way to her chair. The colleague, irritated beyond all gallantry and determined to make his presence known, blew cigar smoke in her face.

She choked. She stared at him as though he were a loathsome insect. Then she rushed to the door, pulled the key out of the lock, as if to prevent further intrusion by this rude, unwanted stranger. Turning around, key in hand, she fell to the floor in a faint.

Breuer rushed to her side, lifted her slight body in his arms, placed her on the bed. He took out his handkerchief, dipped it in a glass of cold water on the table by her bed, and wiped her forehead gently to revive her.

"Will you wait in the parlor for me?" he asked his colleague. After the latter left, Breuer hypnotized his young patient.

"Why did you faint?" he asked.

Her answer was an accusation. "Why did you do this to me?"

"Do what?"

"Bring in a stranger who has no right to be in this room."

"I must go to Berlin to see a very sick patient. I wanted this doctor to take care of you while I was gone."

"I will see no one but you." She was emphatic. "No one."

"Not even if I ask you to?"

"Not even then."

He sighed. "You will just have to wait until I return."

She retreated into muteness. When he woke her from the trance, she would not even say goodbye.

On his next visit to the apartment, six days later, her mother, wan and frightened, met him at the door. She said, "For three days my daughter has eaten nothing but oranges. And she screams in terror, saying she sees snakes and skulls. I'm afraid her father's death has undone everything you accomplished, Dr. Breuer."

"I'll try to get her to eat," he said, as he had the time before. Fed by him, she again ate, and as the routine of his visits was restored, she started once more to move into the world of reality. She improved physically and mentally, though occasionally a symptom would return such as her poor vision.

Breuer thought she might enjoy the beauty of late spring, since she had not been out of the house for nine months. One sunny day in May, when the *Prater* was magnificently aflower, he invited her to ride in his rented carriage. He asked his second oldest child Bertha, then ten, if she would like to go too. She eagerly accepted, honored at the invitation.

As the three rode through the *Prater,* Breuer, gazing at the clusters of violets and primroses, asked his young patient, "Aren't they beautiful?"

She said sadly, "I can see only one flower." She pointed to a blossom the coachman had put in his buttonhole.

Though she had seemed well enough for a ride in the *Prater,* following it she became very depressed. Her mother told Breuer, "My daughter talks of killing herself. She says she no longer wants to live."

After he had hypnotized his patient, Breuer asked, "Why do you threaten to kill yourself?"

"I feel life is useless, empty. I want to die." She spoke as casually as though telling him she wished to bake a cake or write a letter.

It was the first time she had made such a threat. As he left that night, he said to her mother, "It may be dangerous for your daughter to live on the third floor. She could throw herself out the window. A fall might be crippling or even fatal."

"We always moved to our house in the country late in June," said the mother. "Shall I take her now? Her bedroom is on the first floor, just off the garden."

"That seems a good idea," he said.

"Will you still visit her?" the mother asked. "We're more than an hour by carriage from Vienna."

"I can't promise to drive out every evening but I'll come as often as I can—at least twice a week." He added, "It will be refreshing after a day's work."

He could not forsake his young patient at this point. She

needed him desperately, she did not want to live in a world that no longer held her adored father. He had to help her through this most terrifying of times.

7

The Talking Cure

As he drove up to his young patient's summer home on the outskirts of Vienna for the first time, Breuer thought it a comfortable, cool place to spend the hot months ahead. The large house was bordered on three sides by a vast, trimmed lawn, open fields stretched out in the rear.

But his patient was far from comfortable or cool. He found her in a fury because she had been taken from Vienna. Her mother, after greeting him, reported, "When my daughter arrived here, she smashed the window of her room with a shoe. She has screamed incessantly at a temporary nurse I hired in place of her old governess, who resigned. She refuses to eat. And even here she threatens to kill herself."

"That threat is no longer so dangerous with her room on the first floor," Breuer said.

She had once again retreated to her bed. She refused to speak to him, even under hypnosis. Reluctantly, he prescribed chlorol, though unlike many physicians who calmed hysterical patients with drugs, he rarely advised sedatives. He felt drugs did not reach the root of illness, they were temporary expedients. But in this new emergency he resorted to them so his young patient might get some sleep.

He saw her twice a week but inevitably there were lapses of several days when he could not manage the trip from Vienna, for it meant an absence of four hours in the evening. While his wife never complained if a patient needed him, she would be justified if he were away every evening all summer.

Now he found his patient suffering from the return of physical symptoms. Her nervous cough came back in full force, sometimes punctuating every sentence. One day she was almost blind. "I don't know who you are," she told him. "I will know only if I can feel your hands." By touching his hands, the hands that fed her, that lay gently on her forehead when he hypnotized her, she reassured herself, saying, "Now I know you are Dr. Breuer."

At times he would find her in such rage that even under hypnosis she remained mute no matter how persistently he pleaded with her to speak. Other times she spoke of hallucinations. But whereas before her father's death she would become calm and cheerful after telling him of the menacing images in her mind, now she could get no relief. And she no longer created her imaginative, poetic fairy tales. Once in a while she raged at what she felt were indignities inflicted on her by her mother, the nurse, or her brother, who was spending the summer with them.

There were also times she seemed to have drifted into a trance before he arrived and he did not have to hypnotize her. She kept to her odd sleep schedule, napping in the morning and again in late afternoon until she sank into the deep sleep she called "clouds."

Believing she was deteriorating, he made an effort to see her three times a week. Whereupon she once more became what he thought of as "tractable." Her hallucinations subsided. She started to talk coherently of her feelings about her mother and a new governess. She got out of bed, walked around the house, even sat outside.

Sometimes she and Breuer would talk in the garden, where it was cool, or walk along the country road, she limping slightly, for her right leg was again partially paralyzed.

One evening she asked, in English, the language she seemed to reserve for him, "Do I talk a lot when you hypnotize me?"

"You talk freely at times," he replied.

"It's a talking cure," she mused.

He thought that an apt phrase, in keeping with her ability to think in original and imaginative style.

A few days later she commented, as they sat in the garden, "When I tell you everything on my mind, it's like chimney-sweeping," and this too he found an eloquent description.

Slowly, very slowly, for that appeared to be the pace of psychic healing, his young patient lost her physical symptoms though every so often one would reappear. Then one day a new one emerged.

On a hot evening in early July, he drove to the country home to find her mother very upset. "Now my daughter refuses to drink water," she said. "She is dying of thirst but she says she cannot touch a glass of water. She's living on fruit to quench her thirst."

He asked his patient, after hypnotizing her, "Are you thirsty?"

"Very thirsty," she said.

"Why can't you drink a glass of water?"

"I don't know." She shook her dark tresses.

"What prevents you from drinking?"

The nervous cough. Then, "I really don't know."

Perspiration ran down her cheeks, she seemed tortured by thirst. He handed her a glass of water. "Drink this," he said.

She promptly handed back the glass, her face distorted by disgust. "I can't."

The hot spell lasted six weeks and all that time she was unable to drink, getting relief for her thirst by eating fruit. One evening she said to Breuer, "My brother thinks I'm crazy because I can't drink water."

Breuer occasionally caught a glimpse of a round-faced, red-haired young man with a rather morose expression, lurking in far corners of the house as though trying to elude him. He assumed this was her younger brother.

The day the heat broke, she greeted Breuer with a smile, saying, "My brother has gone back to Vienna. Now no one will make fun of me."

After he hypnotized her, Breuer asked, "Have you been able to drink water?"

"No," she said. "And I've a tormenting thirst."

That word "tormenting" again. What tormented her so she could not drink a glass of water even though excruciatingly thirsty?

"What torments you?" he asked.

The words exploded from her parched lips: "That new governess! The one mother hired because she speaks English, so she can overhear what you and I say. I don't like her."

"She seems very pleasant," Breuer said.

"It's that horrid little dog of hers!" His patient's face held the same expression of disgust as when she had refused the glass of water.

"What's the matter with the little dog?" It looked like an innocuous white poodle who would not harm a crawling ant.

"He's a horror!"

"What did he do?" Breuer was puzzled by her intense reaction.

"The first day of the heat wave, the day the governess arrived, I went to her room to welcome her. And—" she paused, looked as though she had seen the most sordid sight possible, "there was this horrid little dog drinking water out of a glass she had placed on the floor!"

"What did you do?"

"I didn't do anything." Her eyes simmered with rage. "I wanted to tell her what I thought of the disgusting little creature. But I held my tongue because I have been brought up to be polite to people, whatever their station in life. Though I felt like throwing something at her and her stupid dog!"

And, with these words, she seized an embroidered pillow with her left hand and hurled it venomously across the room as though it were a stick of dynamite she threw at an enemy.

Then, still in the hypnotic trance, she turned to Breuer, her fury and disgust replaced by a tranquil look.

"May I have a glass of water, please?" she asked. "I'm very thirsty."

Astounded, he stood up, walked into the kitchen, filled a glass with cold water, returned to her, handed her the glass. He expected her to push it away as she had done for the past six weeks as though she were suffering from hydrophobia.

Instead she said, "Thank you, Dr. Breuer," lifted the glass to her lips, daintily sipped the water.

He woke her from the trance, the glass at her lips. She set it casually on a table.

As he drove back to Vienna in the carriage, he thought in

amazement of what had occurred. As the result of an accidental and spontaneous comment under hypnosis, a symptom that
had persisted for a considerable time had cleared up. Or had it
been "an accidental and spontaneous comment?" Was there a
direct connection between her inability to drink water from a
glass and the "horrid" little dog?

It had started when she saw the little dog drink from the
governess' glass, a sight that disgusted and angered her. It was
not until she was able, under hypnosis, to describe the scene,
and speak of her anger and disgust, that she could once again
drink from a glass.

She herself had given the clue when she spoke of something "tormenting" her. He persisted in asking what that torment was, and eventually she told him. Besides describing an
experience, she spoke of feelings she had not expressed because she felt them impolite.

From then on, other symptoms that had returned upon
her father's death, vanished or improved. She suffered fewer
hallucinations. The paralysis in her right leg disappeared and
she could walk without a limp. Breuer thought her mind much
clearer, her judgment improved.

But the talking cure was no quick, magical road to reality.
At times she would stop talking, obviously lost in fantasy. Once
when they sat in the garden talking, in the middle of a sentence she stood up, ran to a tree, started to climb it. He followed and caught hold of her, whereupon she resumed her
interrupted sentence as though nothing had happened. When
he hypnotized her and asked why she had run away, she said
she had seen a large white bird trapped at the top of the tree
and had wanted to climb up and rescue it.

She did rescue one animal. A relative had given her a large
Newfoundland dog to which she became very attached. One
evening as Breuer and she talked in the garden, the dog started to growl, then dashed away from her side to attack a cat that
was part of the household feline menage.

She stood up, walked to the porch, seized what Breuer
took to be a whip and beat off the dog. Breuer could not help
but admire the way in which this frail girl, so beset by tormenting fantasies, quickly came to the rescue of the small victim. He
then noticed that what he had taken to be a whip was her rid-

ing crop. Before her illness she had ridden horseback almost daily, an activity she very much enjoyed, she once told him.

August approached and this meant Breuer would take his family on their summer vacation. He asked a physician who lived near his young patient to substitute in his absence. On meeting this physician, she seemed to like him, not ignoring him as she had the earlier substitute.

On Breuer's return, he found she had permitted the physician to visit her though not to hypnotize her. But in spite of her apparent acceptance of the substitute, she was again plunged in deep depression. She would not talk to Breuer, even under hypnosis. He thought her excessive depression due to the lack of verbal release for her fantasies and feelings.

He told her mother, "I think you should arrange for your daughter to stay in Vienna for a week so I can see her every evening."

Her mother temporarily opened their new Viennese home. It was a different apartment from the one in which her husband had died and her daughter had fallen ill. She had not wanted to remain in the old one with its tragic memories.

Breuer was then able to visit his young patient every evening for a week, encouraging her to talk freely. The depression and rage that had accumulated during the weeks of his absence wore off and the former rapport was re-established.

The summer over, the household returned to Vienna. This meant Breuer would once again see his patient regularly. He hoped this would increase the effectiveness of the talking cure.

8

The Denial

It seemed as though Breuer's expectations might be realized.
She improved so much that very few of her daily experiences,
only the ones he thought of as "striking", now disturbed her.
He dared to believe there would be continuous and lasting improvement.

But this hope was dashed in December. Almost one year
to the very day he had first seen her, paralyzed and mute in
bed, she became overwhelmed by excessive moods. He found
her either extremely excited or gloomy and irritable. She
seemed unable to find pleasure in anything, even when he
could discover nothing disturbing her.

As Christmas approached, she seemed exceptionally restless and uncooperative. For a whole week, even under hypnosis, she would tell him nothing of her current life. Instead,
she described what had happened that day the year before.
She was carried back in memory with such intensity that she
believed she was still living in her former home.

At the end of one visit, she stood up to precede him out of
the room. Instead of going through the doorway, she stum-
bled into a stove that stood against the wall to the right of the
door.

"Are your eyes bothering you?" he asked sympathetically.

"No," she said. "The door . . . where is it? It has always
been right here." She looked in confusion at the stove.

"The door is there." Breuer pointed to the wall to the left

of the stove.

"That is where the bureau stands," she said. "The door is to the left of the window."

He realized this had been true of the room in her previous home.

There were times she realized a year had passed, but he only had to hold an orange in front of her, the fruit on which she had lived the first weeks of her illness, and she would return in memory to the previous year. The only fact she accepted was that her father had died. That she did not deny.

She relived the previous winter day by day. Breuer would only have been able to suspect this had it not been confirmed beyond doubt by a private diary her mother kept.

One evening his young patient said, laughing, "I have no idea why, but I feel angry with you."

He consulted the diary and discovered that a year earlier to the day he had said something that had annoyed her so intensely that she told her mother, who wrote it down. He had informed his young patient he was going on a trip and would not see her for several days.

The diary helped confirm another experience. One evening she said, "There is something the matter with my eyes. I don't see colors correctly. I know I am wearing a brown dress but it looks blue."

Breuer had once brought to the house colored sheets of paper for testing her eyes. Now he took the sheets out of a desk drawer and placed a blue one in front of her.

"What color is this?" he asked.

"Blue," she said.

He shuffled the sheets to a red one. "And this?"

"Red," she said.

He flipped to green. "And this?"

"Green."

"And this?" He held out a brown one.

"Brown."

"Once again, look at your dress and tell me its color."

"Blue," she said.

The disturbance in her eyes related only to her dress. He consulted the diary. He discovered that twelve months earlier she had been making a dressing gown for her father out of a material similar to that of the dress she now wore, but of a different color. The dressing gown had been blue.

She was again living in two worlds of consciousness. As the day progressed, what he called her *absence,* or "alienated state," or *condition seconde* grew more intense. By evening, it took complete possession and she lived in the winter before.

It seemed that even though she admitted her father was dead, she was reliving the previous year in an effort to keep him alive in her mind. It was desperate denial of a truth that held more pain than she could psychically bear.

9

The Third World

Breuer was now confronted by several mysteries. Why could his young patient not live in the present? Why had a symptom —her inability to drink water—disappeared after her recollection, under hypnosis, of the scene of the little dog drinking from a glass?

Because of the way the symptom had vanished, Breuer wondered if each one of her physical symptoms might not be connected to an experience that had so disgusted or alarmed her that she had repressed both its memory and her feelings about it.

Perhaps, he thought, if he could persuade her to remember the specific experience each symptom brought to mind, all the symptoms—her cough, her poor vision, the paralysis of her right arm, her hallucination of snakes and death's heads—might vanish.

But this procedure would take up too much time in the evening sessions, time needed to help her overcome what he thought of as two sets of disturbances—her everyday irritations and her reminiscences of the year before. How could she possibly cope with a third set of disturbances?

He was intrigued, however, by the possibility that each symptom might be related to an experience that had produced an emotional reaction she could not express. It was a theory no one had ever proven, perhaps never even thought of. Breuer made a decision.

He would visit her *twice* a day—once in the morning and once in the evening, doubling the amount of time he was spending with her.

He explained what he wished to do. "I will visit you every morning and hypnotize you," he said. "After you have described whatever has been troubling you, or told a story from your private theater, or talked about your experiences on that day the year before, I will ask you to concentrate your thoughts on one symptom and try to remember the time, or times, this symptom appeared while you were nursing your father." He believed these five months constituted what he called the "incubation" of her illness.

"I will make notes on the morning visit," he continued. "Then, I will return in the evening at the regular hour and hypnotize you again. Referring to my notes of that morning, I will ask you to tell in detail all you remember about the time or times one symptom occurred."

She seemed delighted at his proposal. "I'll do my very best to try to remember," she said.

The next morning he followed the pattern he had outlined. He selected her poor vision, which at times amounted almost to total blindness, as symptom for the day.

"Can you remember the time, or times, while nursing your father, that your vision became blurred or you squinted?" he asked.

She thought for a moment, then said, "There was a night in November when I was reading and my eyes suddenly went so blurry I couldn't see the print. I had to put the book down."

She paused, added, "And a few weeks before that, one night I remember feeling so tired I could hardly see. But I managed to keep awake in case my father called for a drink of water or. . . ." She stopped, blushed.

"Or what?" asked Breuer.

"In case I had to help him to the bathroom."

"Were there other times your eyes blurred?" he asked.

She thought again. She coughed. Then said, "Right after my father became sick, it was sometime in August while we were still living in the country, late at night he suddenly asked the time, and my eyes blurred."

That evening when Breuer returned to the apartment, he

put her in a trance for the second time that day and asked,
"What do you remember about the night your father wanted
to know the time and your eyes blurred?" That experience lay
deep in her memory. Though she had mentioned it last, it had
been the first occurrence of her poor vision.

She spoke slowly, trying to remember. "I was sitting in the
chair next to my father's bed and wondering if he were going
to die from tuberculosis. I couldn't imagine living without my
father. My eyes clouded with tears.

"I thought my father was asleep. Suddenly he asked,
'What time is it?' I tried to blink back the tears. I didn't want
him to see them because he might guess how sick he was. I
picked up his watch from the table by his bed. But I couldn't
see the hands clearly. The tears blurred my eyes."

She coughed, went on. "I tried to see the time through
the tears. I brought the watch close to my eyes. Its face seemed
gigantic. I was conscious of squinting as I looked at it. It was
quarter to twelve."

Tears came to her eyes, as though she were reliving the
sad scene. With her left hand, now quite flexible, she took a
lace handkerchief out of her pocket and daintily brushed
away the tears. Breuer noticed her squint had again become
very marked.

When he returned the next morning he found the apartment in an uproar. His young patient, who always lived in the
previous year at night, had awakened screaming, arousing her
mother, governess, and brother, insisting she had been taken
from her old home to a strange place.

When he entered her room, Breuer noticed that her eyes
looked startlingly clear. The squint had completely disappeared.

"What happened last night?" She looked confused.

"I think perhaps that during my visit your recollections
not only cleared up your vision but also your confusion about
what year you are living in," he said. "When you woke in the
middle of the night, sensing it was 1882 rather than 1881, the
year in which you have been living at night, you found yourself
in what you thought a strange room because you do not live in
the same house as last winter."

"Please hypnotize me every evening as you leave," she

begged, "and tell me I am not to open my eyes until morning. I don't want this to happen again. It's too frightening."

"If you wish," he said, and from then on he did so.

This worked well until one night when she woke crying as though her heart were breaking because she had dreamed her beloved Newfoundland dog had died. But this time when she opened her eyes, even though the surroundings seemed strange, she did not become alarmed. When she told Breuer, he said, "That means you are now living more in the present than the past."

The second symptom whose psychic cause he tried to unravel was her nervous cough. After hypnotizing her in the morning, he suggested she recall the times she coughed at her father's bedside. In the evening, when she was in the trance, he asked, "What details do you remember about the first night you coughed at your father's side?"

She spoke as though in a dream. "I had just started to sit by his side at night and was not as yet used to the strange hours. Or to giving up a night's sleep, which meant I couldn't do anything during the day because I was too tired. It also meant I could never go out at night."

A pause. Then, "I suddenly heard the sound of music. An orchestra was playing next door. Our neighbors were giving a party to which I had been invited. I love to dance. I thought how much fun I was missing. Then I felt ashamed for being so selfish. I started to cough."

The following morning Breuer realized the persistent cough that had plagued most of his visits had disappeared.

He then selected her deafness, what he described as her "passing habit of not hearing." He broke this down into seven categories, explaining, "Your inability to hear holds many variations."

In his first category, "not hearing when someone came in, while her thoughts were abstracted," she recalled a hundred and eight separate instances when this had occurred, remembering the persons involved, the circumstances, and often the exact date. The last experience she mentioned, the one furthest back in memory, was a time she did not hear her father return to his room after he had gone to the bathroom.

For Breuer's second category, "not understanding when

several people were talking," she remembered twenty-seven instances. The earliest involved her father and an acquaintance.

To the third category, "not hearing when she was alone and directly addressed," she thought of fifty instances, the most remote having occurred when her father was forced to ask several times for some wine.

For Breuer's fourth category, "deafness brought on by being physically shaken," she remembered fifteen instances. The furthest back in memory was the night her brother shook her angrily when he caught her listening outside the door of her father's room.

For Breuer's fifth category, "deafness brought on by fright at a noise," she recalled thirty-seven instances. The memory she mentioned last was her terror when her father suffered a choking fit after swallowing some food the wrong way.

To Breuer's sixth category, "deafness during deep *absence*," she spoke of twelve instances. For the seventh category, "deafness brought on by listening hard for a long time, so that when she was spoken to she failed to hear," she remembered fifty-four instances.

Breuer noted that in each case the various experiences were so clearly differentiated in her memory that if she happened to make a mistake in their sequence she would correct herself and state them in the right order. If she did not do this, if he tried to hurry her onwards, she would stop talking.

Many of her experiences lacked interest or significance and were told in such detail that Breuer was certain she could not be inventing them. Some consisted of her reactions and sensations and could not be verified, but those that could he checked with her mother and found his young patient always accurate.

He noticed that when a symptom was being "talked away" it emerged for the moment with greater force. When she was trying to remember the times she could not hear, she became so deaf that for part of the visit he would have to communicate with her in writing.

The first time he had seen her she had been mute, and occasionally thereafter she would again fall mute for a day or so. Breuer now asked her to recall the times this had happened while she nursed her father.

"The first time I could not speak a word was when I had a fight with my mother," she said. "My mother accused me of leaving my father alone in his room for half an hour while I went downstairs to get something to eat in the kitchen. I knew I had been out of the room only ten minutes, and I was beside myself with fury but I didn't say anything."

She mentioned other moments when she held back anger at someone who accused her unfairly. Breuer concluded that she lost the power of speech whenever she felt angry after being unjustly blamed for something but was unable to speak up in her own behalf.

He found that the first cause of a symptom always seemed to be some sort of fright experienced while nursing her father. Often it was related to an oversight on her part, following which she became terrified at the thought her father might die.

Her cough, her disorders of vision, of hearing, of speech, were all "talked away" as she recalled the time the symptom first occurred and relived the feelings of that moment.

Breuer's wife was expecting a baby, their fifth child, and when he arrived half an hour late on the morning of March 11th, he apologized to his young patient.

"I'm sorry I was late," he said. "I was up most of the night. My wife gave birth to a baby girl."

He could not quite fathom the look on his young patient's face, part consternation, part joy, part confusion. She said, "Congratulations, Dr. Breuer. You must be very happy."

"I am," he said. "Happy about the new baby. And happy you are feeling well once more."

He knew that remembering the experiences connected to a symptom was not always easy. There were times when she made a desperate effort, only to fail. No matter how hard he tried to help, she was the one who had to face the pain inherent in reviving buried memories.

But he sensed the greater pain would be in never recalling the memories. Then she would be crippled, perhaps forever, by the symptoms that served to suppress the memories and the feelings they evoked.

10

The Face of Death

One memory refused to emerge. Breuer believed it lay at the root of her entire psychic illness—the hallucination of the snake and the death's head.

A hallucination might seem crazy to everyone else, he thought, but it was, to use her word, "tormenting" to the one who had to endure it. Breuer was determined to discover why the snake and the death's head terrorized his young patient.

One spring morning he hypnotized her and in accordance with their routine asked, "What were the times you saw a death's head?"

She thought a moment, then said, "One night when I was nursing my father, his face turned into a death's head."

Her father's face, then, stood for the death's head in her mind, as well it might, since he lay dying for months before her very eyes, and eventually his face, interred in a coffin, would be no more than a skull.

"Did this image ever occur to you before?" he asked.

She was again silent, as though searching deep into memory. Then she said, "I *do* remember another time!"

Her voice held the exultation that follows the sudden easing of pain, she had unlodged an experience embedded beyond supposed recall.

"When was that?" His voice as always was calm though he shared the exultation.

"Just after my father became ill. I was very tired because I

45

never got enough sleep. I could hardly drag myself around days. But one afternoon I went to visit an aunt. I remember opening the door of a room in her house. Then falling to the floor in a dead faint."

"Why did you faint?"

"I don't know." She sounded puzzled. "I don't remember a thing."

"Perhaps this evening you will recall more."

That night, after he hypnotized her, he suggested, "Tell me about the visit to your aunt's home the day you opened a door, then fell unconscious to the floor."

"I don't remember anything more," she said, as she had said that morning.

Unlike other evenings, she seemed reluctant to explore the memory. But Breuer, sensing this to be the acid test of her treatment, of all the time he had given, of his belief he could ease her torment, persisted as forcefully as a compassionate physician could.

"Please try to remember," he urged. "This is very important."

"My mind is a blank. A white screen with nothing on it." She sighed.

"With all your strength, try to remember what you thought and felt as you entered that room," he insisted.

"I *can't* remember." It was a protest.

"Did you see something? Something so terrible it caused you to faint?"

She made the effort, a tortuous effort, because he asked, he pleaded, he insisted. Because she sensed it meant so much to him. And because she too was courageous.

The words came haltingly, as though spoken by a stranger, a stranger who possessed her, who fought against revealing what lay within.

"The . . . mirror," she said. "It . . . was . . . the . . . mirror. It . . . was . . . in . . . the . . . mirror. It . . ." She gasped, stopped.

"Go on." His words were whispered, he did not want to destroy the delicate thread that connected memory to memory.

A deep sigh flowed from her and now she spoke more naturally, as though telling a story. "When I reached my aunt's house, the maid asked me to wait in the parlor because my aunt was dressing. I opened the door to the parlor. The first thing I saw, facing me across the room, was the large oval mirror framed in gold.

"Gold . . . like his hair, and your hair too, your hair has a golden tint. Not his hair as he was old and dying, then it was as white as the sheets on which he lay. But his hair when he was young, when he would play with me in the country garden and throw me up in the sky, and as I fell into his arms I would clutch at the golden hair for safety."

She stopped. He waited.

She repeated, "It was the mirror." Then was silent.

"What about the mirror?" he asked.

"When I flung open the door to the parlor, I expected to see the mirror and my face reflected in it. But instead I saw the face of my father. His hair was white, his face was twisted in pain, the way it looked so many nights while . . . I . . . watched . . . over him." Her voice broke as though she could not go on.

Breuer's tone was firm, telling her she must. "Was that why you fainted?"

"No."

She retreated into silence. Again Breuer persisted. "What happened then?"

It was caught at last, the elusive, tenuous thread, as she said, "My father's face in the mirror turned into the face of death. A death's head. Leering at me. I screamed. Then I fell to the floor in a faint."

She was quiet, lost in fantasy. But she had remembered the first time she saw a death's head and if his theory was correct, she would no longer be haunted by this hallucination. She had relived the terror and fear of that moment and thus freed herself from its threat.

11

The Last Symptom

She was feeling much better, all physical symptoms had vanished except for the paralysis in her right arm. This had decreased but still prevented full use of the arm.

He was hoping his visits might soon end. He sensed, especially since he had started the twice-a-day visits, that his wife resented the amount of time he spent away from his family. The summer before she had not complained of his long drives to the country. But during her pregnancy she had seemed irritable because he was not home in the evening. He did not wish to upset her even though he felt compelled to see his patient's treatment through to the end. He had been a pioneer in physiological research because of his persistence and now he sensed he might have made an important discovery about hysteria.

He thought his slim young patient very winning, with her expressive blue eyes, flawless white complexion and dark flowing hair. He admired her intelligence, wit, and charm, all of which seemed heightened as she shook off her symptoms. But he was devoted to his wife and five children, he would never dream of an involvement with this young woman, about whom he occasionally spoke at home and about whom his daughter Bertha, who remembered the ride in the *Prater*, sometimes inquired.

He was therefore glad to hear his young patient say one morning in May, "June seventh is the anniversary of the day when I moved to the country last year, and by this June seventh, I am determined to be cured so you will not have to take that long trip."

"Fine." His voice held approval.

Since the June deadline was only a matter of weeks, they concentrated on trying to discover the experience that had caused the paralysis in her right arm.

"It first felt stiff one night at our country home as I was watching at my father's bedside. But I don't remember anything special about that night," she told Breuer.

No matter how often he urged her, under hypnosis, to recall more details, she could remember not one. Her mind seemed like cement hardened over the roots of recall.

It was June 6th, their next to last meeting, and still her mind refused to yield a memory. Breuer thought he might have to admit defeat on this one symptom.

Then he had an idea. "Let's rearrange the room to resemble your father's room in the country," he suggested. "Perhaps the similarity will help you remember what happened the night your arm first felt paralyzed."

"His bed was over there." She pointed to the center of a wall against which stood a small bookcase. Breuer took out the books, placed the bookcase to one side. Then he moved her light bed to the wall.

"His bureau was there." She pointed to the right of the bed, and Breuer, taking out the drawers, shifted her bureau to that spot.

"And I sat here." She indicated a space to the left of the bed. Breuer put a chair there to represent the one she had occupied in her father's room.

She sat in the chair beside the empty bed, he drew up another to sit beside her. Then he hypnotized her.

"Imagine your father lying on that bed," he said. "You are entrusted with his care. You have to make sure nothing happens to him, that he gets through the night without pain. To see he has enough water to drink, that he is kept warm, that he goes to the bathroom if he needs to.

"You sit there hour after hour, a dim light burning. No one else is awake—in the house, in the countryside. You are exhausted. You never get enough sleep. You want to close your eyes. But you are terrified that your father, a man you love deeply, may die if you fall asleep and fail to meet his slightest need."

At that moment Breuer wondered why she had been asked to take on such truly tormenting duties, why had her mother not hired the night nurse immediately and spared her daughter the horror of watching her father die under her very eyes? The family could well afford it, they were one of the wealthiest in Vienna.

His plan had worked, she was returning in memory at long last to that night. She was saying, her voice low, controlled, "I *was* exhausted. I was so tired I couldn't keep my eyes open even though my father had a high fever and needed to be watched carefully. It was a crisis in his illness. The local doctor had called in a surgeon from Vienna who was traveling there that night by train to operate on my father the next day. I had been left alone in the house, except for the maid. My mother had gone to Vienna for a few days. I don't remember why. I think some relative was sick. She was planning to return the next day in time for the operation."

Breuer decided the operation was probably the first time an incision was to be made in her father's back between ribs, to drain the fluid from the pleural abscess so he could breathe more easily.

"The maid had stayed with my father all day while I tried to sleep, though I couldn't. I was too worried. But that night, in spite of knowing how important it was that I stay awake because of his fever, I couldn't help myself. I fell asleep. I don't know how long I slept. But I woke with a start, feeling very guilty."

She stopped, as though it were all too much for her, both the original experience and the telling of it.

Breuer's gentle voice insisted: "What happened when you woke up? There you were, sitting in the chair by your father's bed. What did you see as you opened your eyes?"

She let out a sharp cry. "A snake! A big black snake! It was slithering across the wall. That wall!" pointing to the wall behind the bed. "It was going to attack my father. Bite him! Poison him! Kill him!" Her face contorted in terror.

"What did you do?" Breuer's voice was low.

"I wanted to drive it away, but when I tried to raise my right arm, which I had flung across the back of the chair as I slept, I found I couldn't move it. It was paralyzed!"

There was a soft moan, then, "I just couldn't . . . move my right arm! I turned to look at it, to see what was wrong. Each finger was a little black snake. And each nail, a death's head."

She put her hand to her throat as though choking. "I was powerless to save my father. He would die and it would be all my fault. I tried to pray. But I couldn't remember a single prayer, all I could think of was the lines from an old English nursery song—'All the King's horses and all the King's men, Couldn't put Humpty Dumpty together again.' At that moment I heard the whistle of a train. There was only one train a night and I knew this one held the surgeon from Vienna who was coming to operate on my father.

"I forced myself to look at the wall behind my father's bed. The snake had vanished. My father was breathing naturally. He was all right. The snake hadn't attacked him. Then I looked at my right hand and saw fingers once more. And the nails were no longer death's heads."

She sighed in relief, appearing as exhausted as though she had once again spent the night by her father's bed.

Breuer, concealing his excitement at her revelations, asked quietly, "When was the next time you saw a snake?"

"The following afternoon when I played quoits on the lawn. Inside the house my father was being operated on by the surgeon, who had slept at the inn. He walked into my father's room early that morning, while I was still sitting there, and I was so upset from the night's experience that I didn't even hear him enter.

"My mother had come back from Vienna and ordered me to sleep for a while, then get some fresh air. So I went outside. I threw a quoit into the bushes by mistake. When I leaned over to pick it up, I thought I saw another snake. I screamed. And my right arm again felt paralyzed. Then I realized it wasn't a snake. It was only a bent branch."

"Were there snakes in the field behind your house?" Breuer asked.

"I saw a few when I was a little girl picking wildflowers for my mother. I would always run from them, afraid they would kill me."

"Do you remember other times during your father's illness when you saw a snake?"

"Occasionally I would see something that looked like a snake. A piece of rope on the floor. Or a long curly strand of black hair. And for a moment it would confuse me."

Breuer thought it probable that on the night she fell asleep by her father's bed, she had wanted to drive off the snake with an arm partially paralyzed by the sensation people call "pins and needles," caused by the unnatural position of her arm as she slept. The paralysis of her right arm, spreading later to her left arm, then both legs, became associated with the hallucination of the snake, he believed, a hallucination that became more and more frequent until finally both arms and legs were so afflicted she could not move.

He woke her from the hypnotic trance. "How does your right arm feel?"

She lifted it high above her head.

"It's fine," she said. "There's nothing wrong with it at all."

12

The Final Visit

The next day Breuer visited her only once, in the morning, for the final hour. He did not intend to hypnotize her, there was no reason to now that the symptoms had cleared up.

He looked at her fondly, once again admired her spirit. He felt rewarded for eighteen months of work, but not in money, though he had been paid well. Money had not been the reason he persisted in her treatment, he could have earned the same amount, perhaps even more, seeing a number of patients in the time spent with her. The reward was the inner satisfaction of succeeding against overwhelming odds.

"You should feel proud of your recovery," he said. "You have earned it."

"Thank you, Dr. Breuer." There was new confidence in the eyes that now saw clearly, and her voice was soft and soothing, no longer strained by fear or anger.

She added wistfully, "I shall miss you. It will seem strange not to see you every day."

He would miss her too. They had become close in a way no doctor and patient ever had, for no doctor had devoted that much time and concern to discovering the psychic cause of a symptom.

There seemed little to talk about during that last visit, it was a time only for farewells. Physician and patient shook hands warmly at the door. She walked back to her room, stood at the window and waited for him to descend the stairs,

55

then watched him walk out of the apartment house into the June sunshine and enter the carriage whose two horses were by now familiar with the way to her home.

That night while Breuer was eating supper with his family in his *Brandstätte* apartment, a modest apartment, not nearly as luxurious as the one in which his young patient lived, he heard a knock on the door.

He opened it to see the maid who usually opened the door to him at his young patient's home. She handed him a note. It read: "Please come at once. My daughter is very ill." It was signed by the young patient's mother.

"Wait for me," he said to the maid, "I'll drive you back."

"I have to make an emergency call," he apologized to his wife.

On the street he hailed a one-horse coach, since he had dismissed his regular driver earlier than usual. He had not expected to visit his young patient in the evening any more.

The mother was waiting for him at the door, new sorrow on her face. "I'm so sorry to disturb you, Dr. Breuer, but my daughter is in agony from cramps."

This was a new symptom, he thought, she had never complained of cramps. He walked into the familiar room. The young woman he had left that morning in apparently high spirits was stretched out on the bed, her dark hair wildly strewn about her face. She was muttering words he could not understand, swept once again into her world of fantasy.

Suddenly she started to thrash about on the bed, seemingly gripped by acute pain. And out of her lips came the words, "Now Dr. Breuer's baby is coming! It is coming!" writhing all the while as though giving birth.

Breuer felt a strange panic, nothing like this had ever happened to him and he did not understand it. Not once during the entire eighteen months had she spoken of sex, she had never mentioned falling in love with a man, much less him. He had thought it surprising she did not speak of love. She seemed astonishingly undeveloped sexually in spite of her attractiveness, charm, and capacity for passion. How could she imagine she had become pregnant by him and hallucinate the birth of his baby? It was an alarming idea.

Then the physician in him took over, realizing she was

again in need of his help. Since hypnosis had calmed her in the past when she suffered hallucinations, it should be effective now.

As he had done so many times before, he said softly, "Close your eyes. Sleep . . . sleep."

She stopped the thrashing, shuddered a few times, then lay on her back, still as a wax doll, the blue eyes staring at the ceiling. He repeated, "Close your eyes. Sleep."

Her eyelids fluttered, then closed. In a moment she was breathing deeply.

"When you wake in the morning, you will feel better," he said. "You will realize that what you have just gone through was an imaginary experience."

He covered her with a light blanket, then headed for the door. Reaching it, he turned for a last look at the quiet figure on the bed, the young woman who could not let him go out of her life, the young woman he must now desert.

As he left, he told her mother, who had been waiting for him anxiously, "She is feeling better now. I will send a colleague tomorrow to take care of her. I can do no more."

"I understand, Dr. Breuer." The mother's face, as always, seemed strained in sadness. "You have helped her a lot. More than any other doctor could have."

He sensed she understood his dilemma. He clasped her hand almost desperately, rushed down the two flights and away from his young patient forever. He knew he must not see her again. He had to entrust her future care to others. He had gone as far as he dared.

He could not jeopardize her, or himself, by trying to explore psychic realms no man had ever touched upon. He had been pioneer enough.

- - - - -

Months later, the colleague told Breuer the young woman had become a morphine addict as the result of drugs he prescribed to calm her. A year later, Breuer heard she had been sent to a sanitarium.

He wondered if it would not be better if she died and thus be spared further suffering.

PART II

The Crusader

"If there will be justice in the world
to come, women will be lawgivers,
and men have to have babies."

Bertha Pappenheim
Frankfurt, 1922

1

The Soup Kitchen

She stood, ladle in hand, spooning out soup to starving refugees fleeing the pogroms of Eastern Europe. They had escaped with their lives, but little else, as they streamed westward into the wealthy, centuries-old city of Frankfurt, Germany, in search of shelter.

Old, sick men and women in torn and ragged outfits, undernourished pale children, frail mothers holding tiny, emaciated babies, all homeless, all hungry, lined up waiting for warm soup to bring new strength. They had come to the community kitchen in a house on *Theobaldstrasse* bought as a welfare center by a group of Jewish women. The rest of the house was an orphanage, sheltering thirty little girls.

The young woman ladling out the soup had been asked by a cousin, one of the rich Jewish matrons interested in the center, to volunteer her services for the day. As the refugees flowed past, she noticed a small girl with large brown eyes standing alone, confused, as if not knowing what to do.

"Where is your mother?" the young woman asked the girl, in Yiddish.

"She was killed in the pogrom." The little girl had a blank look in her eyes as though beyond feeling.

"And your father?"

"He was killed too." The blank look.

"How did you get here?"

The little girl pointed to a woman in a shabby grey sweater

standing in line several feet ahead of her.

"She brought me."

"Who is she?"

"She lived up the street from us."

"Where will you live now?"

"I don't know." For the first time there was expression in the large brown eyes—fear.

The young woman ladled out a double portion of the soup, handed it to the little girl, said, "This will warm you."

After all the refugees had been fed, the young woman walked over to her cousin, seated at a desk advising families on where to find housing. "It's unbelievable!" she said. "Imagine these poor people torn away from their homes, and their lives threatened, just because they're Jews."

"Just because they are Jews—no other reason," said her cousin.

"It's not fair!" The young woman's blue eyes flashed anger.

"Whoever said life was fair, Bertha?" Her cousin's eyes twinkled. "You're old enough to know better."

The young woman's name was Bertha Pappenheim. She was twenty-nine years old, and like the refugees, she had just left a country that had been her home. But unlike the refugees, she had not been forced out. Her life had not been threatened, and she had money enough to buy one of the most lavish houses in Frankfurt if she chose.

But when she and her mother moved from Vienna to Frankfurt the year before, on a cold, blustery day at the end of November, 1888, they had been content to rent a spacious but by no means ostentatious apartment on *Leerbachstrasse*. They did not want to flaunt their money. The rich Jews of Europe had learned over the perilous centuries that if they made too much show of their wealth there would be reprisals by those who resented this very small percentage of the population controlling so much money.

Bertha Pappenheim would have been happy to stay in Vienna, where her younger brother, Wilhelm, lived. But her mother, a widow, had wanted to return to her birthplace, the birthplace of her parents and grandparents.

Bertha Pappenheim's mother was a Goldschmidt, one of

the most prominent Jewish families of Frankfurt. The Goldschmidts could trace their ancestry back two centuries, because the small number of Jewish families living in Frankfurt
had remained constant after 1616, when no more Jews
were allowed to settle there. The descendants of these few
families were finally given citizenship in 1812 by local authorities empowered by Napoleon.

Among the Jews who became citizens of Frankfurt that
year was Benedikt Solomon Goldschmidt, Bertha Pappenheim's great-grandfather. Born in 1769, he had had two
wives. The first was Iehe Bella Braunschweig, whom he married in 1796. She died nineteen years later, and in 1815 he
married her sister Zehe Sprinze Braunschweig, living with her
the remaining eleven years of his life. One of the sons from his
first marriage, Meyer Benedikt Goldschmidt, who became a
member of the international banking firm of Benedikt Moritz
Goldschmidt, married Jettchen Shames in 1824. Bertha Pappenheim's mother, Recha, was born six years later. She was the
second daughter in a family that was to have three sons and
three daughters before the mother died at the age of forty-
four.

When she was eighteen, Recha Goldschmidt became the
bride of Siegmund Pappenheim in what was probably an "arranged" marriage. This often happened among the rich Jewish
families of Western Europe, who knew each others' lineage
and exactly how much money each family possessed.

Siegmund Pappenheim was the son of Wolf Pappenheim,
who was born in 1776 in Pappenheim, a small town in southwest Germany near Stuttgart. It contained one of the oldest
Jewish communities in Bavaria, Jews had lived there before
1334. Wolf Pappenheim emigrated to Pressburg, Hungary, now
Batislava, Czechoslovakia. He established a department store
there in 1800, and married Katharina Galman, from whose
brother he inherited a large fortune. They are known to have
had at least two sons—Kalman, born in 1816, and Siegmund,
born in 1824. Wolf Pappenheim became one of the leaders of
Orthodox Jewry in Hungary. One of Kalman's sons, Wolf Pappenheim II, born in 1848 in Pressburg, was later head of the
Vienna Central Bureau of the Aguda Israel World Organization.

As a young man, Siegmund Pappenheim went to Vienna, where he became a wealthy merchant and dealer in grain futures. Like the rest of his family, he was a fervent Orthodox Jew. He was twenty-four when he married Recha Goldschmidt. Of their four children, two survived, Bertha and their only son, Wilhelm.

Siegmund Pappenheim died in the spring of 1881 at the age of fifty-seven. Seven years later his widow decided to return to the city of her youth. Her relatives, most of whom lived in large houses with luxuriant old gardens, welcomed her back enthusiastically, as they did her daughter, who became a close friend of her cousin Louise. Six years her senior, Louise, as it turned out, was also her aunt. In 1872 Louise, who had lived in Prague with her mother, Mrs. Wilhelm Edle von Portheim (Recha Pappenheim's cousin), married her uncle, Marcus Moritz Goldschmidt, who earned his money financing American railroads. They had two sons, who died as infants, and two daughters. Louise gave liberally to charity though she was not personally active as a volunteer.

Bertha Pappenheim soon discovered that some of her female relatives were interested in politics, some in welfare, some in feminist activities, and some in the arts. One of her cousins studied piano with Clara Schumann, then living in Frankfurt. Bertha Pappenheim herself detested playing the piano. She had been forced to practice as a child even though she thought herself utterly devoid of talent. But she loved to listen to music, especially opera, her mind soaring in happy imagery.

In Austria she had enjoyed horseback riding, reveling in the fragrance of the flowers and trees of the Vienna woods, hearing the song of birds, exulting in the feel of the powerful creature beneath her, power she could control with the slightest touch of the reins or the merest flick of a whip. One of her favorite photographs, taken in a studio in Konstanz, Germany, late in 1882, showed her standing on a Persian rug in front of a scenic backdrop of a forest, clad in her black riding suit, crop in right hand, white gloves in left.

Now she had found several cousins who liked to ride in the *Stadtwald,* the forest that framed the city of Frankfurt. The group would gather early in the morning at a riding academy where grooms had their horses ready, then gallop through the woods to breakfast at an inn owned by a former forester. Mrs. Ludwig Edinger, the former Anna Goldschmidt, another of Recha Pappenheim's cousins, was one of the group. Her husband Dr. Ludwig Edinger was an internationally famous neurologist and professor at the University of Frankfurt. He established the Edinger Institute, the oldest such center dedicated to the study of the brain.

Bertha Pappenheim also liked to wander through the Städel Art Institute and to visit antique shops. She collected old glass, china, and rare laces. One day she decided she wanted to learn to tat and organized a small sewing club so that she and her cousins might have the pleasure of handiwork, the feeling of creative satisfaction in watching lace fashioned by their own fingers form before their eyes.

She could have lived, if she wished, like her mother, in quiet leisure, with money enough for endless entertainment and travel. But something within her cried out for a life that held deeper meaning.

She did not know how to seek this kind of life however until the day she stood in the soup kitchen, surrounded by the persecuted men, women, and children. She felt she must help these stricken souls. It was her responsibility as a Jew, as a woman, as a human being.

She knew it as a certainty the moment she asked the little girl with the brown eyes where she would live and the child had replied, "I don't know," with fear in her eyes.

The little girl's eyes haunted her. A child should not have to know such fear—a child should have a mother and father to take care of him, and if a child lost his mother and father because of the barbaric cruelty of man toward man, others must accept responsibility for the child so he could live without fear.

2

The Orphanage

Shortly after that day in the community kitchen, the cousin who had originally asked her to serve there came to call. "Bertha, we need someone to read every afternoon for an hour to the children at our Girls' Orphanage," she said. "Would you do it?"

Bertha Pappenheim thought again of the little girl's eyes. "Yes," she said.

As a child she had been entranced listening to fairy tales, some told by her governess, some by her older sister Henriette, who later died. When she was in school she made up stories or dreamed away the hours as she did housework. She liked to create dramatic situations in which the characters she had brought to life in her imagination solved their personal tragedies.

On her first day at the Orphanage she read from a copy of Hans Christian Andersen's fairy tales. Thirty little girls sat clustered around her on the floor, eyes wide in wonder as she held them spellbound for an hour. When she had finished, they would not let her go, insisting she read on. Her voice had almost vanished at the end of another half hour.

"Will you come tomorrow?" they asked wistfully, as though fearing that she, like their families, would disappear forever. But she returned the next day, and the next, week after week, until she had read all the fairy tales she could find.

She started making up stories of her own. Basing each on

an object found in a rummage store, she described to the little girls what she thought of as the "tragedy" in the life of the owner that had forced him to bring his little treasure to the store. She also spun a contrapuntal story about the store's owner, a man living in deep depression because his wife had deserted him. The saga ended when he discovered a long-lost daughter, who revealed his wife had died and who came to stay with him bringing new hope to his life.

She wrote out each episode, and after the little orphans had asked her to read them over and over, she decided to publish them in a book for other children to enjoy. Called *In The Rummage Store,* the book was privately printed. Instead of signing her own name, she used the pseudonym Paul Berthold, her own initials backward, and the last name a masculine version of her first name. The year was 1890.

She found herself more and more a part of the life of the little orphans. At first they had been only sad, charming, strange faces to her, but now each had become a small person —Helene Kramer and Sophie Rosenthal and Johanna Adler. Most of them had lost both parents, but a few had a mother or father who was unable to take care of them or who did not want them, in some instances because they were illegitimate. Under Orthodox Jewish civil law, an illegitimate child was a pariah, not accepted by the Jewish community, often taken away from his mother and turned over to state- or church-supported welfare institutions, where the child would receive no Jewish religious education.

Her heart went out to these little girls, who had no one to care whether they lived or died, abandoned to whatever fate lay in store in a jungle where Jews were unwanted and persecuted. Little girls without mothers—what kind of mother could give birth to a baby and then desert it, she wondered.

Jewish women in Frankfurt with money and consciences, many of them her relatives, were doing their best to provide care for babies whose parents had died or were unable to support them, or who were illegitimate and unwanted. Traditionally, Orthodox Jewish women with money always looked after the poor Jews in the community. They supplied wedding dresses for the young brides, arranged burials, and took care of orphans. Some of the women gave money, others pro-

vided both money and services, the latter in a well-meaning
but often haphazard fashion.

Bertha Pappenheim became aware that the Catholic and
Protestant women of Germany were far more advanced in
their volunteer welfare activities than were the Jews, who had
been prevented from doing much organizing over the centuries by hostile governments of the countries in which they
lived. The Jewish women of Frankfurt had taken an important
step when they decided to set up the Orphanage.

One day the director of the Orphanage fell ill, and Bertha
Pappenheim's cousin asked her if, in addition to reading to the
children, she would take on some of the administrative duties.
This meant spending more hours at the Orphanage, less hours
riding horseback or enjoying the opera in Frankfurt, Berlin,
or Vienna, where she also went to see her brother Willie. But
she decided that her work at the Orphanage was more important than pleasure. She wanted to learn all she could about
how to help the little girls.

The months passed, then one day her cousin told her,
"Our director has resigned. She's too ill to carry on."

"What will you do?" asked Bertha Pappenheim.

"We want you to be the new director. The children like
you. The staff likes you too, even though at first they were
quite suspicious, wondering why someone with all your
money would want to work there. But your devotion and dedication have won them over."

"I am honored by the offer," said Bertha Pappenheim.
"But I don't know much about running an orphanage."

"You know as much as anyone else."

"Would I have to live at the Orphanage?" The director
had slept in a room on the third floor.

"You could stay there any night you wished, but since you
live so near I don't see why you would need to remain over-
night," her cousin said.

"What about salary? It seems ridiculous for me to accept
money." She had been working as a volunteer.

"You're entitled to a salary," said her cousin. "But you
could always return the money through a donation or buying
something we need."

Bertha Pappenheim was silent, knowing how much the acceptance would change her life, wanting the change, but also recognizing the challenge it would offer. She was not certain she could meet it.

Sensing the indecision, her cousin said, "You would be helping everyone—the orphans, the sick director, and those of us who run the place." She added, "I know you can do the job."

Bertha Pappenheim said quietly, "I will try."

From then on, she walked each morning from the apartment where she lived with her mother, near the center of the city, to the Orphanage about thirty minutes away and put in a full day's work, sometimes staying until late in the evening.

Her predecessor, diligent but uninspired, had kept the Orphanage clean, provided food, and made sure the girls looked presentable, but she had given little thought to their education or future. Bertha Pappenheim looked upon the orphans not merely as her charges for a few years, but as growing girls whose capacity to think, to learn, and to enjoy the beauty that existed in the world, could be developed and enhanced by their experiences there. Thus, in addition to training the girls to be efficient in housework, which meant the chores at the Orphanage were carried out free of charge, she started kindergarten classes for the little girls and classes in history, geography, art appreciation, and music, including weekly singing lessons, for the older ones.

She conducted the art appreciation course herself. She and the girls visited museums, and on Saturday afternoons she invited small groups to the apartment on *Leerbachstrasse* to study the art and paintings her mother had brought from Vienna and to enjoy the rare laces she and her mother collected.

She was learning too—how to run an institution, purchase supplies, take weekly inventory. She discovered that by mending and patching, money could be saved on sheets, pillow cases, underwear, and dresses. Since her mother did not know how to mend, torn sheets and pillow cases had merely been tossed away in her home.

She expected the same discipline of the girls that she asked of herself. She instituted a strict washing, ironing, patching, and sewing routine. She would tolerate no tardiness at classes or meals. She insisted on impeccable table manners, allowed no disorder in the rooms.

She kept meals simple, almost spartan, as though food were the first place to learn control. She realized she might be thought severe but to her, to be severe was to be loving, it equipped one to face life's hardships. And while she might be strict, she would not countenance cruelty. She placed a complete ban on corporal punishment. Any employee discovered striking a girl was fired at once.

She thought of the orphans as her "daughters." But though she felt responsible for their education and their future, she kept an emotional distance. She refused to favor a few in a sentimental manner.

She became an able administrator and she learned also how to convince the women volunteers, who set Orphanage policy, of the need for certain services. They listened to her with respect and tried to make available whatever she asked. They sensed this soft-spoken young woman was gaining faith in her ability to fight some of the world's injustices—racial persecution, poverty, and the stigma borne by a child conceived out of wedlock.

3

The Feminist

One day she picked up a copy of *The Woman*. This monthly publication, begun in 1894, was edited by Helene Lange, leader of the feminist movement in Germany.

In other countries women were waging crusades for the right to vote, for equal job opportunities and equal pay. But in Germany, the feminist movement had been started in 1848 by a group of teachers fighting for higher education for women, and it continued to focus on this.

She read each issue of *The Woman* with mounting excitement. She was finding strong allies in her belief that women had a right to higher education. One of the smouldering resentments of her life was that she, along with all the other young women of Vienna, had not been allowed to continue her education beyond high school. She had attended a private Catholic school. There were no private Jewish or Protestant schools in Vienna, and children from wealthy families went to Catholic schools, which did not attempt to proselytize. After graduating at the age of sixteen, she was supposed to stop thinking, stop learning, and waste time embroidering, playing the loathed piano and indulging in idiotic chatter at boring parties, all the while waiting for some appropriate man to appear on the scene, propose, and marry her, after which she would spend the rest of her life running a house and bringing up children—sons, of course, no Jewish family really wanted daughters.

Discrimination against girls existed in other religions but it was particularly intense in Orthodox Judaism. From the day she was born, a girl was made to feel inferior to a boy, treated as a second-class citizen with no rights of her own. The contempt in which a girl was held was evident at the very birth of a baby. If a visitor asked, "What was it—boy or girl?" and the answer was "boy," everyone looked happy. But if the answer was "Only a girl," faces would fall, and the embarrassed parents could hardly wait until the next birth, this time, hopefully, a cherished boy.

She had watched in envy as Willie went through the University of Vienna, then on to graduate school to study law. Just because she was born a woman, she was thought unworthy of education. She was supposed to do unquestioningly whatever men ordered.

She rebelled passionately against the age-old slavery in which women had been held by the selfishness of man. The unfairness of the Bible toward women suggested to her it had been written by a male genius, rather than at divine dictation. Women had been so exploited for centuries, were so unsure of themselves as a result of that exploitation, that even though a man might be obviously inferior and incompetent in a given job, the women treated him as superior. And men were so vain, so spoiled, allowed for centuries to live without criticism, that if a woman dared object to a masculine act or attitude, she was deemed hostile to men in general. Just to be a man meant to be above reproach.

One day as she read an issue of *The Woman*, she learned of the book that had inspired the feminist movement. *A Vindication of the Rights of Women* by Mary Wollstonecraft had been published in England in 1792, a century before. There had never been a German translation. Bertha Pappenheim decided she would undertake this task at night, after her work at the Orphanage, paying to publish the translation with her own money.

Mary Wollstonecraft not only made a plea for equal education for women, with the State assuming responsibility for the cost, but also championed intellectual companionship as the basis for a happy marriage. She asked that woman be allowed to be man's companion, not merely his plaything.

Bertha Pappenheim discovered that Mary Wollstonecraft had been a rebel in more ways than one. The eldest daughter of an alcoholic father, she had been forced to earn her own living, first as a secretary, then a writer. When she went to Paris to report on the French Revolution, she fell in love with an American, became pregnant and gave birth to a daughter, Fanny, named after her best friend, Fanny Blood, who died in childbirth. Mary Wollstonecraft was abandoned by the father of her child, who refused to marry her, though he offered financial support. This she proudly refused. A few years later, she again violated conventional standards by becoming pregnant outside of marriage, but this time she married the father of her child, the philosopher and political writer William Godwin. Her second daughter, Mary, born five months after the marriage, married the poet Shelley and wrote the novel *Frankenstein*. The first daughter committed suicide. Mary Wollstonecraft died of childbirth fever less than a month after her second daughter was born.

To her German translation, which appeared in 1899, Bertha Pappenheim signed P. Berthold, now using the initial "P" instead of "Paul." She used this same pen name later in the year when she wrote a three-act play *Women's Rights,* for whose publication she also paid.

The play dramatizes the economic, political, and sexual subjugation of women. Its first scene takes place in an unheated attic in which a poor, underpaid working woman lives with her five-year old daughter. The child is starving, but the mother has no food. Other working women enter to organize for their own protection. An argument breaks out among several of them and two, who are prostitutes, inform the police of the forbidden meeting. The police rush to the attic, break up the meeting, and arrest the poor woman who lives there.

The second act takes place in the home of a lawyer. The lawyer's wife asks him for one hundred marks of her own money to give to a poor, sick woman she has just met. The husband, who has control of his wife's property, refuses her demand as extravagant. As the wife leaves the room, a friend of the husband's enters. Bragging about his success with women, he asks the lawyer for a loan and when refused, tries to arouse the lawyer's suspicion that his wife is unfaithful. The lawyer throws him out of the house. The wife finally persuades her husband to accompany her on a visit to the poor, sick woman so he may see for himself that her wish to help is justified.

The third act, a return to the attic room, shows the poor woman, having served her jail sentence, lying fatally ill. She is the one for whom the lawyer's wife wants money. As the lawyer and his wife walk up the stairs to see her, they meet the husband's friend who asked to borrow money. He has tried to rape one of the women workers in the house. When the lawyer enters the attic room the dying woman recognizes him as the former lover who deserted her when she became pregnant. His wife, shocked, tells him that because of their children she will not leave him, but from now on she will refuse sexual relations with him as her "woman's right."

Bertha Pappenheim, in the second act of her play when the wife asks her husband for some of her own money and is refused, made clear the inequities of Jewish civil law, under which a wife could not own property. This was yet another indignity women suffered because of the outmoded Orthodox Jewish attitude.

Like Mary Wollstonecraft, she was convinced the more education a woman had, the less likely she was to accept the centuries-old fantasy that she was inferior to men.

4

The Organizer

Bertha Pappenheim read of other important issues in *The Woman,* the publication proving to be her higher education. In its pages she found much that confirmed her conviction of the need to modernize the welfare work carried on by wealthy volunteers.

The Protestant and Catholic volunteer groups had already put into action the new techniques of professional social work, with its scientific casework methods, its emphasis on human dignity and the right of the individual to get help for physical, economic, and emotional needs. She realized her relatives and friends who were active as volunteers meant well—they had hearts as well as purses of gold. But their efforts to help the needy were disorganized, sporadic, often lackadaisical, devoid of any systematic approach or follow through. "Careless charity" was the phrase she coined to describe this attitude.

Even the money for welfare was given indiscriminately by philanthropists who did not care to what purpose their marks were put. She would ask a donor, "Do you know how your money is being spent?" The donor would look dumbfounded. Wasn't it enough he gave to charity? Was he also supposed to show interest in what happened to the poor?

Wealthy married women with time on their hands ran the Orphanage informally. There was little supervision, few standards, a vague policy.

Bertha Pappenheim needed order in whatever she did.

She believed effort without discipline or direction was wasted. She enjoyed planning, and she set about bringing order to the Jewish voluntary welfare scene. The ideas she found in *The Woman* were her blueprints.

She organized a group of volunteers, many of them her wealthy relatives and friends, into a local Frankfurt organization called Care by Women. This was 1902; she was in her seventh year as director of the Orphanage.

She personally taught the women all the latest social work techniques—the thoughtful investigation of cases, systematic keeping of records, periodic surveys to discover the cause of need, and the relation and incidence of physical and mental illness in a family. She formed special committees to establish nursery schools, find foster homes and adoptive parents for unwanted and illegitimate children, provide travelers' aid at railroad stations, and give women career and family counseling. She instituted "Monday meetings," where as chairman, she presented one case, then discussed the person's needs and how best they could be met.

Slowly, thoughtfully, working with deep conviction, she inspired the women volunteers to give up the old-fashioned way of doling out charity, a way that benefitted neither the donor nor the recipient.

Since a number of her "daughters" were now leaving the Orphanage to go out into the world and earn a living, she organized an educational and recreational center for them and other Jewish working girls. Called the Girls' Club, it occupied several rooms at *Fahrgasse* 146. One room served as a library, another as a dining room where meals prepared according to Jewish dietary law were offered. The club sponsored evening lectures by prominent speakers on world events, art, literature, and social problems; she thought it important to continue the girls' education.

She did not think of the club as a welfare project but rather as a social group supported by the members, a small fee guaranteeing each girl the right to express herself freely. The girls were encouraged to send delegates to board meetings.

This was 1903, the year her brother Willie got married, at the age of forty-two. His wife was a widow, Ida Stern von Herzberg, with a daughter, Marianne, from her previous marriage.

Bertha Pappenheim supposed she should feel insecure because she had not married, while most of her friends had, but she had achieved a kind of security in her ability to lead women to more effective ways of helping the needy. "The road is everything, the destination nothing," she would tell the volunteers.

She realized the Protestant women had organized a national welfare federation that was a member of the liberal feminist organization, the German Federation of Women's Organizations. The Catholic women had also organized nationally, though they did not belong to the Federation. Only the Jewish women volunteers lacked national unity.

She set about convincing the Jewish women in Germany of the need for a national organization similar to those established by the Protestant and Catholic women. In 1904, during her ninth year as director of the Orphanage, she founded such an organization—the Federation of Jewish Women—and was elected president. It was accepted as a member of the German Federation of Women's Organizations. A woman became a member of the Federation of Jewish Women through joining the local voluntary group. In Frankfurt Care by Women was the representative.

From the first, she envisioned the Federation not as a mere conglomeration of clubs and associations throughout Germany but as a spokesman for the world of Jewish women, each with a mission and a spiritual belief in the work she was doing. Its headquarters was in Berlin, where all Jewish organizations were centered. Its goals were to support institutions such as orphanages and hospitals, and to finance the training of Jewish social workers and nurses, urgently needed in Germany.

She wrote of the meeting at which the women decided to form a Federation:

"The German feminist movement gave impetus and direction to those uncertain women who did not know which path to take. For the Jewish women most closely connected with social work, this meeting was one of the highlights of their life."

And Bertha Pappenheim, the once "uncertain" stranger from Vienna, was responsible for the welding of the feminist philosophy with the philanthropic spirit.

5

The White Slave Rescuer

Bertha Pappenheim had never studied geography, girls were not expected to know about the world or to travel, but she learned about it now. She learned other things, too, things she never would have found in a textbook.

One of her very first actions as president of the Federation was to travel to Galicia and see for herself the wretched conditions she had described in her pamphlet *The Jewish Problem in Galicia*. It was written in 1900 before she had actually visited the province, but she had already heard from refugees of the unbelievable poverty to be found in the ghettos. The pamphlet, for whose publication she paid, urged education of women as one way of helping future generations in Galicia. She wrote it because she hoped it would inspire the Jewish women of Frankfurt to give aid to Eastern European Jews.

She signed this pamphlet "P. Berthold," as she had done before, but for the first time she placed her real name in brackets under the pseudonym. She thus publicly acknowledged that she had written *In the Rummage Store*, translated Mary Wollstonecraft's classic, and authored the play *Women's Rights*. She now decided to use her real name for anything she might write in the future.

Galicia was the easternmost province of her native land, Austria. Before the Napoleonic wars, it had been southwest Poland. After Napoleon's defeat, in 1815, Poland, no stranger to partition, was split up into three parts. Russia took the lion's share, what had been Eastern Poland, with its capital, Warsaw. The Carpathian mountains separated Russia from its newly incorporated territory. Prussia received the northwestern part of Poland, and Austria was given Galicia, the southwestern part. For almost one hundred years Poland, chiefly Catholic, had not existed as one country, but it had survived as one language and was essentially still one nation even though its people were divided into three citizenships. Many Jews lived in the Polish part of Russia, though Russia proper did not officially allow Jews into the country. But as elsewhere, if a Jew were wealthy, he would be unofficially tolerated.

Bertha Pappenheim discovered, while in Galicia talking to welfare workers, that Jewish girls from the ghettos were sold into the white slave market by their parents, sometimes knowingly, other times unknowingly. These girls had never learned to read or write or been given the chance to acquire skills that would enable them to earn a living.

The Catholics and Protestants also faced this problem, for girls of all denominations were sold as prostitutes. But there was an additional complication where Jews were concerned, since Orthodox Jewish law permitted a form of polygamy. One group of women likely to become prostitutes themselves, or to sell their own daughters as prostitutes, were the wives of men who had abandoned them to emigrate to America, for this was the era when thousands of immigrants left Europe to work in the growing industries of that Promised Land. A married man with children would set off alone for New York, promising to send for his family as soon as he found work. But he would often never be heard from again.

Under Jewish civil law, a married man who had a child by another woman could consider himself married to her if she were not already married. This made the child legitimate. But it also meant he could abandon his first wife forever and she could never seek a new life of her own, because a wife was not allowed to divorce a husband. Thus a man could have several wives if he wished and not be compelled to get a divorce. But the *Agunah,* the abandoned wife, or the wife who could not prove her husband's death (if he had died on the battlefield, for instance, the death had to be witnessed by a Jew), or the wife who had not received a legally valid Jewish divorce, could not remarry. Bertha Pappenheim had always admired Rabbi Gershon of Mainz for making monogamy legally binding on Western Jews about 1000 A.D., but now she realized loopholes still existed which allowed a man to escape monogamy.

If the wives had any more children after they were abandoned, they could not compel the child's father to support them, since they were still legally married to the first husband. Usually they turned these children over to state institutions. A number of the young wives who were deserted, especially those without children, became prostitutes, got pregnant, and gave the babies to state institutions. Some deserted wives sold their twelve and thirteen year old daughters into prostitution, unable to support them, and the daughters had illegitimate babies which were also sent to institutions. Since the state institutions gave no Jewish religious training, these children were all lost to Jewry.

White slavery had become such a problem for all religions that a German Committee to Fight White Slave Traffic had been organized in 1899 by German feminists, Bertha Pappenheim learned from reports in *The Woman.*

But she also learned, to her amazement, that there was not one Jewish woman on the committee, though studies conducted by the feminists showed there were a number of Jewish prostitutes and madams in Germany.

One evening she asked a relative who was an active feminist, "Why are no Jewish women involved in rescuing Jewish girls from prostitution?"

"That is an extremely unpopular cause among the Jews in Germany," replied her relative.

"Why?"

"Because Germany is such an anti-Semitic country, Jews want to avoid making public anything that might bring disgrace on them. You'll find priests and ministers cooperating with the Catholic and Protestant welfare organizations that work to protect girls from prostitution. But no rabbi will dare show interest in the work of a Jewish group that raises money to help prostitutes or their illegitimate children."

"In spite of the large white slave traffic in Jewish girls?" Bertha Pappenheim asked.

"Yes. And in spite of the fact that many are mere children," said her relative.

"Where do the girls come from?"

"A large number from Galicia and from the eastern part of Poland, now under Russian rule. Some also come from Turkey, some from Greece," said the cousin. Then she asked, "Did you know that Frankfurt is a way station in the white slavery route?"

"What do you mean?" Bertha Pappenheim was puzzled.

"It's the stopping off place for the middlemen and the girls who are shipped to Argentina and the other South American countries, a large market for prostitutes. They have to change trains in Frankfurt to reach the northern seaports."

"What are the middlemen?" Bertha Pappenheim asked.

"They are also called traders. They act as representatives for the men who finance the white slave market, who have become rich from it."

"Who are these rich men?"

"Primarily a group of Jews living in Turkey who pay middlemen in Galicia to do their sordid work. The middleman goes to a family living in poverty in the ghetto and says, 'I have a good job for your daughter in Germany as a maid, or cook, in a wealthy family. She'll have enough to eat and she'll have a chance to marry a man who can support her. I will pay her fare, and I will give you extra money because I get a commission for bringing her to the wealthy family.' Off he goes with the girl. He takes her, along with a few others, by train to the German border. There they must get off the train and slip unnoticed across the border because they are entering illegally, since the girls have no citizenship papers. The middleman then brings them to Frankfurt where they change trains for the northern seaports.

"Some of the girls are saved at the border by agents, hired by Catholic and Protestant religious organizations to alert the police, though sometimes the middlemen bribe the agents. Some girls are also rescued at the railroad station in Frankfurt. If a dealer is recognized by police as he waits for a train going north, he may panic and desert the girls, who are left bewildered, with no idea what has happened. They can't speak a word of German, have no money and no passport or citizenship papers, so that they are here illegally. The police notify the consul of the girl's country unless she is from Russia or Turkey—those countries don't offer protection to a single woman."

"What happens to most of the girls?" Bertha Pappenheim asked.

"The Protestant and Catholic welfare organizations take care of their girls. But there is no one to look after the Jewish girls. The police don't know what to do with them. Sometimes the girls wind up as prostitutes anyhow, for they can't read or write and have no way of earning a decent living in the few fields open to women today. When they have babies, we are supposed to take care of the unwanted children. But we must not admit that there are Jewish prostitutes—or Jewish merchants in Turkey who help finance white slavery."

Bertha Pappenheim was appalled at the thought of innocent girls sold as prostitutes, girls unaware of what was happening to them because they were uneducated. The Jews in Galicia and those living in eastern Poland, part of Russia, were not as educated as the Jews in the Prussian sector, for the latter had been required to pass literacy tests in order to become citizens. Since many of the uneducated Jews from the Polish sector of Russia, fleeing the pogroms, flowed into Galicia, this increased the number of Jewish families there in need of education.

She reported to the Federation on white slavery, pointing out that the numbers of illegitimate children of legalized Jewish prostitutes and of crimes involving immorality and cruelty among Jews in Germany trailed behind those of other religious groups. But she added:

". . . those who are not blind and deaf can see and hear how increasing immorality among the Jews appears on the horizon. This cloud of immorality can do more damage to us than the hate of the people around us. From the steady increase in the number of illegitimate children who become charges of Jewish welfare agencies, we are aware that more and more Jewish girls are becoming involved in extramarital relations. We know that a great number of Jewish girls become prostitutes and that in all the houses of prostitution throughout the world Jewish girls can be found. In the 'traffic in girls,' merchants as well as merchandise are mostly Jewish. We know that family life today is not what it used to be, that the men, both fathers and sons, do not protect themselves and their homes from being soiled and that the dirt cannot be washed away by the tears of deceived and damaged women. Many of the girls who indulge in prostitution know that they have only one value, that of the sex object."

Her life now became a fight on two fronts: she wanted to provide education and training in careers for the orphans, and she wanted to help young Jewish girls in danger of becoming prostitutes, or who were prostitutes, and had become pregnant. To her, the ultimate humiliation was a Jewish girl selling her body because she was uneducated or lacked proper moral training and could find no other way to live.

She seethed with deep scorn at those Jews who swept the dirt under the rug because they feared reprisals, who refused to admit that there were Jewish madams and Jewish merchants engaged in the sordid business of white slavery. Slavery was slavery—whether it involved keeping a woman subjugated by denying her equal education, or the legal rights of voting, divorce, and property, or the right to choose the man to whom she wished to give her body, not for money but for love.

She believed every woman in the world, whatever her position or philosophy, and even if she was unaware of it, was the disciple of those who fought for equal rights.

6

The Fourth Death

It had been seventeen years since her mother and she had left Vienna. But parts of her would always remain Viennese—the gay, dancing part, the sophisticated, elegant part, and the part that still ordered Wiener Schnitzel even in Berlin where they naively served it with gravy and where it tasted no more like the original than machined lace looked like hand-made.

Her mother, in ill health for several years, was now failing so fast that Bertha Pappenheim hired Selma Fliess to live in the apartment as a companion, because she was away so much of the time at the Orphanage, where she was entering her tenth year as director, or the weekly meetings of the Girls' Club and Care by Women, or in Berlin presiding at a Federation board meeting.

Her life had changed from that of a daughter dependent on a mother to that of a mother responsible for the care of many "daughters," some very tiny, others now graduates of the Orphanage and, inspired by her dedication, working to help the needy. She had watched girls like Helene Kramer, Sophie Rosenthal and Johanna Adler grow into sensitive, thoughtful young women who wanted to be social workers, teachers, or nurses. She had been the nearest thing to a mother they had known.

She had always felt close to her own mother. She thought of her mother as kind, wise without being harsh, industrious, able, tactful, and modest. Her mother was "a Goldschmidt in

every way," as the companion phrased it, the companion had
served several families in which Goldschmidt women had
grown old and frail.

Sometimes there was a confusing mixture in her mother—
she could be subtly dominating in the way of a matriarch, but
she could also turn on charm, and then again she could sink
into a contained sadness that defied all contact.

Bertha Pappenheim was very grateful to her mother, and
to her father, for the gift of life, and because they had so
enriched the life they gave her. She thought of them as dignified and loyal human beings, as a link in a chain of worthy
generations, carrying with them the best, as well as the worst,
of the Jewish tradition.

One morning as she was about to leave the apartment for
the Orphanage, her mother's companion rushed down the
hall after her. There were tears in Miss Fleiss' eyes.

"What's wrong?" asked Bertha Pappenheim, though she
already sensed what it was.

"Your mother died in her sleep last night," said the companion. "I just brought in her breakfast and found her lying in
bed peacefully, not breathing."

Even though her mother had been seventy-five years old
and had become more and more frail, and even though she
had not expected her mother to live much longer, the death
was a blow. When her father died, she had gone out of her
mind with grief, but she had been younger then with no one
to think of but herself. Now others depended on her, girls of
all ages, most of whom had never known a parent's love.

She had been fortunate, her mother and father had lived
together until parted by death; they had not deserted each
other nor their children, though she had no illusion their life
together had held perfect harmony or passionate love.

Her mother's funeral was simple. A number of relatives
dutifully attended. She arranged for her mother's marble
headstone to have the years 1830-1905 cut into it and arranged
too that she would be buried next to her mother when her
time came. Her father's grave was in his family's plot in a Pressburg cemetery, her two sisters were buried in Vienna, where
no doubt Willie would be put to rest one day. She and her
mother would lie side by side in Frankfurt.

Soon after her mother's death, Bertha Pappenheim's dark hair turned completely white, an outward sign of her shock at the irrevocable separation. She did not want to remain in the large apartment on *Leerbachstrasse* and, as her mother had moved when her father died, so she moved when her mother died. She found a smaller apartment on *Feldbergstrasse,* near the home of her cousin, Louise.

She moved the gloriously carved antique cabinets, including the black Biedermeier that once held her father's silver and gold goblets, to the new apartment. She also took along the canopied bed, with the year "1705" carved on its headboard together with a cross, the sun, and the letters "H.E.S.", standing for "Jesus" in Greek.

She took the paintings, the china, the bric-a-brac, the rare laces, all still pregnant with memories of her Viennese home.

7

The New Home

She was now free to travel as much as she wished without worrying about leaving a sick, old mother at home. A companion, even a woman who had served Goldschmidts for decades, was no substitute for one's own blood.

The year after her mother's death, she journeyed to the Russian border of Galicia to bring back to Frankfurt a group of children who had lost parents in the pogroms. The girls went to her Orphanage, the boys to another Jewish-supported institution.

But she was thinking of giving up her work as director of the Orphanage for a different, and to her mind more important, task.

Though still moved by the plight of young orphans, she was now even more deeply disturbed by the tragedy of the young unwed mother who had been deserted by her baby's father, or refused to marry him, or, because she was a prostitute did not know who was the father. There was no Jewish institution in Germany to care for such girls, though there were a number of Catholic and Protestant ones.

She wanted to protect Jewish girls from the traders who profited from the sale of their young bodies. She also wanted to help those who had become pregnant and would give birth to illegitimate children, but wished to live a moral life. She was no idealist, she did not believe all prostitutes wanted to marry and raise families. But she believed those who wanted education and moral training should be given the chance to get it so they would never again need to resort to a life of illicit sex.

She decided to build and direct an institution, since she now knew how to run one, where delinquent and feeble-minded girls on the road to prostitution could be educated and trained in work skills so they could avoid becoming prostitutes. It would also serve delinquent girls who had become prostitutes and were pregnant; they would have a place to give birth to their babies and live while they were educated and learned skills. Some could never become more than a maid or cook in a wealthy home but this was far more honorable than the life of a whore.

First she would have to resign as director of the Orphanage so she could spend all her time raising money and planning the new institution. She loved the little girls and would miss them, no child was ever a stranger to her. But she believed, as she wrote to a co-worker, "Who does not want children dries up the fountain; who educates his children badly pollutes the fountain." She had provided education for orphans. Now she wanted to educate young mothers who had gone astray and young girls in danger of going astray, so there would be fewer "orphans," illegitimate children to be brought up in orphanages.

She would not leave the Orphanage without a replacement. She went about finding one, discovering even as she did, that turning it over left her saddened. On November 21st, 1906, she wrote to Sophie Rosenthal, one of her "daughters," who had become a kindergarten teacher in Cologne: "A lady from Vienna arrived yesterday who may be my successor. You can understand how difficult it is to give up my beloved work when I am still at the peak of my ability. Come whatever will come, it is good-bye, and all the old furniture and laces will not help." Sophie would understand she was referring to the solace she received at times from her collection of rare laces and the richly carved antique furniture.

As Sophie grew up at the Orphanage, Bertha Pappenheim had given her guidance and affection. She would always care about this "daughter," and help her in every possible way. She wrote Sophie:

"I am glad you graduates know how much I am one with

you, that makes me very happy indeed. Life lies before you, it will bring you much. You can hope for everything, for the most beautiful things we women may experience. But for me, work and you children are my entire life, a life I had to conquer."

Sophie had written her complaining of added work—taking care of the boys in the morning—as well as teaching. Bertha Pappenheim advised: "It seems your work is not quite what we expected. You know I am not against work, not even against housework, held in so little esteem. But you are supposed to be a kindergarten teacher and for the other employees, too, this must be your position. Most of all you should live well, have enough time for yourself. . . ."

She concluded: "Enough—it may be that we will soon speak with each other, and if you know how to prime, I will be able to talk. Here are the children coming from school, and I have to give them milk."

She told her cousin Louise, with whom she discussed all her problems, that she was resigning as director of the Orphanage.

"I want to build a shelter for unwed Jewish mothers and their babies, where they can be educated and retrained, and also for delinquent and feeble-minded girls," she explained.

"Where will you get the money?" asked Louise.

"I'll donate some of my own and try to raise the rest from relatives and friends," she said. "Once the shelter is built, the Federation will pay the salaries of the staff and the board of girls who are not German citizens. The State will pay the board of girls committed by the German courts as streetwalkers or delinquents. Such government support will give the shelter official standing."

"I'll donate whatever you need to build it," Louise volunteered.

Bertha Pappenheim would never forget Louise's faith in her and her work, or Louise's willingness to talk to her at any time. She always felt welcome at her cousin's house. It was her second home, a place where she sought comfort now her mother was dead.

She looked for land on which to construct the new shelter and decided to buy two acres blooming with fruit trees and wild flowers on *Zeppelinstrasse,* a quiet street in a small town, six miles southeast of Frankfurt, called Isenburg, or Neu-Isenburg. It was about a half hour's twisting trolley ride from Frankfurt. She chose Isenburg rather than Frankfurt because Isenburg was in Hesse, a state of the German Reich that held a more liberal policy towards stateless girls and aliens than the state of Prussia, where Frankfurt was located.

She decided to call the shelter the Home for Wayward Girls and Illegitimate Babies. With an architect's help she planned two houses, three stories high, constructed in the same style as the private homes lining the street. The first house was to hold the dining room, kitchen, laundry, offices of director and staff, classrooms, recreational facilities, and bedrooms for unwed mothers, both those waiting to give birth and those who had had their babies in prison, where they had been committed for prostitution or delinquency.

The second house would shelter delinquent and feebleminded girls who had not as yet become prostitutes or criminals but were in danger of what she thought of as "falling into the habit of vice," infantile or morally inferior girls whose course in life was still uncertain. They tended toward what she had heard described as "moral insanity."

She believed that a quiet life which included education, work, and entertainment would counteract any tendency toward moral deterioration better than unforgiving harshness or hypocrisy or the boredom and complete absence of comfort usually found in state institutions. She wanted only women to staff the Home. She did not believe men had the special understanding necessary to work with delinquent girls. She also wanted women who would not feel superior to the so-called "fallen" girls, women who understood the power of the sexual drive, preferably married women, who would be neither too strict nor too lenient.

As at the Orphanage, conditions would be somewhat spartan. She did not provide central heating for many of the girls would never land in homes with this luxury, and they had to become accustomed to the life they would eventually lead. If they were spoiled now, their future lot would be more difficult. The girls would be expected to do the housework and help with the cooking.

Many homeless adolescents led an uprooted and promiscuous life. They had to be helped to learn self-control, to apply their own limits. Though boys' institutions permitted vacations for some of their trusted youngsters, she did not feel this policy should be applied to girls. It was not openly acknowledged, but it was vaguely implied that these vacations for boys gave silent approval to sexual sprees. If vacations were granted girls, the new morality learned at the Home would be flung to the winds. It was unfortunate but true, she thought, that because of the nature of things the girls are the ones who get hurt, the boys only derive pleasure from the experience.

She watched men pour the concrete and set the foundation, then saw walls, ceilings, and windows rise as the two houses of the Isenburg Home came into being, a shelter for lost and frightened young women.

She would take care of the girls and their babies, she would try to persuade each girl to marry the man who had made her pregnant, but if that were impossible and a young woman did not wish to keep her baby, the Home would help find adoptive or foster parents.

She made arrangements for the younger girls to attend school in Isenburg, a friendly community, and for a local doctor to serve the Home without fee. She also arranged for twenty medical specialists, most of them professors at the University of Frankfurt, some of whom she knew personally, to be consultants free of charge. They agreed to do so out of admiration and respect for her.

The day the doors of the Home officially opened, she felt the special thrill that stirs in the heart of anyone who has created something new. She planned to commute by streetcar from her apartment in Frankfurt though there was a room at the Home where she could sleep if she worked late or a baby needed care through the night.

She wrote Sophie, still unhappy in Cologne, "Don't worry if not everyone there understands what's right; do your duty, and listen to your conscience." Then realizing Sophie might be more comfortable at the new Home, she offered her a job, saying, "Isenburg is really a world in itself." She was delighted when Sophie promptly accepted. She paid Sophie's salary because at that moment the Federation was short of funds.

She had lost her spiritual home when her mother died, but she had found another home, one she built to shelter others who were homeless too.

8

The Third Little Bird

Within a year the Home was running smoothly, and she had more time for other activities, including a trip to America. In New York City she visited relatives, among them her cousin Felix Warburg, who had worked briefly for her grandfather's banking firm in Frankfurt. While in New York she toured Manhattan's Lower East Side, at the Henry Street Settlement discussed the problem of immigrants who had deserted their wives and children in Europe.

As the time came for her to sail back to Germany, she realized she admired much in America but could never feel at home there, her roots were now in Isenburg.

After her return to Germany, she resumed her duties as president of the Federation. Since one of its goals was to sponsor the training of social workers, she decided to investigate the situation in Galicia, where they were in particularly short supply.

On her way there, she stopped in Vienna to see her brother. As she sat in the parlor of his apartment looking over charts that traced their maternal ancestors back several centuries, she was intrigued to find herself related to Gluckel von Hameln, whose family had rescued oppressed Jews two centuries earlier and whose seven small books of *Memoirs* had gained a measure of literary fame.

When she returned to Frankfurt Bertha Pappenheim read the *Memoirs* carefully. She was fascinated by the parallels with her own life. Gluckel's father, like hers, had been a leader of the Jewish community. And, like herself, Gluckel knew Yiddish and was deeply concerned about the needy Jews of eastern Europe.

Born in Hamburg in 1646, Gluckel was three years old when the Cossack leader Bogdan Chmielnicki led a savage pogrom against the Jews of Poland and Russia. Tens of thousands were massacred and many more perished from starvation, disease, and exposure. Some managed to flee to Germany and found their way to Hamburg, where Gluckel's father housed ten who had caught a contagious disease and were refused treatment by hospitals. Gluckel and her grandmother, who insisted on visiting the sick refugees four times a day, caught the disease. The little girl recovered but her grandmother died.

Centuries before most women dreamed of careers, Gluckel was running businesses with her husband, including a stocking factory, trading in seed pearls, and conducting financial transactions in the Hamburg Exchange. She wrote the *Memoirs* after her husband died, "to stifle and banish the melancholy thoughts which came to me during many sleepless nights," and because she wanted her children to know "from whom you are descended."

Inspired by the life of her ancestor, Bertha Pappenheim decided to translate the *Memoirs* into German. Her brother encouraged her, offering to pay for the printing.

As she translated her ancestor's life, Bertha Pappenheim felt the centuries draw close. She lived with the heroic Gluckel through her dreams, her conflicts, her joys, her sorrows. She saw Gluckel as the three-year old girl falling dangerously ill, as the wife losing the husband she adored, as the widow marrying a rich man for comfort but finding only bankruptcy and distress, as the old lady spending the last years of her life with a married daughter.

Gluckel, who liked to wear several strands of coral or seed pearls around her neck, described how, when she sat for her portrait, she had worn a fur coat, lace cuffs, and a lace cap, the cap signifying she was a married woman. According to Orthodox Jewish custom, when a woman married she had to cut her hair and wear a wig or a cap.

Bertha Pappenheim thought of the daguerreotype she had seen of her mother as a young woman, her only adornment a lace collar, her long dark hair parted in the middle and swept behind her rather prominent ears to a bun in the back. Her mother, a member of an assimilated Jewish family, had been freed from the punitive Orthodox tradition of the wig or cap over a shaven head.

As Bertha Pappenheim translated her ancestor's memoirs she felt close to Gluckel in carrying on the family tradition of helping the poor and persecuted. She had not given birth to thirteen children of her own, as Gluckel had, but there were thousands of children in the world whose mothers had failed or abandoned them and who needed help.

She particularly liked a parable Gluckel related in the *Memoirs,* of a bird flying over a raging river during a severe storm, carrying his little birds one by one from their precarious nest to safety. As he flew with the first little bird, the parent-bird said, in mid-river, "You see how hard I struggle to carry you to safety. Will you do the same for me when I am old and weak?"

The little bird replied, "Of course, dear Father," whereupon the parent-bird dropped his baby into the swirling torrents below, saying, "A liar shouldn't be saved."

He did this to the second baby bird when it gave the same answer. But in reply to his parent's question, the third baby bird said, "Dear Father, I can't promise you that. But I promise to save my own little ones."

Bertha Pappenheim often told this story to colleagues and friends, laughing merrily. She enjoyed the honesty of the third little bird, an honesty that had saved its life. In her own way, she too was living a promise to save her own little ones.

9

The Journeys East

She was driven, almost fiercely, to inspire Jewish leaders of Eastern Europe to form a league to protect girls from white slavers. She visited a number of countries during 1911 and 1912 to ask the cooperation of these leaders. She also wanted to learn how white slavery operated and how extensive it was.

She had become somewhat of an authority on the rapidly growing problem. She gave a speech at the International Congress to Fight White Slave Traffic in London in 1910 and early in 1911 presented a report to the German National Committee Against White Slavery. She pointed out the existence of this very profitable but sordid "business" operated by wealthy Turkish Jews, a business the Jewish community would not expose because it feared repercussions. Some of the Federation board members, embarrassed by her revelations, predicted she would be sorry when there was retaliation against the Jews. Her answer was always the same: "To know of wrong and to remain quiet is to share the guilt."

She went to Greece, Turkey, Jerusalem and Egypt in 1911 to visit brothels, slums, and institutions that took care of humanity's wreckage. The following year she traveled to the part of Poland incorporated into Russia, then to Russia proper, then west to Galicia.

Along the way she wrote letters to a group of women on the board of the Federation and the Home whom she called her subscribers.

The Year 1911

March 9, Budapest:
She interviewed the secretary of the Burial Society, a very wealthy organization; she had once met him at a conference in London. "Do you have a women's committee set up to investigate white slavery?" she asked.

He answered, "God protect me, as long as *I* have anything at all to do with it, no woman will have any say in this organization."

"Have you no concern for young Jewish women who are exploited by the white slave traffic?"

"It is completely outside my duties."

A leading feminist of Budapest took her to meet the chief rabbi there, a tall gentleman dressed in Hungarian clerical garb. After keeping the two women waiting a long time, he finally allowed them to enter his office, then sat like a stone, she thought, saying not a word, turning his aristocratic profile to her as she explained her mission.

After describing the Jewish involvement in white slavery, she asked, "Will you help us organize a league in the interest of the individual girl and the entire Jewish community?"

"I'm not interested in such matters."

The feminist leader objected, "But you are chairman of the Society for the Protection of Children."

"Yes, but only children up to twelve or thirteen. Older ones are not my business."

Trying to restrain herself, Bertha Pappenheim struggled to speak quietly, "But—"

The head of the Jewish congregation of Budapest, raising his hand forbiddingly, interrupted, "I do not allow myself to be converted."

Once more she was hearing the traditional Orthodox Jewish attitude towards women as inferior creatures, the denial of the problem of white slavery, the refusal to be involved. It was infuriating, it was humiliating, it intensified her anger at Orthodox Jewry and at men—perpetrators and perpetuators of the crime of illicit sex, both those who used it for momentary physical release, giving no thought to the future of the baby that might be conceived as a result of that one moment of lust, and those who made fortunes by selling Jewish girls into white slavery.

April 2, Saloniki, Turkey:
The Secretary at one consulate said, "What do you care? The Jews sell their children like chickens!"

She visited a brothel. She had been told there were a number of unusually beautiful prostitutes in Saloniki. She met one, a twenty-one-year-old girl named Jolanthe whom she thought the most beautiful Jewish woman she had ever seen.

She felt deep sorrow that this lovely young girl was destined to such a fate. She could understand how a man might risk his marriage or his reputation to be with such a woman, but she could not understand how this strikingly exotic woman could sell her body in such sordid fashion. Of course, Jolanthe could not read or write, so there was no other way to earn her living. But she had a mother in Saloniki and how could a mother let her daughter demean herself so?

As she fell asleep that night, she thought she might dream of the beautiful Jolanthe. But instead, she dreamed that she wanted to melt down her rubbers because they felt too heavy. When she woke, she thought that her father would have scoffed, "Chalaumes!"—the Hebrew-German word for "dreams."

April 8, Constantinople:
She thought of her father again as she listened to music at a service in the Moschee of the Doves, an Islamic Temple. The melodies reminded her of those she had heard as a girl in the Viennese synagogue of which her father had been co-founder. Called the *Schiffschul,* the synagogue had been named in honor of a Viennese scholar, Schiff, who had lived two centuries before. She wondered what her father would think of his daughter visiting brothels, busy with pursuits for which he and her mother did not even know the words. Her father had wanted her to be "happy," which to him meant "married."

She visited the chief rabbi to discover how much he knew about the white slave market in Turkey. "Do you realize that there are Jews in Turkey who have become wealthy on their profits from white slavery?" she asked.

"Yes. There is even in this city a synagogue for the white slave traders where prostitutes purchase honors for their procurers," he told her.

"What do you mean?" She was puzzled.

"The white slave traders give money to the synagogue, for which they are honored. This money is earned by the Jewish girls who sell their bodies."

"Why don't you close this 'House of God'?" She could not keep the irony out of her voice.

"If we tell these merchants, 'We don't want your money, it's dirty,' our orphanages and our hospitals would close for lack of funds."

"What percentage of the girls in prostitution here are Jewish?" she asked.

"About ninety percent," he said.

"And what percentage of the dealers are Jews?"

"About ninety percent."

"And you can do nothing?"

"Nothing."

It was the same everywhere.

April 26, Aboard the Czarevitsch:

Because there were no railroads in Asia Minor, she had to sail around the Mediterranean to Jerusalem, where she was going to find out if white slavery existed and the extent of poverty.

She sat at the Captain's table on this Russian ship. The man assigned to the seat next to her, whom she thought of as a playboy from Prussia, asked her in a contentious tone, "Why are *you* taking this trip?"

"I'm hoping to establish a league to protect Jewish girls against white slavery," she explained. "This is one of the ways poor, uneducated girls are exploited—not only Jewish girls but Catholic and Protestant as well."

"Bah!" he sneered. "Feminist propaganda. That Helene Lange. Ought to be deported, putting such crazy ideas in the heads of women. Ought to ban publication of that sheet of hers. *The Woman.* It's an outrage!"

You are the outrage, she thought, and it would take a

Helene Lange to put you in your place. She said quietly, "It's about time women took action in their own behalf."

The man on the other side of her, a rather handsome, earnest, stolid man, bronzed as though he spent much time in the sun—as well he might, for he was an inspector of lighthouses—asked her, when he could get a word in, "Are you married?"

"No," she said, feeling amused, as she always did when people asked this, as though she were something of a freak to be single at fifty-two. She could have married, there were men over the years who had proposed, but she had felt no need to marry, her need was to help the persecuted and the exploited.

"It's not too late," the lighthouse inspector said gallantly. Then he asked, as though she might be eligible for him, "How old are you?"

"I'm fifty-two."

"I don't believe it!" He looked amazed.

"I have my birth certificate to prove it." She produced it from her purse.

He looked at her appraisingly. "You know, if you dyed your hair, you could pass for thirty."

"Thank you." She knew he meant this, she had been told her face looked remarkably youthful.

After dinner they talked, and she explained the purpose of her trip. He walked her to her stateroom but seemed reluctant to part. "I am bound for Beirut," he said. "Please leave with me when we get there tomorrow and stay until the next Russian boat arrives in about a week."

He added pleadingly, "I could show you a lot of depravity for your survey."

She laughed, said, "Thank you very much. But I have to go on to Jerusalem."

Alone in her stateroom, she mused that if she were not so utterly without practice and experience as far as men were concerned, and if she had not produced that birth certificate to prove her age, the trip might have had a sudden, romantic ending.

That night she had a puzzling dream. It started with her telling her mother she had tamed two small jackals. Her mother would not believe her, so she showed them to her. Though previously she was quite sure they were jackals, sud-

denly she saw two cats on the leash. She became very angry.
She pulled the leash. Then the cats turned into two men.
Whereupon her mother graciously asked them to sit down in
the dining room of her apartment on *Leerbachstrasse*.

When she woke, her stateroom seemed to smell of real
jackals. The ship itself reeked of goats and chickens, onions,
cheese, dirty laundry, seawater, fish raw and fried, tobacco,
and things she dared not define. That day, the day the inspector of lighthouses left the ship at Beirut, it rained endlessly.

May 4, Jerusalem:

She visited orphanages and hospitals and the founder of
Schaare Zedek Hospital, a German doctor, told her that in
Jerusalem the Jews were "morally pure," for piety and early
marriage were great protection against prostitution. He said he
had lived there for twenty years and knew of no illegitimate
children.

The scarcity of water seemed a problem; only rain water
was available for drinking. When someone complained about
the lack of street lights in a community, she said, "If the owner
of each home would hang out a lamp, the community would
be lit," thinking, My disastrous brain always has to breed plans.

She admired the buildings in Jerusalem and the warm cli-
mate, which she thought made poverty less painful than in
northern Europe. She told a woman from Galicia, who con-
stantly pointed out the incredible poverty of Jerusalem, that
everything in Jerusalem was better than Galicia, adding, "I
think you have plenty to do in your own country." She had
recently sent several of her "daughters" to Galicia as educators
and nurses, their salaries paid by Care by Women. There was
unbelievable ignorance, as well as poverty, in Galicia. When
she helped establish a Jewish hospital in Przemysl, she discovered that, as well as being poor, Galician women were incredibly ignorant in the ways of the rest of the world. She had
brought in two Jewish nurses from Frankfurt to train Galician
girls and had suggested the young students wear white uniforms similar to those of their teachers. The mothers, seeing
the uniforms, believed their daughters were being trained as
Catholic nuns and threw rocks at her as she walked down the
street.

At sunset one day she climbed the Mount of Olives, where she could see the city from one side and the mountains, the Dead Sea, and a sliver of Jordan from the other. On a tour conducted by an Arab guide, she went to the Wailing Wall, then wrote her subscribers:

"I am cured forever. What I saw was neither prayer nor devotion. Professional beggars fighting among themselves. Professional prayers I found, but nobody who was truly mourning the past. I saw anti-Semitic Germans with spiteful faces and Englishmen with Kodaks, and I wished that around this only authentic Jewish holy place there was a wide fence! . . . It is most interesting to have been in Jerusalem for a short time. Its landscape is very strange, wild and barren, but I do not want to live here forever, even as a social worker. If Frankfurt is the German Jerusalem, it seems to me Jerusalem is the Oriental Frankfurt."

She had met a woman who had opened a music school and commented to the subscribers, "It would be fine if all the Russian geniuses would come here instead of Germany."

Summing up her impressions of the Holy Land, she wrote, "Tomorrow I will leave the Holy City without tears and without hammering a nail into the stones of the Wailing Wall to ensure my return."

May 13, Jaffa:

She wrote her subscribers:

"Haifa and Jaffa, and no end, you will say. But I have forgotten to take notes on Haifa and I will catch up on this duty. The word 'duty' is one I like. It means a very good and necessary equivalent to my fantasy, which goes on at a galloping pace as if there were no duties. Duties which you have taken on of your own free will are laws you have given yourself and are no burden. What is for you 'duty', may be for me 'sacrifice', which to me means destruction of everything I do gladly out of a feeling of duty."

May 23, Alexandria:

She followed a police officer through the streets of Alexandria as people from many countries wearing a variety of costumes brushed by. The police officer turned into a narrow street, nodded in the direction of a drab, stone building, and said, "There's one." He pointed across the street to an equally dismal structure. "And there's another. This alley is full of them."

As they trudged onward into the dusk she welcomed the dark, for it brought a certain relief from the heat of the day.

The police officer, faithfully keeping his promise to show her the brothels of Alexandria, suddenly stopped in front of one grimy house and asked, "Would you like to go inside?"

"Yes, please." She had not traveled thousands of miles to stare at brothels from the outside.

In the darkness they slowly climbed narrow, dank stone steps to a flimsy wooden door. The police officer knocked. A woman's voice called out in Arabic, "Come in."

The police officer said to Bertha Pappenheim in English, "I will act as interpreter, since you don't speak Arabic and they don't speak English."

He opened the door, led her into a room kept cool by the stone floor. Delicately patterned blue drapes shaded the windows. In the center of the room sat three girls at a large round table above which hung a lamp. They were dressed in colorful gowns and shawls, strands of beads and coins encircled their necks.

She noticed that two of the girls seemed close friends, for each wore in her right ear one of a pair of earrings. These two were vivacious, like curious children. The third girl sat in silence, she seemed a stranger to the others.

The two lively girls gestured to her and the police officer to join them at the round table. There the five of them sat, the three colorfully dressed prostitutes with jewelry clinking, the kindly police officer, and she, investigator from a foreign country.

"What would you like to know?" the police officer asked her.

"How old they are, why they are prostitutes, and if they would have returned home if someone made it possible."

He asked each girl the three questions. Only the vivacious two answered. The third listened intently to his questions but did not reply.

The police officer turned to Bertha Pappenheim. "The two

girls who answered said they were sixteen years old and ran away from home out of boredom and love of adventure. If someone had been here to advise them when they arrived, they would gladly have returned home. They said they would have been received with open arms, especially if they brought back twenty francs. They think they would have married soon after."

"Thank you. What about the third girl?"

"She won't answer. I don't think she understands Arabic. I don't know where she comes from."

Bertha Pappenheim looked across the round table at the third girl, who sat quietly but with a certain dignity. Her bare arms, neck, and shoulders were deep bronze. Her face was immobile, the dark eyes looked haunted.

The police officer stood up to indicate that the visit was at an end. Bertha Pappenheim rose and shook hands with the two talkative girls. One of them spoke to her in Arabic.

"What did the girl say?" she asked the police officer.

"She said not to bother to shake hands with the third one. She doesn't count."

Bertha Pappenheim walked over to the girl with the haunted eyes and put out her hand. The girl hesitated, uncertain whether to respond, then timidly offered her own hand. A warm clasp was exchanged between the two women, the silent young whore from Alexandria and the fifty-two year old stranger from another continent.

As Bertha Pappenheim and the police officer started to leave the darkened room, the girl who had been silent suddenly stood up, tall and slim. She spoke a few words in Arabic, in a low, sweet voice, pointing at Bertha Pappenheim.

The police officer explained, as they groped their way down the dark stairs, "The tall girl pointed to you and said, 'She shall be blessed, and her family also, for no such woman has ever spoken thus to us.' "

Bertha Pappenheim shuddered and thought, This is a summons to, and an accusation of, the women of the world.

The Year 1912

May 4, Lodz:

A woman told her of "a place near the Russian-Galician border where Jews sell their children without any scruples."

She wrote in answer to a letter from her subscribers telling news of the Girls' Club in Frankfurt, "I am glad L. C. helps in the library, it is a good, healthy beginning in social work for her. How happy are present-day girls! I remember how difficult people made it for me at this age, trying to keep me from the way that was right for me."

She met the sister of a Polish rabbi and commented, "This woman is a true to life Gluckel von Hameln. It's wonderful how she talks, her faith, her common sense, her naiveté. . . . She asked about my mission and grasped with incredible speed what it is that I want to achieve. She looked at me doubtfully, with raised eyebrows, and said, 'So, a swallow wants to drain the sea?' "

May 10, Warsaw:

In a burst of frankness, alluding to some strong differences of opinion between several members of the Federation board and herself, she wrote the subscribers:

"The assurance by you that you think a great deal about me, that my absence seems much longer than it appears by the calendar, that at times I am missed by some of you, this is all very kindly said and felt . . . .

"I am necessary for nothing and to no one. This is not an accusation, probably it is all my own fault. It is a fact of my life, and it makes it easy for me to live like a nomad. Sometimes, it is true, I am homesick. But this is only a kind of longing for my apartment, my writing desk, my lamp, my funny silhouettes, my colored antique glasses and, most of all, my laces, the wonderful variety of creations made of a simple linen thread. If I were not an enemy of all poetic comparisons, believing such comparisons wrong, I would say our lives should also be made of such fine, true fabric, be of such weaving—sometimes simple, sometimes complicated, sometimes aesthetic, sometimes ethical. This is the only longing I have: to live such a life. I hate the clumsy fingers that disturb my beautiful planning and tear my threads or destroy them. I have often thought that if one has nothing to love, to hate something is a good substitute. . . . I believe it doesn't make any difference whether you are burned at the stake or whether you are the one who sets the fire, the important thing is to fight with true conviction."

May 24, Moscow:
     She felt happy just strolling along past the forty-times-forty churches, their brilliant gold and silver cupolas glinting in the bright sun. She had been invited to the home of a countess who ran night shelters for the city of Moscow on a grant of two million roubles from the government. Over the telephone, the Countess had offered to show her these shelters, as well as privately run ones that she wanted abolished because conditions in them were so sordid.
     The Countess lived in a house set somewhat back from the street. Bertha Pappenheim rang the bell. A man-servant opened the door, led her up wooden stairs covered with disheveled rugs, to a narrow hall crowded with trunks, and into a large room full of china cabinets, pictures, and furniture, old and new. She saw a large, modern desk with a phone, and thought, There is no better sign of the victory in the feminist movement than the disappearance of the ladies' desk. If she had to wait to see a woman—and she always had to—and there was a ladies' desk and furniture in slip-covers, she always discovered undeveloped female brains when the woman finally appeared.
     But here was a big, solid desk, and the Countess, who did not make her wait, proved to be a woman with a soft face, who dressed simply and did not speak German, only English and French.
     "I have no time for women's problems like the protection of prostitutes because I am too busy running the night shelters of Moscow." The Countess spoke frankly. "I will be glad to show them to you this evening. I suggest you wear an old, short skirt because of the vermin. Be here at seven, and I will drive us there."
     Bertha Pappenheim returned promptly at seven, and the two women set out in the Countess' car, talking on the way.
     The Countess said, "I have no sympathy for the feminists, nor for the Catholic league for the protection of girls, because the women active in these causes have an attitude different

from mine. I have respect only for people who live according
to their convictions."

Then she asked, "You're Jewish aren't you? The woman
who phoned me to ask if you could visit me had that unmistak-
able, disgusting Jewish accent." She added, "The Russians will
never integrate with Jews. They are completely different."

"Not integrating, but tolerating is the issue," said Bertha
Pappenheim, who felt anger but kept her voice low.

"Definitely not!" said the Countess. "I suppose one
might understand and pity the poor Jews of Wolhynia who live
so crowded together that they need religion to keep going.
But the wealthy and intelligent Jews are atheists and anar-
chists. I know of no Jew who is well off and still dedicated to
any ideal for which he would live and die, or sacrifice anything. Every Jew thinks only of his own benefit. Whereas we
Russians have an ideal, our people, the Mushik, for which we
live. We do everything to help our people."

"But Jews think the same way. They want to help their
people," Bertha Pappenheim said, thinking, the Countess
speaks with devastating fire and fury, she is typical of thousands who think as she does.

Then the Countess said, as though in apology, "I don't
mind, for once, meeting an individual Jewish woman. The
director of my shelter, a physician, is a Jew."

"Why a Jew?" asked Bertha Pappenheim.

"Because I could find no completely non-political physician, of whom the government would have approved, who
was not Jewish. And this Jew is a good doctor. He knows his
business and has no political leanings whatsoever."

Then, as though to retract her apology, the Countess
said, "But I find that in talking with Jews, a Christian—
whether Russian Orthodox, Catholic, or Protestant—soon arrives at the point where he can go no further, for Jewish ethics
and aesthetics are completely different."

"Christian ethics are Jewish as well," said Bertha Pappenheim.

"Never, never!" said the Countess heatedly.

Bertha Pappenheim thought she could never convince the
countess of the existence of Jewish ethics or idealism, and she
did have to admit that if one considered the ethics, the crook-

edness—yes, that was the word—of the Jewish race, she should keep silent, for there the Countess was correct. The Countess would never understand the tragic Jewish history, one of persecution and suffering, which hampered the honest facing of some moral issues.

The two women were both so violently angry by now that had they not been restrained by education and civilization, had they not been talking in a speeding car, but perhaps in a wilderness or a desert, they might have fought physically. As Bertha Pappenheim wrote to her subscribers, the Countess would have been victorious, perhaps spiritually as well as physically, for the Countess, her enemy, was right—the Russians worked for the betterment of their people while the Jews merely watched "the demoralization, annihilation, and the destruction of their people with a happy grin."

The Countess drove to the building she had erected with the two million roubles, the night shelter of the Moscow community. Its three floors could accommodate fifteen hundred people on wooden cots in large heated rooms. There were about three hundred women and girls among the men. The Countess told her that peasants flocked to Moscow and other large cities looking for work, and the government built this shelter to house them until they found jobs, wanting to protect them from the privately run shelters where hooligans robbed the men and raped the women. The nightly rent at the government shelter was five kopeks. Good, inexpensive food and tea were sold. No alcohol was available.

But the lack of alcohol on the premises did not keep the guests from getting it elsewhere. As the Countess and she stood on the staircase, a drunken man was dragged down it by two guards.

Bertha Pappenheim asked, "Don't you try to combat alcoholism?"

"No, that's not in our line," said the Countess.

"Would you let an organization distribute anti-alcohol propaganda leaflets?"

"I would not object," said the Countess. "But it's not my job. I concentrate only on the shelter."

Bertha Pappenheim conceded that the shelter made a good impression. Its worst feature was the presence of ama-

teur prostitutes, who obviously slept with a number of the
men. No one took care of the children and minors. The
countess told her, "That's the business of individual case
workers from the organizations I don't think much of—
suffragettes, women's groups, and the like."

Giving credit to what the Countess had achieved, Bertha
Pappenheim said, "You are proof of how well a woman can
work."

"I am doing a man's work as a member of the community," stated the Countess.

"True," said Bertha Pappenheim, thinking the Countess
could do much more if only she were interested in the education of children and adults.

The Countess then drove to the sordid shelters she wanted to eliminate, large houses of two to three floors in the worst
neighborhoods of Moscow, operated by the owner at a profit
of sixty percent. Bertha Pappenheim thought of Gorki's *Lower
Depths* as she heard drunken men and women scream at each
other and shriek with obscene laughter. She was pushed ag-
gressively, she inhaled the foul air, she saw bodies dumped in
heaps in the basement, the bodies of those killed in the fights
that waged through the night.

As they left one of the houses, they almost stepped on a
drunken girl lying in the street. She looked about fourteen
years old. Bertha Pappenheim asked the Countess, "Can't
you help this child?"

"No," said the Countess. "And even if I could, it would
be too late."

Bertha Pappenheim thought, It would be better if this
child never woke up.

May 30, Lemberg, Galicia:
    She wrote her subscribers:
    "Today I met the head of the art gallery, Mrs. D., painter,
feminist, friend of the late poetess Konognitzka. A gray, interesting man's head—most sympathetic. Funny, I think I disappointed her—she had expected a big, strong, black person,
and met a slim, small, white one."

June 12, Stanislaw, Galicia:

She had watched certain changes in Galicia over the past ten years, at least in the larger cities. Houses were now three and four stories high, one even planned running water. Quite a few people had gold-filled teeth. The children of the poor wanted shoes and the children of the rich wanted to go bare-foot or wear sandals, believing this fashionable.

She thought, All this is a sign of progress but what does it achieve if the moral level is not raised? Her fight to start a league to protect innocent girls from white slavery was, she sensed, a lost cause.

10

The Great War

February 27th, 1914, was her fifty-fifth birthday. She had lived five years past the half-century mark, and though she did not feel old, for the first time in her life she was slowed down by the aches of her body.

She was starting to dislike cold weather, which formerly had invigorated her. Now the cold caused rheumatic pains. There were times she felt out of breath when she climbed stairs, and she wondered if she had a weak heart. But worst of all, every so often a sharp pain would stab her in the abdomen.

Her personal physician gave her a complete physical examination and told her the acute pains were caused by her gall bladder but the condition was not sufficiently serious to warrant an operation.

But no matter how ill she felt, thoughts always flowed through her mind in an unending stream, and following her last visit to Galicia on the way home from Moscow, she wrote another pamphlet about the province. This was entitled *Struggles*. It described the latest Russian pogroms and the opposition to refugees in Western Europe.

She further dramatized the situation in a trilogy of plays, *Tragic Incidents*. This she wrote for the girls at the Home to present as a drama project. She put into the plays her feelings about Zionism, crystallized after her visit to Jerusalem, as a young Jew in the play says to his father:

"With a thousand threads I feel bound to the culture that

has grown and has been inherited through centuries in Western Europe, the culture that has resulted from the collaboration of Christians and Jews. I need the books, the paintings, the stage, the newspapers, the struggle between opinions and interests, urban industry with its technical facilities. I cannot play the role of a peasant . . . . I cannot, father."

But all thoughts of Judeo-Christian cultural development fled upon the emotional shock of June 28th, 1914. One of the staff rushed into her office to report in a tone of horror that Archduke Franz Ferdinand, heir to the throne of Austria, had been assassinated in Bosnia. By August 4th, the leading nations of Europe, entangled in the intricate webs of their alliances, were at war with each other.

Running the Home had become more complicated. The two acres now held five buildings. A house stood in each corner of the rectangular lot and the fifth rose along the rear border.

The third house had been constructed for children under six. Upon reaching six, girls were transferred to the fourth house, where they could stay until they were sixteen, and boys were sent to an institution in Frankfurt. The fifth building, a small one, held living quarters for the staff and an "isolation station" for the treatment of children with high fevers, bad colds or contagious diseases.

It was fortunate that the Home could provide its own vegetables and fruit, for as the war progressed, she found it more and more difficult to get food. Meat became a luxury. Most staples were ersatz, and the children complained of the taste. She had to keep up a steady appeal to the wealthy Jews in Frankfurt to donate any flour and sugar they could spare.

Soldiers might die by the thousands but children still had to be fed. No child at the Home starved, but there were days when she knew, as she looked at the wistful young faces in the dining room, that nothing would have made them happier than a second piece of bread or a second helping of gelatin.

One day a three-year-old boy got up from his chair, slowly walked over to her. He stood by her side, his eyes fastened hungrily on a potato she had not as yet eaten.

She stood up, her plate in her right hand, led him by her left hand to his seat at another table. There she transferred the potato from her plate to his empty one.

She would have traded all the potatoes she had ever eaten for his shy smile of gratitude.

She had finally allowed the installation of central heating, but the scarcity of fuel now made heat an academic question. Household supplies became scarce, pots and pans were used until the bottoms wore out, and the sheets had been mended so often they contained more patches than original fabric.

She had been elected to the board of the German Federation of Women's Organizations, which meant she was now both director of the Jewish Federation and on the board of the liberal, feminist organization to which the Jewish and Protestant federations belonged. All the national women's organizations cooperated in the war effort.

She wrote Sophie, "Care for the poor Jews and certain branches of war welfare work take all my time, and I forget my somewhat miserable body. Today I ordered myself to bed because it is Saturday, but I'm not very relaxed. I am thinking of the many thousands of soldiers in the field or, if seriously wounded, in bad need of help."

She urged Sophie, who had resigned from a social work job in Galicia to serve the Berlin Organization of Jewish Nurses, to remain a nurse, saying, "Nobody will insist you return to Galicia while there is still war." She told her Helene Kramer had left her institution in Galicia when it closed, and that other of her "daughters" serving with the Red Cross had not been heard from in months. She ended the letter: "But all individual stories are of no importance, we have to remember all people."

Three months later, on December 8th, she wrote to Sophie, who was thinking of offering her services to the Red Cross, that while she could not "forbid" Sophie to do this, she believed that since Sophie had been trained by the Berlin Organization of Jewish Nurses, she should stay with that organization. She warned, "You know you are prone to asthma attacks and will be no good in a field hospital. If one knows he has a weak spot, it is egotistical to take a job where one will very possibly fail . . . . I can understand that under the influence of the loss of your brother you are very upset and may decide things which are not right. I want to keep you from

doing this, in my old motherly loyalty. I believe I can understand you, but I cannot agree with your plans."

She was saddened by the sight of the Girls' Club, which
had moved from its original small quarters at *Fahrgasse* 146 to
more spacious ones. The new rooms had fallen in disarray
because the landlord failed to keep up the premises, which
served a double function since he rented them as offices during the day. The flowered wallpaper was torn, the walls themselves were covered by ugly file cabinets hiding the fine paintings donated by Frankfurt artists, and knobs were missing from
most of the doors. But the books were still stacked on the
library shelves and the evening lectures were as always well attended.

The Federation was asked to help in the care of young
women brought to Germany as part of an imported labor
force. They came from areas that had once been Polish and in
which the number of Jewish unemployed mounted as the Germans ruthlessly destroyed the industrial plants. Since Germany
lacked workers to replace men who had gone into the Army, it
started to import labor for war industry, though this was
against international law. Unemployed, starving Jews were
eager to accept this recruitment, it meant escape from the
forced labor imposed on them in the occupied zones. They
had to sign up for "the duration of the war," and once in Germany there was no return, anyone leaving his assigned place of
work was hunted by the police.

Bertha Pappenheim wrote Sophie on August 18th, 1917:

"In the next few days at Griesheim and Hoechst, about
two hundred to three hundred Russian Jewish girls are expected as munition workers. They are supposed to live in two bar-
racks—at present we know of only one. Care by Women will
look after these girls in a friendly but strict way and we need
somebody who understands their language, Yiddish, and their
ways. We may have Johanna Stahl [Johanna Adler had married]
for some of the girls (she arrived here in good health some
time ago) and for the others I would like to suggest you. This,
of course, will be a really well-paid job. I believe we have a
right to ask you, because it doesn't make any difference
whether you go to Eastern Europe or whether, unfortunately,

as it is now doing, Eastern Europe comes to Germany . . . With common sense and good will we will learn how to supervise these girls without hurting their selfrespect . . . ."

Sophie did not accept the offer, and Bertha Pappenheim, for the first time that she could remember, felt displeased with one of her daughters. But she did not relay this feeling to Sophie and when she heard that Sophie had other offers she wrote that she was glad to hear this and would do nothing to hinder Sophie's progress.

But she was aware that she was sometimes possessed by moods of disillusionment, though she refused to give in to them for long. She insisted that the women on her staff and boards rise above their "moods" and physical ailments, and she required the same of herself.

The bitterness she felt inside often took the outward form of irony. When Martin Buber, following a conversation in which she told him she was looking for interesting topics, sent her one of his books to discuss with the staff, she wrote him on May 17th, 1918, that she could not discuss the book because "Just as I do not understand much of it, the girls, too, would not understand and I would not be able to answer their questions." She added, "I imagine it would be even worse if one of the young girls did understand it!"

She thanked him, saying, "Maybe you will have a . . . dissenting smile for my remarks. Anyway, I owe you many thanks for your book. I am grateful to every one who offers me food for thought."

Not long after, she met Martin Buber on the street. It was raining and they stood under her umbrella and talked about the book as the rain streamed down.

"You use such complicated words," she complained. "I do not understand the use of big words for such obvious concepts. They are words thousands of Jewish women like me do not know."

He smiled, tolerantly, she thought, and she went on, "I miss something in your book. Something has not been explained about Jewish social work philosophy. You do not stress compassion enough."

She knew she could be candid with him and they would

always be friends. They had been through much together, as Germans, as Jews, as planners.

On November 11th, 1918, the Great War, as it was known in Europe, came to an end. She hoped she could once again devote all her time to those she had chosen to help.

11

The Celebration

It was December 23, 1919. She was alone in her apartment on *Feldbergstrasse*. The Great War had been over for more than a year and her health had been declining steadily, as well as her money. Most Jews had put their money in investments and banking and lost fortunes in the nightmare of runaway inflation that followed the war. The needs of the poor could no longer be met by wealthy German Jews, who could hardly survive themselves.

Fuel was extremely scarce, as it had been for five years, but because it was Chanukah she decided to use more charcoal than usual—enough to start a small fire in her stove. It soon heated the room, not really enough to keep her warm but enough for a Chanukah celebration. She pretended the stove was the Pappenheim family fireplace, and she stood in front of it warming her hands at the flames, as she had done so often at Chanukah when she was a girl in Vienna.

The lamp on the table in front of the antique couch glowed gently. The yellow vase next to it sparkled like precious amber. The bouquet of real flowers was wilted, but she did not care, wilted fresh flowers were preferable to artificial flowers which she detested.

She gave in to what she considered an economically criminal urge to light three of the electric candles on her big brass lamp. The candles were very small and it was the last eve of Chanukah.

She walked over to her desk intending to write a letter to her subscribers, the intimate group of women who seemed to enjoy knowing her thoughts. She took out paper and pen.

But before she put down a word, she looked with pleasure around the softly lit room, enjoying the memories it stirred. One wall, its gray broken into squares framed with delicate black woodwork, provided a serene background to what she called her beloved junk collection, small miniatures displayed in a little cabinet lined with red velvet. They were not the fragile miniatures connoisseurs would envy, they were rather ugly, but she loved them, particularly the tiny baby dressed in old-fashioned swaddling clothes.

She turned to the wall at her right, decorated with small silhouettes, Daumier-style caricatures of political figures. She did not know who had cut them out but she admired the artist who could bring a piece of black paper to life. The little figures in their small frames had a personality all their own, they were full of dignity and earnestness.

She laughed as she looked at the blue wooden clock with the carved eagle atop. It had stopped years ago, perhaps it had never worked, but its color matched the pastel blue background of the manor house in white silhouette beside it.

Presiding above the blue clock and white manor house hung a painting of Maria Theresa, Empress of Austria from 1740 to 1780. Bertha Pappenheim felt herself more tolerant than this imperial anti-Semite in her stays and court dress, for she had flanked Maria Theresa with portraits of two priests to save her soul. And out of the same ironic compassion she had placed a painting of six elegant Viennese girls close to the portrait of the Emperor Franz Josef as a young man. As her eyes rested on the painting of the six Viennese girls, she thought of her old home in Vienna, a city once so gay, now full of cold and hungry people like the rest of Europe.

Her eyes turned to a painting of Mary Wollstonecraft, a woman of courage, which she had placed to watch over the funny cherubs sculpted by Pestacowski. The portrait of Mary Wollstonecraft recalled the years of her feminist zeal, she felt pleasure in the knowledge that German women had at last been given the vote.

She looked at the beautiful carved chest loaned by her

dear cousin Louise, and thought, Beauty belongs to all; it may give joy for generations when shaped in precious material. The color and grain of the wood were exquisite. But common materials could also be precious, she had some iron necklaces and brooches that had been artistically forged into graceful patterns. The result was a combination of charm and strength. She wished women might combine these qualities, usually believed to be opposites, then thought how Mary Wollstonecraft had united them harmoniously.

Her eyes wandered to the bell-pull with its parrots embroidered in beads. She admired and envied the woman who had time enough for such elaborate embroidery. Above the couch she had placed more bric-a-brac, including an oddly shaped piece of beeswax. She was not sure what it represented but it was close to her heart even though no one else might like it.

And last, but most important—the black cabinet that once held her father's collection of silver and gold goblets. Ever since childhood the cabinet had over-awed her, but now it was her "comforter." It stood empty. For the last three years she had not had the time, energy or leisure to place her many china knick-knacks in it, where she could have touched them fondly every so often. She used the fear of bombings as an excuse, but it was a silly one.

And how sad, she thought, that for five years she had not seen her laces, her greatest treasure, creations of feminine artistry, taste, and culture. Fearing they might be destroyed, she had stored them in a vault. She planned eventually to bequeath them to the Viennese Museum for Arts and Crafts where she would go to catalogue them. She sighed, wondering when that would be.

Then she took up the pen, to write her subscribers about her private Chanukah celebration. She ended the letter:

"What longing one can have for dead things. Maybe because my life has left me lonely."

The fire in the stove had gone out. She extinguished the three candles in the brass lamp. It was time to bury memories, the tasks of the present were overwhelming enough.

12

The Aftermath

One night she slept in the bedroom that was hers whenever she wished to stay at the Home. She had to leave Isenburg at 7:30 the next morning on a mission to Crumstadt, some twenty miles to the south.

Crumstadt was a small Jewish settlement of sixteen families, with six children, three of school age—a dying community, in which nevertheless the Home had managed to place several children with foster parents. One placement had not worked out, and she was going there to bring back a little girl, Irmchen Weingart. The foster father, a man named Gruenebaum, was reported to be mistreating his wife.

There had never been a rail connection between Isenburg and Crumstadt, and the trip, usually taking a few hours, involved going northwest to Frankfurt and then south to Crumstadt. Her visit had been arranged in advance, several families knew she was coming, including the Bergens, who had a foster child, Arthur, and the Bruchfelds, in whose hardware store sixteen-year old Lina, a former charge of the Home, had been working for a three-week trial period.

Before the war Isenburg boasted a train that went to Frankfurt, or rather, as far as the border of the state of Prussia, from which a short trolley ride took one into the city. But the French, who now occupied the industrial Ruhr Valley, had taken over all trains, not permitting any to go beyond the border of the occupied zone. Isenburg was outside the oc-

127

cupied zone, its former railroad station had become a shack in the woods.

She first had to decide how to travel the six miles from Isenburg to Frankfurt, then from Frankfurt she could go on foot to the nearest railroad station in the occupied zone. From there she would take a train south to Pfungstadt, the nearest station to Crumstadt. Mr. Bergen, a teacher, had said he would meet her with a car at Pfungstadt, drive her back to where she would pick up Irmchen, then drive her back to Pfungstadt so she could return to Isenburg that evening. The Gruenebaum family had been alerted and were expected to have Irmchen ready.

She left the Home promptly at 7:30, taking with her only a briefcase containing a newspaper and some articles from journals she wanted to read. She had a companion as far as Frankfurt, a three-year old girl named Emmy, who was on her way to a foster home in Holland, accompanied by a young helper. They had to walk about a mile through the woods to a car waiting to drive them to Frankfurt. One of the local men who did repair work at the Home had offered his car if they would meet him at the end of the path.

The weather was dreadful that November morning, snow mixed with rain. They had the choice of walking through underbrush, roots, holes, and fallen leaves, or taking a longer but smoother path. She selected the longer path because little Emmy had to be wheeled in a baby buggy—its lack of tires or a hood accounted for the Home having received it as a gift. Little Emmy seemed to enjoy the bumpy ride as the young helper pushed, and Bertha Pappenheim pulled over the worst spots.

Her shoes were soaked and she thought ruefully that rubber soles serve no purpose if water pours over the top of the shoes. Whenever she or her charges had to take this path at dawn or dusk, she wished Poincaré, the Premier of France, were forced to walk with them. They finally reached the path's end and heaved a delighted Emmy into the waiting car. The driver took the dignified old woman's arm saying, "With a few hops you'll get in, too, Granny!"

At Frankfurt she said goodbye to Emmy and the young helper and continued on her way, an hour's walk to a station where she could catch the train to Pfungstadt. She was cold when she boarded the train and even colder on it, for no heat reached the car in which she sat. As she rode, she realized that the faces in the fourth class car epitomized living conditions in post-war Germany, tired, worn, angry faces. All the talk was about inflation. "We slave away, but we earn nothing at all. All those millions of marks buy nothing, a loaf of bread costs 600 billion marks."

She sat next to a pale and sickly woman, who jumped up and repeated in a desperate voice, "Six hundred billion!"

They complained about young folks who earned money but wouldn't help their parents, who used the money for cigarettes and sheer stockings. They complained about peasants who hid potatoes and fed them to livestock or sold them for dollars.

She expected venomous remarks about Jews but heard none. These people seemed too preoccupied with their own problems to hurl anti-Semitic invectives.

She knew how much misery the downfall of Germany had added to the plight of the East European Jews as law and order collapsed. There had been a revolution which, after short-lived success, ended with the murder of many of its leaders, including Kurt Eisner, Rosa Luxemburg, and Gustav Landauer, all Jews. Returning soldiers, embittered by defeat, were very susceptible to anti-Semitism, especially when they found their former jobs held by Jews.

The dismissal of forced labor imported from other countries added to the chaos. The newly founded states of Poland, Lithuania, Latvia and Estonia did not welcome the masses of returning Jews. Many Jews did not want to go back to home towns destroyed or devastated by war. The number of foreign Jews in Germany at the end of the war included about 90,000 from eastern Europe who had lived in Germany before 1914, about 35,000 from Russia and Poland imported as forced labor, and another 35,000 prisoners and civilians interned during the war—a total of 160,000. They were joined by refugees fleeing the pogroms raging throughout eastern Europe, trying to find refuge in a country shattered by defeat and revolution. Actually there had been an influx of fewer than 100,000 Jews since 1914 into a country of more than 63,000,000.

When Bertha Pappenheim changed trains at Darmstadt for

Pfungstadt, she did not find the occupants of the second train as restrained as the first. The "parlor" car, fourth class, was jammed. The seats ran the length of the car and men and women huddled on the floor in the center corridor. As she entered a laborer stood up to offer her his seat.

She soon realized that a red-haired Galician Jew sitting in the center was the target of angry taunts. He was a peddler of material; two large packages, apparently bolts of cloth, lay on the floor next to him and a yardstick was pushed into one of his boots. He was being assaulted by violently hostile words. His answers, in Yiddish, drew angry laughter.

One man, who seemed the ringleader, demanded of the group, "What did we pay for potatoes in peacetime?"

"Three marks for a hundred pounds!" A chorus.

"What did we pay for material for aprons?"

"Eighty pfennigs," roared the chorus.

"And this dirty Jew today asks one hundred pounds of potatoes for one meter of apron cloth!"

A roar of anger. A woman cried out, "But Junghans asks just as much!" Junghans, another peddler, was not a Jew.

"He's even worse than a Jew," yelled a second woman.

"You should be strung up!" This shriek from a third woman was directed at the Galician Jew.

"All of them should be strung up. A stone round their neck, dumped into a river, all the *Mischpoche!*"

Then another burst of angry laughter. There was a certain humor underlying this tragic scene, she thought; it was a coarse joke which could easily turn ugly if touched off by something in the atmosphere, a drop of alcohol, for example.

She left the train at Pfungstadt, where the teacher Bergen was supposed to meet her with a car. But there was no sign of Bergen or his car; the station was quite deserted. She waited a while in the sharp wind, then decided to walk to Crumstadt. She asked a man for directions. He said it was a two-and-a-half-hour walk and advised her against it, looking at her as though she would never make it, underestimating her strength.

But she took his advice and decided to phone the Bergens from the station. The phone did not work. It was then fifteen minutes past noon.

"Are there any Jews in Pfungstadt?" she asked a kindly looking woman.

"Plenty," the woman said. "Blum lives nearby." She pointed to a store down the street. "That's his. He lives behind it."

Bertha Pappenheim walked to the Blum General Store. It was locked. She crossed a yard to the rear, and finding a mezuzah on the back door she felt reassured.

She knocked and a young woman opened the door, wearing an impressive wig—obviously still a slave to the Orthodox custom that forced women to cut their hair and wear wig or cap when they married. Bertha Pappenheim resented this, as she did all exploitation of Jewish women by men. She had written as one of her "Memoranda" half a year before, on April 8th, 1923: "If there will be justice in the world to come, women will be lawgivers, and men have to have babies. Will Saint Peter keep his job?"

The young woman, realizing the stranger standing in the yard looked very cold, took her at once to a heated room where the family had gathered for lunch. Bertha Pappenheim introduced herself and explained why she was there. As so frequently happened when she met a stranger, the grandmother remembered her as director when her late husband's sister-in-law's cousin lived at the Orphanage. The young wife had met her in Cassel, a town in Germany where the Federation once held a conference. Looking at the family's youngest child she thought, ironically, that little flower in the baby buggy does not know me yet, otherwise it would not be sucking its thumb so happily.

In five minutes a plate of hot vegetable soup was placed before her, and a phone call was made to Max Bruchfeld III at Crumstadt in his hardware store to find out why teacher Bergen had not appeared. Mr. Bruchfeld explained that the French no longer permitted anyone to meet trains and suggested she board the mail coach leaving at four o'clock for Crumstadt, where Mr. Bergen would meet her.

She had several hours wait, so she explored the Blum General Store, asking about pots and pans for the Home. "So many of ours are bottomless," she explained.

"There's a plant here in Pfungstadt that makes enamel pots," said one of the Blums. "Why don't you call the Jewish partner, Kaatz?"

She dialed the number given her, introduced herself, and asked, "Are you the Mr. Kaatz who has an aunt and a sister in Kattowitz?"

"Yes," he said.

"And is your brother-in-law Councillor Wiener?"—a man she knew who also lived in Upper Silesia.

"Of course! Please come over."

She thanked the Blums for their hospitality and walked to the plant where Kaatz, a genial man, promised he would try to get her cheap or second-hand pots and dishes for the Home. He made her a gift of a rug to keep her warm the rest of the trip. She thought, Bless him whose kindness offsets my carelessness. She thanked him. She was beginning to wish she had had the foresight to have put on a sweater or two under the military coat she was wearing; it was stiff and heavy but not very warm.

She walked to the inn to wait for the mail coach. There she saw the red-haired peddler who had been the target of abuse on the train. He sat in silence for a few moments, then left. Several Germans who were drinking beer spoke about him in the same derogatory way as before.

One sneered, "Jews who exploit Germany's poverty should be treated the way they say in Munich and Bavaria." The nucleus of Hitler's Nazi party was making no secret of its hatred of Jews.

She remained silent, thinking herself a coward not to defend the Jews, having twice that day heard vicious attacks, but also realizing that there was no hope of convincing any of these bitter people in the few minutes she had.

She recalled a prayer she had composed:

"Time, ancient and revered source of help and of healing, Thou hast built and bestowed upon me so much; brought to life the heritage of my ancestors, which has enriched my life, has revealed to me the pulsating filaments which bind together the very essence of life. Time, thou all kindly time, confer upon me at the ripeness of old age, mildness."

Mildness was of little use in combatting the hatred she saw around her, but she did not know how to fight it; words were of no avail.

She stood at the window of the inn waiting for the mail coach to arrive. Finally someone told her the open cart with the sorry-looking nag standing outside the inn was the mail coach. Mail was now carried in a potato cart, drawn by whatever horse could stand on its uncertain feet. The French had confiscated all the healthy horses.

It was four-thirty in the afternoon as she climbed into the cart, after paying a fare of 1 billion marks. She sat down on the board that served as a seat, shivered, tried to wrap herself into kindly Mr. Kaatz' rug. Then the red-haired peddler climbed in and sat next to her. Soon the driver appeared, seized the reins, and the nag started to jog slowly away from the inn.

Darkness closed in; the landscape looked grim. The wind was icy, and a freezing rain began to fall. The three passengers were joined by a fourth, picked up along the way.

She noticed the red-haired Jew wore odd glasses; his eyes seemed too large for a face that was rather vacant. She wanted to question him about the price of potatoes and aprons, needing both for the Home, but did not dare because she thought the two Aryans might turn on him.

Instead she asked in a low voice, "Did you feel badly about what happened this morning on the train?"

"No, I'm used to it," he said.

"What is your name?"

"Kupfermann, from Frankfurt."

"Do you live in Stadelhof?" A slum area of Frankfurt.

"Yes."

"I've heard of a Mr. Kupfermann in Frankfurt who has a sick wife who underwent surgery a few days ago, and three small children," she said.

"That's me." His large eyes showed his distress.

As they drove along quietly in the dark and cold, she noticed that her and her companion's eyes watered but not those of the Aryans. She made a mental note of this, wondering if it was a racial characteristic. After a ride of almost two hours, the cart suddenly stopped.

She heard someone call out, "Miss Pappenheim!"

They had arrived in occupied Crumstadt. She climbed down from the cart and into the welcoming arms of teacher Bergen, while the carriage sped on its way, taking the persecuted peddler with it.

"Do you want to take a detour to my house or climb over a wall?" Berger asked.

"Let's climb the wall." Anything to get out of the icy cold.

Within minutes she was warming herself in the living room of the Bergen home. Mrs. Bergen was excited at meeting a very prominent guest, though Bertha Pappenheim thought she must be a rather pitiful sight after the long, cold ride.

Mrs. Bergen set the table with her best china. Supper was noodle soup with meat; Bertha Pappenheim set aside the meat for them to use later, aware there was a sick grandmother in the house. She had brought little Arthur a slate as a gift from a worker he had known at the Home, and he happily unwrapped it.

"Where will I spend the night?" she asked. It was obviously too late for her to pick up Irmchen.

Mr. Bergen smiled. "The Bergens and the Bruchfelds tossed dice for you, and the Bergens won."

"I'm glad." She felt at ease with them.

"You'll have to sleep on the couch, if you don't mind," he said.

"I could sleep on a rock tonight." She was so exhausted she wanted to go to bed that very moment, but the Bergens talked on and on.

Finally Mr. Bergen stood up and said, "We'd better let you sleep. Don't worry about Irmchen. Gruenebaum will not dare refuse to let her go."

"I don't think he will, either," she said.

But it was hard to imagine what a man who was reported to have beaten his wife two days before she was to have a baby was capable of doing. It was certain, however, that Irmchen could not remain with such an unstable foster parent.

"One must love a child to keep it these days," Mr. Bergen had said. "Your Frankfurt office pays so little and so late for foster care."

He was right; money was not available. She wished she owned a Jewish mint; then she could print endless money to pay foster parents and to see that children in institutions lived just as well as the French were living in Germany.

Before she went to sleep, still cold, she thought of a way to keep warm that she wanted to try out in the morning to see if it worked. When she woke, she took the newspaper she had brought with her and, fashioning a vest, placed it underneath her dress. She felt warmer, even though the stuffing did not protect her lower limbs. She intended to recommend it to her friends who liked winter sports; unfortunately those who lived in the occupied zone could not take advantage of this idea because no newspapers were allowed.

Mrs. Bergen served her ersatz but tasty coffee, delicious homemade bread and jam. She refused the pat of butter and the cream that Mrs. Bergen proudly offered, knowing the family would need it.

Little Arthur, seeing the butter and cream, asked his foster mother, "What holiday is it?"

Mrs. Bergen pointed at Bertha Pappenheim. "Our guest is the holiday."

She felt honored and resolved to be worthy of the tribute.

Before Mr. Bergen left to teach in a neighboring community, he told her where the Gruenebaums lived and where Bruchfeld's hardware store was located. She thanked the Bergens for their kindness, clasped her rug and briefcase under her arm, and walked to the Gruenebaum home.

She knocked on the door. A stocky man opened it, obviously Gruenebaum. She said, "I'm from the Home at Isenburg. I've come to get Irmchen."

He grunted, then led her inside but did not ask her to sit down. There was no sign of Mrs. Gruenebaum; she was probably still in bed recovering from the beating, Bertha Pappenheim thought, and wondered where the baby was and whether it had lived.

"Got any dough?" Gruenebaum's tone was as sullen as his face.

"No." She realized he was owed several weeks pay for foster care.

He stared at her for a minute, then shrugged his shoulders, as if giving up. "You can have it. It has nothing to wear anyway." He did not even dignify Irmchen with a "she."

Little Irmchen walked in, a smile on her face, carrying a large cottage cheese sandwich and apples for the trip and a small cardboard box bearing her few belongings. She announced happily to the room at large, "I will never come back here."

"How is your wife?" Bertha Pappenheim asked Gruene-baum, trying to keep up amenities.

He nodded at a closed door to the rear of the room, muttering, "She's in bed." He said no more, not even goodbye.

She and Irmchen walked out of the house and over to the Bruchfeld store to see Lina, who greeted them cheerfully. Her cheeks looked plump, as though she had been eating well, and she said happily, "There's everything to be had here." The hardware store sold items only for French money or for grain and potatoes as barter.

"Do you think I should stay?" Lina asked.

"As you say, there's everything here," she replied, thinking, Everything except an inside toilet.

The Bruchfelds invited Irmchen and her for a lunch of preserved meat and beans. They discussed the various ways for her to return to Pfungstadt, including the mail coach and a ride with friends of his. At the last moment he decided to drive her. He rushed them into his small open carriage and got them to Pfungstadt ten minutes after the train had departed.

The next train left in two hours. She told Mr. Bruchfeld not to wait and thanked him for his hospitality. The station agent informed her that her fare would be ninety centimes, no German money accepted. So, loaded down with briefcase, rug, Irmchen's cardboard box and Irmchen, she walked to a nearby inn to exchange German money for French—a franc was worth 100 centimes.

At the inn she ordered a cup of coffee. But when it arrived, she found it unpalatable and refused to drink it, thinking in triumph, German's poverty has not subdued me yet; I was born in Vienna; I have kept my Austrian passport, the symbol of a spirit that refuses to accept horrible coffee even if a cup costs 100 million marks. Or a billion!

Though she did not enjoy the coffee, she did enjoy Irmchen who chattered the minutes away. At one point she stared at Bertha Pappenheim and predicted, "You will soon die because your hair is so old."

The next minute she asked, "Do all your children at Isenburg have a bed of their own?"

"Yes," said Bertha Pappenheim.

"Where is your husband?"

"I have none."

"Were you ever married?"

"Never." She was amused by the child's curiosity.

"Oh!" Irmchen sank into thoughtfulness, then confided, "My mother never married either. I never had a father. My mother gave me away because she wasn't married."

Bertha Pappenheim halted further inquiries into marital matters by buying Irmchen a cookie. Finally, feeling she was overstaying the time at the Inn to which the purchase of a cup of undrinkable coffee and a cookie entitled her, she exchanged German money for French, and they walked back to the station. There she bought the tickets with centimes.

The station was unheated. As they sat waiting for the train, Irmchen shivered and pleaded, "Please warm my hands; they are cold." Bertha Pappenheim covered the child's hands with her own. She was happy that her newspaper vest had proved successful in keeping her warm from the waist up; she wondered if the French, noticing a slight rustle as she walked, would search her and find the forbidden newspapers she carried so innocently.

The train finally chugged in. They boarded it, and she showed the French conductor her Austrian passport, half expecting him to make a derogatory remark, though he did not.

On arriving at the last station in the occupied zone, after the change at Darmstadt, she had to decide whether to take the hour's walk to Frankfurt with the tired child, the box, briefcase, and rug or try to get a cab at the cost of a billion and a half marks. Outside the station, sitting in his horse and carriage waiting for fares, she saw an old man from Frankfurt, a talkative widower who had raised seven children. He offered to give her a lift if she would wait half an hour for passengers from the next train.

At Frankfurt she paid the old man, then walked Irmchen to a friend's house where she knew there was an extra bedroom. "I will pick you up in the morning and we'll go to Isenburg," she told Irmchen.

There was no room in her apartment for the little girl because she had been obliged to take in boarders to pay the rent. The tenants were an uncouth couple who talked in loud voices and cursed often, so she no longer thought of her apartment with pleasure.

Her bedroom was unheated—there was never enough fuel—and she found herself unable to fall asleep in the beautiful canopied bed with its carved cross. Thinking of her experiences during the past two days in the occupied zone, she seethed with rage at the French. Leviticus 19:34 came to mind: "Be loving to the foreigner for he is as you were, a foreigner in Egypt." That was the way her friend Martin Buber had translated it. People behave as savagely as ever, she realized; the wars that have torn Europe apart for centuries show man does not love but hates the foreigner.

She heard the clock strike midnight, then one, then two. She could not get warm or fall asleep even though she was exhausted. Finally she felt so frustrated and forlorn that she cried, something she rarely did, and the tears released her tension.

Just before she drifted into sleep, she thought, why need I, a lonely old woman of sixty-four, wake up in the morning? Then, another, more realistic thought, I am afraid of the day when I won't have the strength to go to Crumstadt.

At the suggestion of Louise, she wrote a description of her trip to their mutual cousin Felix Warburg, in America, hoping he might send funds to the impoverished German Jews as he had in the past.

She dated the letter "23, November, 1923." Then added, "In the year of manifold misfortunes."

She began: "A few days ago I told Louise in my sanitarium on *Praunheimstrasse*, [the street on which Louise lived] about an inspection trip I took to see children in foster homes. She felt I should write a record of my trip as characteristic of the year 1923 and send it to you."

But she doubted, even as she mailed the letter, that America, at a comfortable distance from war-torn Europe, could possibly understand the suffering of Jews in occupied Germany and the hatred against them that was being fed by Hitler's propaganda.

13

The Voice of an Unknown Woman

Somehow she managed to struggle along, her life made easier by the gift of a small house in Isenburg almost across the street from the Home. It was given her by a wealthy dealer in scrap iron, Henry Rothschild, who had taken care of her finances over the years and who admired her. He realized that if she lived near the Home, she would be saved at least an hour's commuting each day between Frankfurt and Isenburg.

The house was indeed small but it had charm. From the front windows she could see the buildings and gardens of the Home. From the second story, the mountains of the Taunis Range north of Frankfurt were visible. Once again she had packed her precious possessions and moved, sensing this would be the last time.

She also received another gift, one of more intangible a nature—the gift of friendship. A young woman, Hannah Karminski, graduate of a course for kindergarten teachers at the School of Social Work in Hamburg, had been hired as director of the Girls' Club. Bertha Pappenheim was so impressed by Hannah's warmth and graciousness, as well as her effectiveness with the board and the girls, that she proposed Hannah as executive secretary of the Federation, to work in the Berlin office.

Hannah was a tall young woman with a sweet face and quiet manner. She understood the younger members of the board because of her age—she was thirty-eight years younger than Bertha Pappenheim—and often smoothed out difficulties that arose between the aging pioneer leader and the younger women.

When Hannah went to Berlin, they wrote each other almost every day. Bertha Pappenheim felt a closeness to Hannah that she had never felt for a younger woman. Even though she did not believe social work should be done by professionals, she thought a salary took away dedication, she respected Hannah, who had attended graduate school.

But she did not feel possessive about Hannah. She tried to find her a suitable husband. She almost succeeded with one wealthy Jewish bachelor until he snobbishly decided Hannah did not have the proper social credentials.

She also admired another woman who was proving to be one of the most faithful, dedicated volunteers she had ever known. Mrs. Jenny Wolf lived only one block from the Home with her husband, Alfred, owner of a leather goods factory, and her two-year-old son. On Chanukah, 1922, she had come to the Home with her little boy, carrying gifts for the children. Earlier, she had sent one hundred pounds of flour.

Bertha Pappenheim watched Mrs. Wolf kneel to help her son light the first Chanukah candle. Then she walked over to Mrs. Wolf and asked, "Would you like to work with us?"

A look of sheer delight had come over Mrs. Wolf's face and the look had never left. Mrs. Wolf would say at times, "I love working here," and Bertha Pappenheim would reply, "I am happy as a king to have you."

That spring she strolled the grounds with Mrs. Wolf, admiring the blossoming peach trees and the red berries on the bushes. They sat by the fountain which boasted a hen and her chickens sculptured by Benno Elkan. She remarked to Mrs. Wolf, "If the hen gives her little chickens enough confidence so they can make their way in the world, she will have done her job."

Bertha Pappenheim met a new relative by marriage whom she liked and respected. Dora Edinger, a young woman who had earned her doctorate, magna cum laude, in history from the University of Heidelberg, had married a physician, Dr. Friedrich Edinger. His father was Dr. Ludwig Edinger, the neurologist, and his mother, the former Anna Goldschmidt, a second cousin of Bertha Pappenheim's mother.

Dora Edinger, after she moved from Berlin to Frankfurt with her husband in 1923, worked with Bertha Pappenheim as a volunteer board member at the Girls' Club and also lectured on current events once a week for the staff at the Home. Bertha Pappenheim admired her young relative's intelligence, sensitivity and spirit. She readily accepted her into the family.

One evening she said, "Since you are now part of the family, you should know a little more about it."

She took out the chart showing her ancestors and explained the various intermarriages. She also mentioned some who had emotional breakdowns, some who had committed suicide, and some who had died before the age of eighteen and were therefore not recorded on the chart.

The letters she had sent to her subscribers in 1911 and 1912 were often praised and in 1924 she decided to subsidize their publication in a book entitled *Sisyphus Work*. She felt the task she had set herself in the journeys was as hopeless as that of the greedy King of Corinth, doomed forever in Hades to try to roll a heavy stone up a mountain. As she explained in the preface:

"To excuse the publication of these travel notes I want to say that having looked over them twelve years after they were written, I was struck by how little of what I hoped for so confidently has been fulfilled . . . . When I traveled to study the miserable conditions of the Jewish people and to improve the protection of women, girls, and children, I wrote only to a small group of women from Frankfurt who were 'subscribers' to my letters, hoping my notes would be the start of some movement. Nothing happened. I have discovered that *one* voice, the voice of an unknown woman, is ineffective. Today I believe I have not quite done my duty. Nobody is allowed to remain quiet if he knows that somewhere wrong is being done. Neither sex nor age nor religion nor party can be an excuse to remain quiet."

She kept busy as always in many ways. She read from her translation of Gluckel's *Memoirs* at a conference where Dora Edinger spoke on "Ethics of Social Work." She led study groups on volunteer social work at the *Lehrhaus,* where Martin Buber was director. She traveled to conferences, sometimes with Mrs. Wolf.

She knew she shocked Mrs. Wolf on a trip to Mannheim. When they got off the train at lunch-time a vendor in the station called out, "Ham sandwiches! Ham sandwiches!"

She asked Mrs. Wolf, "Will you have a ham sandwich?"

Mrs. Wolf's mouth opened in wonder. "No, thank you," she said hastily.

"I shall have one," announced Bertha Pappenheim and bought a ham sandwich, confiding to Mrs. Wolf, "I wouldn't eat this at home."

She kept up her extensive letter-writing, expressing in her open way precisely what she thought. A friend in Bern, Switzerland, Mrs. Bertha Guggenheim, wrote to her saying she had just learned she could not have a baby and was despondent. Bertha Pappenheim answered her on November 6th, 1924, one year after she had made the trip to Crumstadt to rescue little Irmchen Weingart:

"I understand how sad you are, that perhaps the highest happiness of women may be denied you. But I want to give you some comfort. Though you may not accept it now, as time goes on it will become more vivid. Women who have to miss the happiness of real personal motherhood may have a chance of spiritual motherhood if they take the unheralded way of helping children and adolescents whose actual mothers have failed them—partially, or completely. You can influence these young people's destinies, so you should give yourself to them with all your heart and vitality. Do important work but also the small but holy work of details. Then you will be able to learn to bear your fate and maybe understand it in a larger, though painful, context. And remember that however old I may be, I am there for you if, at a particular moment, you may need me in your work."

She was happy when Mrs. Guggenheim did as she suggested and founded a vacation home for children at Heiden, on Lake Constance.

She decided to have her portrait painted by Leopold Pilichowski, posing herself like Gluckel in her fur coat, lace cap, and lace cuffs. She had never owned a fur coat, not even when she could afford it, believing it too ostentatious, so she borrowed one from a member of the board of the Home, Mrs. Clem Cramer. She selected lace cap and cuffs from her collection. She asked the artist to be sure to place her hands, of whose slender fingers she was very proud, in a prominent position.

Though she was suffering gall-bladder pains she journeyed to Russia again in 1926, at the age of sixty-seven, to observe the Jewish colonies developing the land along the Crimean Sea with American money.

On her return she learned that Sophie, who had married a man named Mamelok, had lost her husband and had visited Frankfurt in her absence to see her. She wrote Sophie on October 2nd:

"I was sorry I missed you when you were in Frankfurt because I wanted to tell you how sad I am that your happiness was so short-lived. Though the catastrophe was not a surprise to you, your life will be quite empty now. But the thought that you made the life of a man who was important in his field happier and richer should be a great help to you."

Again she had a job for Sophie. She told her that the Federation had just bought a house to be converted into a thirty-five bed orphanage at Wyk, on an island at the far northern border of Germany, near Denmark. Sophie was asked if she wished to be director.

Bertha Pappenheim reported she had returned from her trip to Russia anxious "to do with my shaky health what has to be done. Part of it is Wyk. Therefore, I expect to hear from you soon and ask you to consider my suggestion and, if you refuse —which I would regret very much, indeed—find somebody else. I hope you are in good health and that you have the strength to build a new and worthwhile life." Sophie wrote back, accepting.

Her concern with white slavery was still as strong as ever. On September 21st, 1924, she had taken part in a special conference of Jewish participants at the World Congress Against Vice in Graz, Austria. When called upon to state her views, she said, "The Jewish people have never shown a desire to cooperate in solving the problem of white slavery, though everyone is aware of the large percentage of Jewish dealers, goods, and consumers. For instance, in the brothels of Pera, in Constantinople, forty percent of the prostitutes are said to be Jewish women.

"Jewish religious leaders will not involve themselves in

this problem, though Protestant and Catholic clergymen have. Since we have no religious representation in this work, we must create an organization with the goal of being effective all over the world so that this blemish may disappear from Judaism. This small gathering should be its beginning."

Two years later she reported on white slavery to the Secretariat of the League of Nations in Geneva. Though many of her written appeals to prominent Jewish leaders of the world asking support in the fight against prostitution went unanswered, she succeeded in having a resolution, signed by a number of prominent Jews, sent to the League requesting the release of material on the complicity of Jews in white slavery.

It was with deep pride she attended the 25th anniversary celebration of the Girls' Club on March 19th, 1928. This had been her first social work project and she told the audience, "If you have been here at twenty-five annual meetings, you heard at every one of those meetings complaints by older members who said, 'We don't know what to do with the greenhorns. They disturb us; they always want something different.' Two or three years later, the 'greenhorns' were the ones to complain that the new members were greenhorns and did not understand; and so it went through the years. It is possible that today's greenhorns are a little greener than they were twenty-five years ago. I don't remember. As you grow older and have your memory firmly under control, you will remember only the things you want to remember and be able to forget the rest. I find this a very practical talent, ladies, and I recommend it to you."

But she could not tolerate one "greenhorn" who appeared at a board meeting of the Home. The woman showed up with her fingernails painted a shocking bright red.

Bertha Pappenheim said to her before the meeting officially started but in a voice all the other members could hear, "I do not approve of the color of your nails. It is not appropriate."

The new member did not reply but never appeared again, she had attended her first and last board meeting. Bertha Pappenheim noticed a slightly shocked look on the face of the board's secretary, Mrs. Jenny Wolf. But Mrs. Wolf should know how she felt about frivolous women. When Mrs. Wolf remarked that one of the Isenburg housewives wanted to teach her bridge, Bertha Pappenheim told her emphatically, "A woman like you, with a fine husband and two lovely children should not play bridge!"

She thought Mrs. Wolf's assent was rather uncertain, as also was her look when Bertha Pappenheim instructed her, in accordance with the feminist philosophy, "You are Jenny Wolf. You are not Mrs. Alfred Wolf."

The ranks of the *Agunah,* the deserted wives of men who immigrated to America, were now swollen by an estimated 20,000 wives of men who had joined the Jewish labor force in Germany during the war and never returned home. Still fighting against the Jewish civil law which prevented these women from getting a divorce and remarrying, Bertha Pappenheim wrote a statement on July 29th, 1929, which the Federation sent as petition to the General Assembly of Rabbis and Scholars convening in Vienna.

The petition asked the Assembly to take action on behalf of the *Agunah,* "these weakened, intimidated, helpless ones . . . women trampled upon by fate, who have not yet found the desperate courage to seek help for themselves . . . neglected by Jewish law and its interpreters and judges."

She pointed out that under this law healthy young women had to choose either to repress their natural instincts and live moral but lonely and rejected lives, or give in to their instincts and become prostitutes. In accordance with the justice "that is a pillar of the Jewish world," these 20,000 women should "not be buried alive, adding to the large number of victims, male and female, that the world has already claimed from us Jews," she said.

She managed once again to take a crack at rabbis, saying, "The prevailing attitude of orthodoxy has already caused a decrease in the respect for, and influence of, the rabbis."

These days, instead of tatting lace as she once did, she kept her fingers busy stringing tiny beads of myriad colors bought during her travels, intricately fashioning delicate necklaces for which she had found artistic clasps.

She decided she wanted to study the Greek philosophers; philosophy had been another educational subject denied her because she was a girl. So in 1930 she started private lessons with Margarethe Susman, a philosopher and poet.

That year she attended a conference of the summer school the Federation sponsored at Bad Durkheim, Austria, where she was part of a panel on abortion. She told the women:

"It is a woman's privilege and duty to have children. She becomes blessed through having children. She becomes immortal through her children. She should do nothing to interfere with giving birth, whether she is married or not. Abortion is a crime against the human race. If a woman becomes pregnant, she was meant to be."

A member of her Federation board, a woman who was also a physician, Dr. Rahel Strauss, defended the opposite point of view.

"If a woman does not wish to have a child, she should not be forced to have one, married or not," said Dr. Strauss, the mother of several children.

"Abortion is murder," said Bertha Pappenheim in her rebuttal.

"It is also murder, in a sense, if a child is brought up by a mother who does not want him, either because there is no father around, or if she is married, because she cannot handle another child," retorted Dr. Strauss.

Bertha Pappenheim soon had a chance to prove her convictions. One day Mrs. Jenny Wolf paid an unexpected visit to the Home as Bertha Pappenheim was sitting in her office going over bills. She noticed an excited look on Mrs. Wolf's face.

Without preamble Mrs. Wolf said, "Do you know that Mrs. Betty is pregnant again?"

It was the custom to call every young woman who had given birth, "Mrs." Mrs. Betty, the young, pretty cook had had two illegitimate children and Bertha Pappenheim had kept close watch on her, susceptible as she was to masculine charm.

Bertha Pappenheim stared at Mrs. Wolf, stunned. "You must be mistaken. Mrs. Betty hasn't left the Home in months."

"My maid went to the kitchen to ask for her recipe for chocolate cake and told me Mrs. Betty looked pregnant. I went to see for myself. She is quite pregnant, I think."

Bertha Pappenheim sent at once for Mrs. Betty, who entered the room wiping her hands apologetically on her apron.

"Mrs. Betty, are you pregnant again?" Bertha Pappenheim came right to the point, even though she knew the answer from the bulge behind the apron.

Mrs. Betty looked embarrassed. "Yes, ma'am."

"How did you *get* pregnant?" Bertha Pappenheim asked in wonder. "You haven't been off the grounds in months."

Mrs. Betty blushed, replied, "The house painter, ma'am."

Pregnancy was a sacred state to Bertha Pappenheim. Reading of the conviction for murder in Berlin of Lieschen Neumann, an adolescent girl who was pregnant, Bertha Pappenheim wrote her on February 7th, 1931:

"During these past few days I have often thought about you. Not because I felt you had become a special, 'interesting' person because of your serious crimes, nor because I felt you had become a famous person in your own right, though in a repulsive way you have, since your name has appeared frequently in the papers. No, my dear L. N., I did not think of you as one individual L. N. Quite the contrary. I thought of the many girls like you. Girls running around Berlin, just as you did a short time ago, eager to do, at any moment, what might be very dangerous for them and for others; dabbling with dirt, forgetting there are clean things, too. These many Lieschen made me think—as, no doubt, many other silent friends of young people are doing—how does it happen that all those heavily made-up, greedy, clothes-conscious, lazy Lieschen are running around in Berlin without giving a thought to their families, ready to listen to the brash words of young men, until the situation suddenly makes them do something which shows how desperate, how meaningless, their lives have become?

"During your trial one of the investigators spoke to you with kindly interest. And you said, 'Everything would have been different if anyone had ever spoken to me in this way.' L. N., I am willing to concede you may have believed at that moment what you said, for just then you may have realized what a mess you had made of your life. But, truthfully, did you really believe, during the short period you are able to remember, that if someone—a teacher, a social worker, a minister, an employer, your parents—had said, 'Control yourself, work, try to be kind, enjoy all the chances for education Berlin

offers young people,' you would have done so? Would you
not have jerked back your head saying, 'I won't let anyone interfere with my life. I do as I please'? Do not think that I mean
to accuse you—it is an important principle that those still at lib-
erty do as they please. You would have gone on asking your
young boy friends for favors they could not possibly afford. It
is not the worst thing to have made love with a boy friend in
adolescent passion; it is much worse that you exploited sex to
get what you could not possibly get in a decent way. If someone had talked to you when you first went to U's [a brothel],
then again and again, would it have made any difference?
Deep down you surely knew it was wrong. But, be truthful,
who could have followed you in your dark hidden ways?
Would you have listened to warnings? No more than the other
fifty girls who frequent U's, I fear.

"I think that much has been said to excuse you, but I feel
that the final, most important things have not been mentioned. That is my reason for writing. You have killed, or at
least, helped to kill—not knowing, or rather, not remembering
that there is a commandment beyond time, beyond politics,
beyond all religions, 'Thou shalt not kill.' It means, have rever-
ence for life; it means everything: love, beauty, goodness—all
without end. But, for me, your greatest guilt is not that you
took part, whatever your share, in such a crime, but that what
you did, you did in U's house as an expectant mother feeling
the heartbeat of your unborn child. A holy mystery of nature
did not prevent you from offering your young body to filth.
This was your greatest crime.

"But everything may still come to you from this child, dear
L. N. He may help you build a future life over your dark,
serious crimes. Do not forget them, but build your life around
being a true mother to your child. When you conceived this
child, you were neither better nor worse than thousands of
women who fell between right and wrong. No science can
predict that bad parents will not have good children. You are
still so very young.

"I hope you will give birth to a healthy child. That you will
be able to nurse it. That in the seclusion imposed by the verdict you will gain the strength, thinking of your child, to develop your capacities for good. Let your child influence you, so

that he may, when he learns your fate, pity his mother but not despise his origins."

She signed herself "An old friend of young people."

She also spoke frankly yet with understanding to three of her board members in a letter addressed "Dear Women" in which she chastised them for being "caricatures" of volunteer workers. She said:

"You overdo things—that's it, in brief. Your minds and your bodies suffer from overwork.

"It's a pity that ambition grows so close to kindness and the will to help. Their stems and branches intertwine; one cannot tell which root brought forth the flowers, which the fruits; they look very much alike. My dears, you are restless, over-excited. You know, since God's voice speaks within your conscience, that you are not taking care of your bodies, your minds, your homes, as you should. You try to hold on stubbornly to what is beyond your power. If you were not essentially good, and your husbands kind . . .

"And now, dear women, let me say what worries me especially. Was I wrong to help you step outside your house? I often ask this of myself. Thinking it over quietly today, I believe that I was not wrong to point out a way to a fuller life. You used to listen to my advice; please, listen again."

The Home at Isenburg celebrated its 25th anniversary, the Home that had been her temple, her fortress. She had conceived it, nurtured it, watched it grow. And most important, she believed that because of her faith and work, at least fifteen hundred young girls and babies had been given the chance to live happier lives.

At times the question arose as to whether the girls, many of them emotionally disturbed, their delinquency and pregnancy obvious and blatant signs of the disturbance, should receive psychological treatment. Psychoanalysis was coming into prominence with the publication of the works of Sigmund Freud.

At one board meeting the problem of what to do with a young girl named Manya was discussed. Manya was a Jewish farm girl from Poland who had been abandoned by a white slave dealer at the railroad station in Frankfurt when he fled the police. A Care by Women volunteer, assigned to work with the police at the station in the rescue of Jewish girls, brought Manya to the Home. The girl had no passport, no citizenship papers, no money, and could speak no German. The Home took care of Manya for weeks as some of the staff tried to teach her German so she could go out and try to find a job. But she was unable to learn one word of the new language. The staff thought she might be emotionally disturbed and had asked Dr. Josef Minkel, an Isenburg physician who treated the children at the Home without fee and was Bertha Pappenheim's personal physician, to examine her. Dr. Minkel, a man for whom they all had much admiration and affection, had confirmed what they had sensed.

At this conference a member of the board, the wife of a doctor with adolescent children of her own, suggested, "Perhaps we should take Manya to see a psychoanalyst."

Bertha Pappenheim had been sitting quietly in her chair, her fingers busy stringing the delicate beads, but her mind as attentive as ever. On hearing the suggestion she abruptly stood up and said, her voice emphatic, "Never! Not as long as I am alive."

A hush fell over the room. The other women did not understand her dramatic reaction but realized she spoke out of deep feeling.

Then she said, "Let's go on to other matters," and sat down.

14

The Enemy Within

She sat in her little house with Mrs. Jenny Wolf listening to Hitler's first harangue in 1933 broadcast over the radio. Along with many other German Jews, she thought it would be possible to weather the anti-Semitic storm by withdrawing into the Jewish community.

She kept struggling to maintain standards at the Home even as the Nazis staged their boycott on April 1, 1933, smashing windows in stores owned by Jews and beating Jews on the street.

Death was not too far from her thoughts as the pain in her abdomen grew more intense. After paying a visit to her mother's grave in July she wrote a prayer, concluding, "May I retain the strength to serve, in speech, in silence, and in action, as long as I live, so that I may preserve my right to the small plot of earth next to your grave, Mother! Amen."

In a more humorous vein, she prepared her own obituary as five different periodicals might have written it:

"*Family News:* She was a woman who for decades stubbornly fought for her ideas, the ideas of her time. But she went about it in a way that was not to everybody's taste. What a pity!

"*Israelite* [a Jewish Orthodox publication]: She was by descent and training an Orthodox woman, she believed herself separated from her roots—obviously under the revolutionary feminist influence. She was often hostile—but never denied her origins. She should have done more for Orthodoxy—let us

remember that her father was a co-founder of the *Schiffschul*
at Vienna. What a pity!

"*C.V. Journal* [a patriotic German-Jewish publication]:
. . . a woman of real gifts, indebted both to the Jewish tradition and German civilization; yet she remained consciously
outside our ranks because she sternly rejected ideas she did
not like. What a pity!

"*Jewish Review* [Zionist publication]: An old and active
enemy of our movement, though one cannot deny that she
was aware of her Jewishness. What a pity!

"*Blatter des Judischen Frauenbund* [a monthly publication
of the Jewish Women's Federation]: In 1904 she founded the
Jewish Women's Federation; its importance is not yet fully understood. The Jews of the entire world, men and women, owe
her thanks for this social achievement. But they withhold it.
What a pity!"

The Home was more and more in need of food and supplies. Whenever anyone sent a gift that was useful, she wrote a
letter telling how much it meant. She was irked when a gift arrived that had no value and would write asking the donor just
what purpose he thought it would serve.

She tried to find a use for everything, no matter how
senseless it seemed. One day a gift package arrived which contained wide, worn-out elastic strips. She threw the pieces to
the floor, remarked to Gertrud Ehrenwerth, a new member of
the staff, "How can anyone send such a worthless gift?"

She went home, tossed in bed that night, berating herself
for throwing away anything in this time of need, thinking,
Waste not, want not. Suddenly a use for the elastic occurred to
her. She checked her impulse to call Miss Ehrenwerth and tell
her to save the elastic, knowing she would frighten her if she
phoned at midnight.

She called at seven in the morning when she woke, asked,
"Did you keep those strips of worn-out elastic that arrived yesterday?"

"Yes," replied Miss Ehrenwerth, puzzled.

"Don't throw them out. I thought of a use."

"You did?" Surprise in the voice.

"We can tie the house linen in bundles to keep it neat,"
she said.

Miss Ehrenwerth, who had applied for a job when dismissed from an administrative position as a municipal social worker because she was a Jew, had seemed shaken at first by what was happening to German Jews, but was proving efficient.

They were both delighted when there arrived one day the gift of one hundred pounds of sugar and one hundred pounds of flour sent by Eugene Kamberg, a man with a law degree, who was in the grain and flour business. He was the husband of a spirited young woman whose maiden name had been Anne Nathan, and who was now a member of the board, after first joining Care by Women in 1925 as a volunteer.

Bertha Pappenheim asked the secretary of the board, Mrs. M. Posen Prinz, to acknowledge Mr. Kamberg's gift by letter. Then she signed her own signature, adding the word "Strudelfabrikantin," meaning a manufacturer of strudel.

"How I wish we could use the sugar and flour for strudel," she said to Miss Ehrenwerth. Both women knew the flour would become bread and the sugar added in small quantities to cereal.

That Tuesday afternoon she left the Home early, as she did every Tuesday, to prepare supper for a group of young women, mostly unmarried, she called her "Tuesday guests," or sometimes jokingly, her "Girls Coffee Club."

She intentionally chose Tuesday for this evening of entertainment and talk because it was the day twice called "Kitof," or "good," in the history of creation. She thought of the young women as her "Kitof people." Usually, it was the same group though she would often ask them to suggest additional guests.

That evening she planned to serve fruit salad, the fruit picked from the garden, and a coffee cake she made herself from a recipe originally from Vienna. She prepared the salad, set the table in her dining room with one of her most exquisite lace tablecloths and napkins. She arranged fresh flowers in a centerpiece.

The young women arrived promptly, as they always did, and at seven, she served the light supper. It ended with the indispensable black coffee, prefaced by a cube of sugar dipped in the coffee which, for her, was always a festive moment. She would rather forego coffee, as she had done on the journey with Irmchen, than drink coffee improperly brewed.

After dinner, she showed the group the latest necklace on which she was working. One of them would eventually receive it as a gift in a "raffle." No money was paid in this raffle, her way of avoiding favoritism.

The women discussed conditions in Germany, where it was becoming more and more difficult for Jews to live. One of the young women asked, "What are you writing, Miss Pappenheim?" knowing she was usually at work on a memoranda, or a report for the Federation, or a fairy tale for the children.

"A survey for the Federation on volunteers in social work," she said.

Then she added, "Children, I now tell you something in strictest confidence—which means, 'Pass it on!' "

They laughed merrily, knowing this meant she wanted whatever she said to get back to the board members.

"Some women do not understand what they do when they advocate the use of professionals in social work," she said. "They are cutting their own throats. It means back to bridge tables, beauty parlors—the useless life for them. No one will want them. It's a shame!"

At the end of the evening she was gratified when one young woman thanked her, said, "Every Tuesday is like a holiday at home. I feel so enriched when I leave here."

There were times over the years when, as president of the Federation, Bertha Pappenheim had quarreled with board members who refused to do as she wished, who objected to certain projects, who did not move as quickly as she desired. She had resigned once in 1924 and stayed away from the jubilee festivities in 1929 after disagreements. In 1934 she again resigned, this time for good, though she remained on the board representing the Isenburg Home.

She sent the board a handwritten letter explaining why she was resigning: she could not tolerate what she considered a "chain of lukewarm feeling, misunderstanding, non-understanding, and procrastination," and her conscience did not permit her to deviate from what she believed important. She mentioned sterilization, which she strongly opposed, and the "deportation" of children without their parents to Palestine. She added:

"I know you will object that the Federation was not responsible for either of these actions. Granted, but the opposition in our circle was weak, united only as long as I was present. I cannot accept responsibility for this attitude . . . also the ogling at the Central Welfare Office and the Reconstruction Help goes against my grain. It is possible there is no other way, but this is no reason for me, knowing I cannot get my conviction across, to remain on a committee, grinning in a friendly fashion."

The Central Welfare Board had been her idea but it had been taken over and run by men who were eliminating volunteer workers, replacing them with professionals. This was completely at odds with her philosophy. She thought it beneficial for the housewife to do something besides play bridge, that though volunteers might not always be as efficient as professionals, they were devoted and dedicated.

Then came the Nazi book-burnings about which she wrote Hannah on July 29, 1934, saying that, as she had often confessed, books did not mean much to her as an educational yardstick:

"I know books can actually disturb me if I feel I am being forced to read them. Hunger for books, swallowing everything printed . . . seems to me spiritually acquired gluttony, degeneration of the blessing of the art of printing . . . my desire for the daily paper is something utterly different from reading masses of books . . . . The fleeting, developing, unfinished political, social, and economic relationships and consequences interest me in the daily newspaper, the finished book much less.

"Let's try to make a list of books one really 'needs.' I do not mean technical ones. I can well understand that this list may be entirely different for different people. The average person certainly does not need 'beloved books.'

"Today's book-burning is a sign of overall barbarism emanating from over- as well as under-evaluation of books. Please don't think, dear Hannah, that I don't respect your bookshelf. On the contrary, I have too much respect for the knowledge I know I do not have. I believe I'm so afraid of books because I know so little, because I am so uneducated. On the other hand, I believe that I grew into what I am, and into what I am not, through this lack of spiritual food—spiritual under-nourishment, I call it.

"Very large libraries which care more for quantity than quality I understand well, both as storehouses of knowledge and as ways to knowledge, to education, and as mere collections. But journalists and literati are not full of respect for knowledge, though they yell loudest for books. I do not believe that people who own many books and have read many books are smarter than others, nor that they are better. (I wonder whether a lifetime is long enough to read all the books a well-to-do boy gets for his *bar mitzvah?*)

"Not all bibliophiles are spiritual princes—just as not all kleptomaniacs are thieves, they are only driven to it. If I think of an unborn child, if I see a newborn baby in its crib, all I might learn or read envelops this growing being whom I want to raise to the spirit which lives in books—a diaspora of the spirit."

She was now seventy-five and starting to give up some of her duties as director of the Home, though not the title.

She used her spare time to compose an essay, "The Jewish Woman," which she mailed to her co-workers. It contained her philosophy about social work, women volunteers, and Zionism. She discussed the historical role of the Jewish woman, charging that no adult education "can repair today the sin committed against the Jewish woman's soul and thus against all Judaism by excluding the ignorant woman, keeping her from developing her whole being, cultivating only her physical strength for the service of man. The wife of the Jew in family life was supposed to carry bricks as a beast of burden, her spirit was expected to remain dull. Her lovesong was sung along with the serving of gefilte fish!"

She concluded:

"We are responsible for each other. It doesn't matter where one stands individually. We have a communal fate. For us German Jews, the third notch is the terrible boycott staged on April 1, 1933. How it hit us! How will we survive? How will we bear the hatred and misery? By the suicide of individuals? By the suicide of the community? Shall we forget the past? Shall we lament or deny? Shall we emigrate and change our economic status? Shall we wait? Shall we carry on philosophically or foolishly? Everyone—man or woman—should do what he has to do, out of his strength or his lack of strength. We Jews should always remember that wherever we are in the world—the diaspora—and even Palestine—is exile, yet we may see the summit of Mt. Sinai in the distance."

She decided to go to Vienna to catalogue the collection of laces she had given the Museum for Arts and Crafts. She spent several days in the Museum, took time out to walk through the old lanes to "browse around," as she called it, in the second-hand stores, searching for a piece of precious old lace or antique glass for her collection. She also visited, as she usually did when in Vienna, an old, faithful friend who had been in her class at the parochial school. They tried to recapture the spirit of the days when they were sixteen as they sat talking in the splendid apartment of her friend, now a Baroness. She noticed her friend's mind did not seem as alert as it used to be. She did not stay as long as usual because she needed her strength to continue cataloguing the laces.

She knew this was the last time she would see Vienna, smell the lilac and jasmine of spring, taste wine from the vineyards of the villages skirting the city.

She visited Willie and his wife, thought of the time she took Marianne, the wife's daughter, to *Fidelio,* finding the excitement and sense of suspense of the youthful audience in the gallery heartwarming—such naive participation, such feeling for the artistry of the opera, was lacking in the youth of Frankfurt and Berlin.

From the Pension Vienna, where she stayed, she wrote Miss Ehrenwerth:

"It seems terribly long since I left Isenburg, and since then many little things have kept me busy. But it has to be this way; others have to take over the responsibility. I imagine that you and Mrs. Haas have much to do. I would be happy to hear that Dr. Minkel has no more than sore throats to keep him busy. How are the babies who were vaccinated? And Lena's rupture? And Marga? And what else has happened? Has Erna run away again, or anyone else? You carry your snail's shell always with you."

There was a postscript: "Dr. Minkel, cordial greetings. I write at night, and I'm not so eager to write as usual."

She decided on her way home to stay a few days in Ischl, a resort in the Austrian Alps where, as a girl, she had enjoyed vacations. At Ischl she was stricken by such severe intestinal pain that she was rushed to the Jewish hospital in Munich, just across the border. There she was operated upon.

On the sixth day in the hospital, when she felt the ache of her body subsiding after the surgery, she asked the surgeon, "Did you remove my gall bladder?"

"No," he said. "It wasn't necessary."

"Why not? Wasn't that causing the pain?" It was a quiet demand for the truth. She must always know the truth—how else could she fight? A fight waged without truth was a fruitless fight.

"It wasn't serious," he said. "Nothing had to be removed."

"Am I dying?" she asked, suddenly suspecting Dr. Minkel had been lying to her, that she had cancer, not a rebellious gall bladder.

"You'll enjoy many more years."

She sensed he was not telling the truth but for the first time in her life she did not argue against what she felt to be a lie.

She had thought herself invincible, no outside enemy would ever strike her down. Instead she had been attacked from within, her own body had betrayed her.

She asked for a pen and paper to write Miss Ehrenwerth, whom the hospital had phoned the day before. She started the letter, "Munich, Fifth (?) July, 1935, Friday":

"I had you phoned yesterday long distance so that all of you in Isenburg would know where I am and why. It is not at all sure whether the surgery helped, but I was in such pain in Ischl that I submitted to the claws of Aesculapius. The surgeon told me my condition might become better. Please give my regards to Dr. Minkel and tell him that I'm very angry with him; he will know why."

Two days later she wrote Miss Ehrenwerth and Mrs. Haas jointly:

"Many thanks for your report and for your interest in my *Schlemiehlerei* [bad luck]. It had to happen, and I'm very skeptical whether surgery really helped. I cannot say when I'll be

back, because who says A has also to say B. Later I will write to
Dr. Minkel and complain about my fate. I am glad that everything is as usual in the Home, since it means that nothing especially disturbing has happened . . . .

"As 'very important' I have noted the news that you are
busy canning, so I must put into writing that the berries in the
yard of House 4 are mine!!! If not all of them, I want to keep
the larger part for myself. The older girls may learn how to can.
You see what worries I have. It is very fortunate that Miss
Kramer and I are away at the same time so that you all know
everyone can be replaced and that there are potentials in
human beings which grow only if given a chance.

"The doctor was just here and said that I might travel on
Tuesday . . . ."

She went home on Tuesday and two months later she was
traveling again—to Amsterdam to meet Henrietta Szold, the
American Zionist leader, at a Youth Aliyah convention. Miss
Szold had come to Germany to organize the emigration of
Jewish adolescents to Palestine. She wanted to rescue as many
German Jewish children as possible from Hitler. Though this
meant separating them from their parents, the separation was
justified by the threat of extermination confronting German
Jewry, Miss Szold maintained. Bertha Pappenheim fought the
breakup of families, believing, as did many of her contemporaries, that the Jews should quietly wait out the anti-Semitism. The two women, both the same age, both unmarried,
both serving their people in their own way, fought hard, but
neither could change the other's convictions. Following their
confrontation they had supper with several women. Bertha
Pappenheim sat in stony silence and Miss Szold looked deeply
depressed.

That November she learned of the death of two educational leaders at the Beth-Jakob Seminary for Girls in Cracow.
She had been very interested in helping to plan the Seminary's
curricula and in sending a number of her "daughters" there
for further education. Worried by the effect the two deaths
might have on the Seminary, she went to Cracow and pleaded
with the board to add to their teachers-training functions a
program for the training of social workers and nurses, very
much needed in Poland. She promised to return in a few

months, as the board requested.

The acute pain in her abdomen came back when she reached home. She tried to ignore it as she worked with Dr. Kathe Mende, a social worker who was evaluating what had happened to the illegitimate children after they left the Home.

In the work with Dr. Mende, she came across copies of letters she had written over the years to "indignant parents" of unwed mothers, or grandparents, hoping to persuade them to adopt an illegitimate baby. She had tried not to moralize, nor to reproach, either the girl or her parents, but to make a plea for the child's adoption. She had pointed out the blessing that forgiveness would bring to everyone, and the joy of having a child in the home.

Dr. Mende, reading her letters, said, "You have such a warm, alive feeling for every mother and child. You do not see numbers in a file. You see human beings, created by God."

During this study Bertha Pappenheim would not take the drugs Dr. Minkel advised to ease the pain, because she wanted to stay fully alert mentally.

When Dr. Mende's full report had been written, Bertha Pappenheim wrote her:

"It is exactly what I had long hoped for: treatment of difficult material, clear, well-organized, intelligently understood, warm, womanly, and Jewish. I want to thank you. With this partial study you have given a great deal to many and to me a great and dear gift. I am not able to thank you as I really want and as I should. But I know you don't want any thanks or recognition, you are satisfied, and I hope, secretly, that your study will smooth the way for others to try similar tasks. Then we both will be quietly happy for a longer or shorter period, as our fate and 'our time' will allow. Once more, I thank you very much."

She was not sure how much her "fate" and her "time" would permit her to do, but she kept working as hard as she could. German Jewish children had been forbidden by the Nazis to attend German schools, and she wanted to convince the organizers of new schools for these children of the need for an added year of training to prevent the children from leaving their families too soon. Her appeal was published in May, 1936, in the *Blatter*. She maintained that a ninth year in school, or a pre-apprenticeship, was necessary for the transition between the insecurity of the present and the insecurity of the future.

She spoke particularly of girls and their failure to perform "simple, everyday tasks." She blamed it not "on the intellectualization of the education of young people . . . intellectualization is such a flattering expression where intellect is lacking," but on the failure of mothers.

"It is their own pampering which makes mothers unable in many cases to bring up their daughters," she wrote. "Therefore . . . one sends daughters into institutions where they don't learn any more than they could have learned at home from their mothers."

She urged young girls to learn to be homemakers by remaining at home rather than going to an institution "where girls live as on an island." Any pre-apprenticeship plan "must allow time to the girls to fulfill their tasks in their own homes . . . . it is wrong if mothers say 'I can do it better and faster myself.' It is the duty of mothers to teach what they know (and truly, they know very little) even if things run badly and unpleasantly for a while.

"These suggestions are for the few who have sense."

The only concession she made to pain was to stay in bed a few hours later each morning, though she always called the Home for a full report on what had happened during the night. At eleven she crossed the quiet street, her first stop the house where the babies were sheltered. She stopped by each crib, murmured a few words to the baby in it, she had known each one from the day it was born. Little Eddie was crying and she asked for a bottle to feed him. Little Wanda was gurgling and Bertha Pappenheim stooped over and gently swung the golden agate she wore around her neck on a crocheted strand back and forth as Wanda's small hands reached out for it in delight. Little Ethel seemed cold and Bertha Pappenheim went to the closet, got out an extra blanket and covered her. Little Tommy looked listless and she took his temperature. It was normal, otherwise she would have called Dr. Minkel at once. She always stayed with a baby who had a high fever until the doctor arrived. And she always accompanied Dr. Minkel on his visits to the babies, the older children, and the girls, wanting to be sure they all received the medication he prescribed.

She went next to the house where the toddlers lived, and as always, they raced towards her as fast as they could on little feet they were just starting to manipulate, crying out what sounded like "Miss Papahome, Miss Papahome!" A few almost strangled her trying to hug her as she sat down in a chair for a moment, in sudden pain.

She ate lunch in the dining room with the girls, the staff and the children, then went to her office to answer letters. A few of the children walked in, as they always did, knowing they were welcome, to say hello shyly or tell of some need. Helen asked for a warmer sweater and Marsha wanted to know if they could have chocolate ice cream as a treat on Sunday.

In the afternoon she sat with the older girls, helping them with their needlework, as she strung her beads. Frances, a newcomer, had never used a thimble and Bertha Pappenheim showed her how.

After supper the children clustered around her, each wanting to sit next to her as she read aloud from the latest *Dr. Doolittle* book. She stopped at times to ask if they understood a difficult word, or if they could guess what came next.

On Purim the children provided her with surprise entertainment. They acted out a fairy tale she wrote for them on the birth of a hazelnut cake. Eight-year old Jean played the part of the confused cook, the star role, and other children played "sugar," "butter," and "flour," as they marched into the kitchen one by one to be stirred as batter into the "pot," a large crate the children had carted to the center of the stage.

In rare hours when she felt free from pain, she would put on one of her old, elegant satin dresses and in front of company would stride around the room in high spirits, pretending to be a model showing the latest fashion. At times when she felt nostalgic, she would sit at the piano in the Home and play remembered passages of Hayden and Mozart. Much as she had loathed practicing as a girl, she was now glad she had learned how to play.

At one board meeting a member, noticing she seemed in great pain, asked, "Didn't you have that bothersome gall bladder taken out in Munich?"

"No," she said.

"Aren't you going to have it out?" The board member looked surprised.

"I've lived with it almost seventy-seven years and I don't expect to have it out now," she replied.

That was all she would say. She had never sought sympathy.

15

The Final Fight

She wanted to return to Cracow as she had promised in February, 1936. The Beth-Jakob Seminary depended on her to help plan the education of Jewish girls in Poland. But Dr. Minkel said "No!" Behind his back she consulted a specialist in Frankfurt. He too advised against the trip.

She accepted the verdict stoically. If the end was to come, she would rather go down fighting at Isenburg. An extra day of life might mean the difference between tyranny and freedom for her charges.

She faced such a day. She received a summons from the Gestapo to report to the local headquarters in Isenburg. Maria, a mentally retarded girl, had stared with her sad, vacant eyes at a photograph of Hitler in a newspaper and said, "He looks like a criminal." An Aryan employee in the Home had reported this to the Gestapo. There were informers on one's very hearth, Bertha Pappenheim thought, as she prepared to face the Gestapo, who believed Maria's words mirrored what she was taught at the Home.

Helene Kramer, now her assistant, insisted on going with her, knowing they were both risking their lives.

"I will not allow you to go alone," Helene said.

Side by side in the winter cold, they walked the few blocks into town, the sick old lady leaning heavily on her "daughter's" arm. On the way they saw enlarged photostats of articles printed in *Der Sturmer,* the Nazi paper, posted on street corners. The articles quoted Bertha Pappenheim's reports exposing the involvement of wealthy Jews in the white slave traffic. This was exactly what the cautious had warned would happen when she had called them hypocrites and cowards for not defying the white slave traders.

She had not been afraid of the criminal middlemen nor of the merchants who trafficked in the bodies of young girls, and she was not afraid now of the thugs who had taken over Germany. One had to fight them too, for they were thieves and murderers. As she once wrote Sophie, "Don't worry if not everyone understands what's right; do your duty and listen to your conscience."

As she faced the uniformed storm troopers at Gestapo headquarters she stood erect as always, though she was in pain.

"One of the children you are responsible for has called Hitler a criminal." This was the accusation. It might mean death to them all, the children, the girls, the staff.

Her voice was matter-of-fact. "It is quite possible Maria said this. But you can't take her seriously. She's retarded. No one can be held responsible for what comes out of a defective mind."

She was so calm, she convinced the Gestapo. They let her go. Though perhaps, she thought, they realized she was dying and their murderous work would soon be done for them by nature.

The two women walked back to the Home, silent, each contained in her own thoughts. Bertha Pappenheim knew now that German Jews could not successfully hold out against the Nazis. What would become of them? The problem could not concern her personally much longer, but what about those who had followed her example? What about her children?

She had tried to fight the enemies in her life. It seemed her entire existence had been a fight, perhaps that was what life was all about, a fight to help those with less strength. She had fought for what she believed, with her money, her energy, her time, her wits, her pen, and all the passion in her. Her money had run out, her energy and time were running out, but she still had her wits, her pen, and her passion.

Because she felt so intensely, she had made many enemies

along the way. She knew she was wilful, that she insisted on getting her way even though sometimes it might be the wrong way. She had been told she was flying in the face of what was progressive and liberal when she fought for the volunteer social worker against the professional, when she fought against Zionism, and against psychoanalysis. But she knew the only way she could live was to defend her convictions.

She had asked a lot of herself, believing if one asked much, first and foremost of oneself, then from others one might hope for some success.

She knew people thought her severe at times. Once, after a visit to her mother's grave, she wrote a prayer:

"Wind blows over the graves, sunlight lies on the stones. Drop by drop, memories trickle through my thoughts. I lay a small stone on the beloved spot, and I, childless, wish for myself small memorial stones placed on the rim of the red stone, with the inscription:

" 'She was very severe.' "

She had filled her life with her work, her writings, her travels. In sad, reflective moments, she might wonder why she never married, never had children of her own instead of caring for the forsaken. But the sadness soon passed, there was always too much to do—finding the right woman to head a new orphanage or staff the Home, fighting at board meetings for what she believed right, and ever since the Great War, obtaining enough food and other necessities for the Home.

Once, only once, had she given in to deeper feelings. It was on her seventieth birthday, and the Federation board had surprised her with a table laden with gifts for the Home. She had been so moved she could not speak at first.

Finally she said with tears in her eyes, "Excuse me, please. I'm so little used to love that I am quite overwhelmed."

16

The End

She lay frail and helpless, a tiny figure on the canopied bed, the bed in which her mother had died.

Set in a corner of the room, the bed was framed on two sides by a Gobelin tapestry which reached from floor to ceiling. It pictured two roosters fighting, and she would tell visitors, with the hint of a smile, "That's Willie and me." Willie was still alive and living in Vienna but she had not seen him recently. It was impossible for her to travel, and Willie did not seem to realize her strength had vanished.

She had been confined to the canopied bed for several weeks, imprisoned in the little house she loved, the house that held all her treasures. She had been stricken following the summons to Gestapo headquarters.

Remembering that scene, she thought of something she wanted to do. She asked Hannah Karminski, who was staying with her, to invite to her home the president of the Federation, who lived in Bochum, about one hundred miles northwest of Frankfurt. Bertha Pappenheim had something she wished to say to Ottilie Schoenewald.

When Mrs. Schoenewald arrived, she tried not to show how shocked she was at the sight of the sallow face and listless limbs. She sat numbly in a chair by the canopied bed.

Bertha Pappenheim said, "Mrs. Schoenewald, you were right about the Nazis. I always thought you were a coward. But now I know what we are up against."

169

Mrs. Schoenewald handed her a bouquet of tea roses she had brought from Bochum, knowing how much Bertha Pappenheim loved fresh flowers.

Very delicately, with her long, graceful fingers, Bertha Pappenheim lifted the yellow roses, placed the soft petals against her cheeks. The May sun streamed through the window, shining on her white hair.

She said softly, "How very nice."

Then added, "They match my complexion."

Even in death the humor was there, the humor that kept her from false sentiment, that enabled her to fight on at moments when otherwise she might have lost hope.

One of her prayers spoke of it:

"It is senseless to cling to this bare life, which according to eternal law must pass away. But to fill life's cup and be allowed to carry it so that its dew and rain overflow as a blessing for many is a gift from God. The dregs of the cup are tears.

"May liberating laughter remain for me. It is the spice of life and as indispensable as bread and salt."

But laughter was becoming more difficult as pain overwhelmed everything, even humor, and reluctantly she took the pain-killers Dr. Minkel had prescribed. To Hannah she dictated a final prayer:

>*"Softly, softly without ado*
>*passes the time,*
>*Softly, softly without ado*
>*I am ready*
>*to walk with you.*
>*Softly, softly, without ado*
>*one must be ready*
>*for time and forever.*
>*Who is it—You?*
>*Let me rest."*

Late in the afternoon of May 28th, 1936, two weeks after Mrs. Schoenewald brought the yellow roses, Hannah Karminski sat by the side of the canopied bed. Four members of the board were also in the room, Mrs. Stephanie Forchheimer, Mrs. Ella Werner, Mrs. Paula Nassauer-Niedermayer, and Mrs.

Jenny Wolf.

The women talked in low voices, not wishing to disturb Bertha Pappenheim but wishing her to know they were near when she needed them most.

Suddenly they saw the white head turn slowly from the rays of the sun to the dark side of the room. The lids slowly closed over the blue eyes.

And the hands that had once warmed little Irmchen's shivering fingers grew cold.

17

The Tributes

At her request there were no eulogies at the funeral service. But two weeks after her death the board of the Federation held a memorial meeting at the Home for co-workers, members of the board of the Federation and of the Home, relatives, and friends. Mrs. Schoenewald announced that almost all condolence messages mentioned that German Jewry had lost its most prominent woman member at a very critical time.

Martin Buber's message said of Bertha Pappenheim, "I not only admired her but loved her, and will love her until the day I die." He added:

"There are people of spirit and there are people of passion, both less common than one might think. Rarer still are the people of spirit and passion. But rarest of all is a passionate spirit. Bertha Pappenheim was a woman with just such a spirit.

"She had to become severe—not hard, but severe, lovingly severe, demanding much, full of passion—because all was what it was and remained what it was. She lived at a time when people could not bear the white fire; they did not see it, did not even believe that it still existed.

"But it did exist. This white flame burned in our days. Now it is extinguished. Only her image survives, in the hearts of those who knew her.

"Pass on this image. Pass on her memory. Be witnesses that it still exists. We have a pledge."

Max Warburg, Felix's brother, who had given money for

Bertha Pappenheim's projects, wrote, "Her life was an example for many, and her goals should be kept as she intended. I always admired her, even though I opposed her at times because I favored different approaches."

The board suggested that Bertha Pappenheim's achievements be written up by Hannah Karminski. Mrs. Schoenewald proposed that this be done at a later date, when Bertha Pappenheim could be seen in true historical perspective. For the present, the Federation decided to put out a memorial issue, a "Gedenknumner," of its monthly publication.

This special issue of July/August, 1936, edited by Hannah Karminski, described the local, national, and international social work achievements by Bertha Pappenheim, as well as her literary and artistic interests. It also contained tributes from board members, co-workers, and "daughters."

An interesting analysis of her personality was presented by Cora Berliner, a leading Jewish educator and a member of the Federation board. She titled her tribute "Fight."

After quoting from the handwritten letter Bertha Pappenheim had sent to the Federation executive board when she resigned as president in 1934, Cora Berliner wrote:

"Letters in this and in an even stronger tone are not rare in Bertha Pappenheim's correspondence. Twice she turned her back on the Federation which she founded. In 1924 she resigned from the presidency with similar arguments and also stayed away from the Jubilee festivities in the year 1929 at the 25th anniversary celebration . . . . She also attacked other organizations and individuals in a similar manner.

"One wonders, where does this acrimony come from? It is surely in part a matter of her temperament. A volcano lived in this woman; it erupted when someone angered her. Was it that she enjoyed a fight? In part this, too. For when the person who was attacked resisted and tried to defend his point of view, reproaching her as being unfair or even self-righteous, she was not in the least hurt or angered. On the contrary, she felt a certain satisfaction in having goaded the other person into taking a stand and did not notice the wounds she had inflicted. But a qualification is necessary. She fought only about things that were involved directly with her ultimate aims. She could lash out without mercy at what she saw as indifference, weakness, or untruthfulness, and she could never be convinced that her opponent might have realistic reasons for his attitude. But if she had the feeling that she had slid off factual ground and hurt the other person in a personal sense, she would unhesitatingly apologize and turn back her assault.

"But it would be wrong to try and explain her attitude toward people and institutions by only considering her temperament and joy in battle. She painfully felt the tragedy of these fights. The battle itself was never the purpose per se. She only brought out her heavy artillery when her mission—the exercise of her ultimate aims—was threatened. No matter how much she should resent and scold, disdain and withdraw, if the same mission demanded it, she also found the way back to people. She loved people and needed them, but she did not permit herself to escape the educational task to which she felt called.

"In the autumn of 1934 she left the board because she did not agree with the attitude of two chairmen toward many of the demands she made on the Federation. Though it was immensely difficult for her, she stayed away from the convention of the national board at Nauheim, probably because she believed that her stepping out and staying away would have more success than an open attack. It probably hit her hard that this did not happen, that the women, though shaken and perplexed when they learned of her resignation, simply entrusted themselves to the existing leadership without investigating her reasons for resigning. But she did not—and this was perhaps the greatest quality in her—bury herself in her sorrow and annoyance; she found the way back to what she felt was her mission. The words she expressed a year later at the convention of the main committee in Berlin about the free, charitable work of women (not as civil servants but as volunteers) were also extremely aggressive but they were said out of deep conviction, not to destroy but to summon up strength and to build . . .

"Battle was her life element and the expression of her strength. She used a sharp rapier and did not spare the opponent, but she never misused the fight for small or personal reasons. Battle was as holy to her as was social work."

    Another perceptive tribute was given by Margarethe Susman, the poet, who had tutored Bertha Pappenheim in Greek philosophy and who knew her for the last ten years of her life. She wrote of "Bertha Pappenheim's Spiritual World":
    "We all know that with the death of Bertha Pappenheim a great woman, a real fighter, a true Jewish person, has left us, that a life is gone which will not reappear in Judaism for generations, because of the drastically changed living conditions. We know her life was interwoven with a wide and fateful web of Jewish and German influences, that she lived through the developments of our times with an alert and passionate mind, never yielding her original position, no matter how intensely the changes of the era affected her. Her personality, her life, were from the beginning to the end a single flaming protest against the religious and moral dissolution of the time in which she lived. In the middle of all the uprooted, wavering, and tumbling lives in our world, she always stood erect and always progressed. For she possessed the highest gift that can be bestowed on a person, particularly those living in the chaos of enormous upheavals: a *way*. And this way was also a road for others. She led the way, pointing out the goals. She was gifted with great strength and the capacity to bring order to lives, to arrange them, to lead and to train people . . . . This delicate woman took on the world . . . .
    "Her unshakable faith in the law and in everything lawful, which governed her entire life, was evident in a sphere which seemed farthest from her being: in her relationship to *beauty* and *art*. This faith, which on the one hand brought about her severe sense of justice produced on the other hand her deep and singular relation to art—to any kind of art, but mainly to the fine arts and architecture. This, too, was not a mere side interest in her life, but absorbed her fully and earnestly. Art was for her, in a way, a genuine proof of life. In one of her memoranda, she called art 'the highest emanation of the human mind.'
    "It shows the great impartiality of her thinking that she disputed the belief that the Jewish mind has the prophetic expression of art, this highest emanation of the human mind. 'There is no Jewish art,' she exclaimed more than once. 'There

are perceptions where hate and love meet.' In one of her most moving memoranda she states in what sense, and from what viewpoint, she denied the Jew's artistic talent: 'No Jew could have conceived the idea of the Cathedral of Cologne, because we lack the finesse and power to express form and the technically productive qualities of patience and perseverance, but also because the Jewish idea of God transcends the vaulted arches of a cathedral!'

"Certainly her sense of humor, her knowledge of beauty, the charm and melancholy of her smile, her delicate, airy art, and her memoranda were only sketchy expressions of form, light arabesques of a life that at its deepest was always attached to *reality* and its changes . . . .

"The deepest expression of her life, where she heard God's will and brought it to consciousness, is found not only in her deeds but in the prayers which she wrote, particularly in the later years of her life.

" . . . She hardly ever created poetry; lyric was alien to her. She believed in the mind, but she did not believe in the word. Lyrical words probably seemed to her too ecstatic, creating smoke that covered truth with a screen and thus obliterating truth, about which one had to make decisions. . . . And for a closely related reason she mistrusted love for a single person. As the word veils pure truth, she felt love for a single person veiled love for mankind.

" . . . Her alert mind questioned to the end, but her heart knew that great tranquility came from it."

Ottilie Schoenewald, the new president, wrote:

"Bertha Pappenheim had the nature of a fighter in the highest sense of the word, a fighter for everything good and beautiful. Her aim was never, 'Victory,' but progress, development towards something better, improvement of people and conditions. She was entirely without pathos, without sentimentality, her thinking crystal and her soul not to be bribed. But in times of emotion she could develop a pathos that carried you away—fiery eloquence, prophetic vistas.

"The Federation and Isenburg—these were the buttresses on which her life's work rested, the poles between which the spark of her mind leaped from idea to deed, from planning to fulfillment . . . .

"Her occasional turning away from the Federation was not fruitless rebellion. As a sharp plow opens up the earth and prepares it to receive new seed, so the reproaches and criticisms by the spiritual leader, which were often felt painfully and bitterly, spurred her co-workers on to self-examination and fuller devotion. Under the effervescent richness of a mind that always gave itself anew, the hierarchy lost all importance . . . . She was always the center, guide, and unattainable example. Even during one of our last meetings of the Executive Board, which she attended as representative of Isenburg, she told us: 'I feel that I cannot tear myself away from any place in Jewish women's work, without giving up a part of myself.'

"In thousands of Jewish women's hearts, Bertha Pappenheim has stirred the hidden and often extinguished spark of God, the all-embracing motherly responsibility, the preparedness to help and sacrifice, the wrestling for highest spiritual goals. These sparks unite in our Jewish Federation to form a pure flame of aim and effort, a flame we pass on to coming generations, and thus forge the invisible chain which connects a life's work to eternity."

Two of Bertha Pappenheim's "daughters," women who had known her since the days of the orphanage, told of their feelings. Helene Kramer described what had happened to Bertha Pappenheim when she became director of the orphanage: "It meant a complete change in her life. With generous devotion and with complete renunciation of her former way of living—she had been spoiled in Vienna in every way, leading there the life of a daughter of the wealthy—she fulfilled the multi-faceted demands in a field of work that up to then had been alien to her."

The other "daughter" was Johanna Stahl, who concluded her tribute:
"The brilliance of her personality shone above all, above her work and above her words. The deepest, most vital parts of this personality were only felt by those who were with her in the rare quiet hours, and her words to me remain a beacon on

my road."

The tribute written by Helene Hanna Thon, a leader in the Zionist movement who had met Bertha Pappenheim in Palestine in 1911 and had admired her, was titled, "Her Picture on My Desk." Mrs. Thon said:

"In these days of sorrow and suffering in Palestine, every person who feels bound to his brothers and sisters who need help is driven more than ever to the dwellings of the poorest in the country who—as everywhere in the world—are affected first by the misery of the times. When, then, I come home depressed from the sad experiences in the Jewish streets of the old town of Jerusalem and other districts of the poor to continue the work at my desk, there stands before me Bertha Pappenheim's picture, and as I study her features, the depression of the day falls away, and there remains the recognition that beyond the harshness of our Jewish fate there is eternal immortal spirit.

"The eyes of the woman in the picture before me have all their life looked deep into human suffering, human weakness, and immorality, until a reflection of all human sorrow, and above all, of all Jewish sorrow, resided in them. But they looked through this suffering, as through a transparent shell, until they reached the core of things: recognition of the immortal life of the Jewish people and of the immortal strength of Judaism.

"When years ago I visited Bertha Pappenheim in the company of an eleven-year-old Palestinian boy, the child said, upon our leaving the room, 'She looks like Deborah,' so strongly had he been moved by the nobility of this face with its silvery white crown, resting on the delicate shoulders of the equally noble body."

An eloquent tribute was later paid by Dr. Rahel Straus, the woman physician who was a member of the Federation's board, a Zionist who left Germany in August, 1933, to live in Palestine. In a book she wrote called *We Lived in Germany*, she spoke of Bertha Pappenheim, saying she had not only admired but loved her.

"One often gets very discouraged, if one fights for the good, one very often gets bitter. Bertha Pappenheim had become bitter and sometimes, it would seem, hard. But I felt how soft and warm she was inside as I saw her with the children in Isenburg. There were moments also when the whole of her dammed-up warmth and kindliness could be seen."

For the biography, to be published at a later date, Hannah Karminski sought information from the only living member of Bertha Pappenheim's immediate family, her brother Wilhelm. He told her that no written records existed of the almost thirty years his sister spent in Vienna. He died one year after his sister.

Hannah never wrote the biography. She left all the material she had collected in a trunk in the basement of the Berlin house of a Swiss man she knew; the house was bombed and completely destroyed. Hannah could have fled the Nazis by escaping to her sister's home in Switzerland, but she chose to stay in Germany and try to help Jewish families escape, as did Cora Berliner.

On June 21, 1942, Cora Berliner wrote to Dr. Hans Schaffer in Berlin, former Secretary of the Ministry of Finance who lost his job because of the Nazis and who later escaped to Sweden: "Tomorrow I and a number of my friends, among them Franz Eugen [Franz Eugen Fuchs], will start on our journey." This meant they were being deported to a concentration camp. " . . . I don't know when I shall meet you again. Hannah will give you news . . . . There have been times lately when I felt that I kept too much outside reality. Now there will be new impressions and new possibilities to prove one's mettle."

Four days later Hannah wrote Dr. Schaffer:

"I feel that a letter to you will help me to get over this sense of infinite loneliness . . . . They went off on Tuesday night, a group of the best of our people. Not to be one of them was very painful . . . . It is hard to be here now, and the morphine of work will have to help sustain us . . . .

"When I saw Cora for the last time, on Tuesday, she was very disappointed that I did not bring her a letter from you. 'Usually it always worked out,' she said. And she wants me to assure you that she believes with all her heart in a reunion."

One month later, on July 24, Hannah wrote:

"Alas, there is no longer any satisfaction in this work: it has not much to do with social work as we knew it, but where it is a question of human beings, not of real estate or monies, liquidation is particularly difficult. Since we *are*, however, dealing with human beings, there are still moments when 'still-being-here' appears meaningful and makes sense—and that must suffice as 'satisfaction.'

"C. and the other friends took books along . . . . As far as I know, C. took Faust, Part I. When I went to see them on the last day before the departure, they were sitting in the court-yard in the sun reading Goethe . . . .

"Yesterday Mrs. Frankel came to see me . . . . Here is another person who tries to overcome loneliness by helping others . . . ."

Dr. Leo Baeck, President of the Organization of German Jews and friend of both Hannah's and Cora's, wrote on November 27, 1942, to Dr. Schaffer:

"Our dear friend Hannah is no longer in her home; she is about to go to a concentration camp . . . .

"I need not tell you that she is bearing her fate with dignity. Wherever she may be, she will be a source of strength to the people around her. Her firm willpower will also mean a great deal for her health, which has lately improved after weeks of ups and downs. We are confident of a reunion in better days and of renewed common work . . . ."

The two women were never heard from again. Hannah, then forty-five years old, was put on a train in Berlin with a group of other social workers. No one knew where it was going, no one ever heard of its arriving anywhere, and all the station masters along the route denied seeing it.

Dr. Baeck was deported to the concentration camp at Theresienstadt two months later. He survived. His letter and the last letters of Hannah and Cora Berliner appear as "documents" in the *Yearbook II,* 1957, at the Leo Baeck Institute of Jews from Germany.

Helene Kramer served as director of the Home for several years, then emigrated to the United States, where, now in her nineties, she is a resident of the Daughters of Jacob Home for the Aged in the Bronx, New York. A few of the children were sent to Israel but mostly it was too late to save them or the young girls, who either were forced by the Nazis to become prostitutes or sent to concentration camps.

"The fate of the girls was so sad nobody would speak of it," says Dora Edinger, who tried to find out the details. Her son, Lewis J. Edinger, a member of the Department of Public Law and Government, the European Institute and the Faculty of International Affairs at Columbia University, visited Isenburg after the war to take photographs of the restored home for his mother's biography of Bertha Pappenheim. He asked a neighbor what had happened to the residents of the Home but the man refused to say.

The board was forced to sell Bertha Pappenheim's home. Her private possessions were taken to Federation headquarters in Berlin. Her little house and the four buildings of the Home were burned by the Nazis in the pogrom of November 9, 1938, and almost completely destroyed. One house was rebuilt and today serves as a shelter for retarded children.

Bertha Pappenheim was spared the sight of the Nazi pillage and wreckage of the institution that meant so much to her and of the burning of her home. She was spared, too, the knowledge of what happened to the ninety-three students at the Beth-Jakob Seminary when they heard the Nazis announce they would turn the seminary into a brothel.

The girls took baths, then all swallowed poison. A letter written by one of them and smuggled out held the lines:

> "Death does not terrify us; we go out to meet him.
> We served our God while we were alive;
> Pity oh merciful Father! Oh pity the people
>   that knew Thee!
> For there is no more pity in men."

In 1954, after the defeat of the Nazi party, after pity in men was partially restored in the world, a stamp in honor of Bertha Pappenheim was issued by the West Bonn government at the suggestion of Dr. Baeck. It was one of the series, "Helpers of Humanity."

Bertha Pappenheim wrote one prayer that she did not date, perhaps waiting for a date to be put on it, the date of her death, May 28, 1936:

"When I descend into eternal darkness, and when the

waves of creation and of nothingness close over my head, let me, unbroken, have willed only the right—without detour and without rest."

PART III

The Woman

"Hysterics suffer mainly from reminiscences."

Sigmund Freud
*On the Psychical Mechanism
of Hysterical Phenomena,
Preliminary Communication, 1893.*

1

The Case of Anna O.

For five months after he had concluded the treatment of his young hysterical patient Dr. Josef Breuer told no one of her amazing "talking cure."

Then, on November 18, 1882, he spoke of what had happened to a close friend, a young physician in whom he had great faith as a research scientist. The younger man's name was Sigmund Freud.

Breuer described how his patient's paralysis, poor vision, cough, muteness, and headaches had all disappeared under hypnosis as she talked about experiences related to each symptom. She was able to recall the first time the symptom had appeared and the emotions it provoked in her even though she had lost all conscious memory of the event and the emotions.

Though Freud knew nothing about the treatment of hysteria by hypnosis, he was fascinated. He asked questions, and together they discussed the implication of such a cure. He believed Breuer had made a revolutionary discovery in treating hysteria and should inform the medical world. Breuer disagreed, said he had enough of hysterical women, they were an ordeal and he was giving them up.

Freud was twenty-six, only three years older than Breuer's young patient. In 1880, when Breuer first visited his patient, Freud was a teaching assistant in the research laboratory of the Vienna Institute of Physiology, headed by Dr. Ernest Brücke.

He was pursuing research in histology, that branch of biology concerned with the microscopic study of the structure of tissue.

Freud received his medical degree on March 31, 1881, almost on the very day—actually the day after—Breuer's patient first stepped out of the bed in which she had lain paralyzed since December 11th. In the summer of 1881, when Breuer was visiting his young patient at her country home, Freud was studying the nerve cells of the crayfish under a microscope.

As Breuer's patient ended her treatment in the spring of 1882, Freud met and fell in love with nineteen-year-old Martha Bernays, who lived in Vienna and was a friend of Breuer's young patient.

Freud first met Breuer, then a distinguished teacher, at the Institute in the late 1870's. From the first they found they shared common scientific interests. Freud often accompanied Breuer on visits to patients. At times Breuer loaned small sums of money to Freud, who was then penniless.

Freud became secretly engaged to Martha Bernays on June 17, 1882, and on the advice of Brücke gave up the financially unrewarding research—which he had hoped to make his life's work—in order to prepare for general practice. He then became an intern at the Viennese General Hospital, one of the most famous teaching centers of the world. As a junior resident physician in May, 1883, he transferred from the department of medicine to the psychiatric clinic run by Dr. Theodor Meynart, who had impressed Freud in medical school as the most brilliant man he had ever met. According to general medical opinion Meynart was the most astute brain anatomist of that era, though not an outstanding psychiatrist. But Freud's study of the mental disorder called "Meynart's Amentia"—acute hallucinatory psychosis—made him aware that hallucinations might be related to wishes that the patient did not consciously realize he had.

Freud now became very interested in studying neurology. There were few neurological specialists in Vienna, but in the distance "glimmered the great name of Charcot," as Freud put it, and he went to Paris on October 11, 1885, to study under the famous Professor of Pathological Anatomy at the Salpêtrière, a mammoth institution, just outside Paris, housing thousands of the chronically ill, aged, and insane. It was a "great asylum of human misery," to use Charcot's words.

Freud studied for four months with Charcot, watched him induce hysterical symptoms in a hypnotized patient, then remove the symptoms during a second hypnosis. A man in a hypnotic trance was told his right arm would feel paralyzed when he came out of the trance. Awakened, the man found he could not move his right arm. When asked why, he said he did not know or made up a false reason. Then he was again hypnotized, and the suggestion made that his arm would be normal when he woke, which it proved to be.

Seeing this occur time after time, Freud concluded there was a part of the human mind outside awareness that was more powerful than the conscious, that could in fact control the conscious. The "unconscious," referred to by philosophers and poets of the past, had now, by way of hypnotism, come alive before Freud's eyes.

He recalled Breuer's young patient and told Charcot of the "talking cure." But Charcot seemed unimpressed. "So," Freud said, "I never returned to it and allowed it to pass from my mind." But only for the four months he remained in Paris. When he returned to Vienna on April 4, 1886, after spending the month of March in Berlin studying pediatrics, the memory of the "talking cure" once again haunted him. In his words, he "made" Breuer tell him "more about it." And he persuaded Breuer, who for four years had practiced only internal medicine, to resume treatment of hysterical women.

Ten years after Breuer had last seen his young patient, Freud finally persuaded him to co-author an article about the "talking cure," referring to the case from notes he had kept when he saw her. By then Freud had cured several of his own patients of hysterical symptoms. He had moved from the *Suehnhaus,* a palatial apartment house facing the *Ringstrasse,* to *Bergasse* 19, near the University of Vienna. Breuer still lived at *Brandstätte* 8.

The two authors gave their article the formidable title, "On the Psychical Mechanism of Hysterical Phenomena, Preliminary Communication." In preparation for the article Freud wrote three "memoranda," the first in the form of a letter to Breuer dated June 29, 1892. In it he says, "I am tormented by the problem of how it will be possible to give a two-dimensional picture of anything that is so much of a solid as our theory of neurosis." It is interesting that Freud uses the word "tormented," the very word Breuer's young patient used to describe how she felt, the word which first led Breuer to question her further.

In the memoranda Freud refers to a "second state of consciousness." This is believed to be the first time in his published scientific work that he mentions the unconscious.

The "Preliminary Communication" appeared in 1893, in two issues, January 1st and January 15th, of the periodical *Neurologisches Centralblatt* [the principal German neurological journal], which came out fortnightly in Berlin. The article was immediately reprinted in Vienna in the *Wiener Medizinische Blatter* [The Vienna Medical Journal].

The authors refer to the hysterical young woman as "one of our patients," and describe her as "a girl who, while watching a sickbed in a torment of anxiety, fell into a twilight state and had a terrifying hallucination, while her right arm, which was hanging over the back of her chair, went to sleep. From this there developed a paresis [paralysis] of the same arm accompanied by contracture and anesthesia [loss of sensation]."

They report that in this "highly complicated case of hysteria" all the symptoms, "which sprang from separate causes, were separately removed." They also found in other cases "to our great surprise," that every hysterical symptom immediately and permanently disappeared "when we had succeeded in bringing clearly to light the memory of the event by which it was provoked and in arousing its accompanying affect [emotion], and when the patient had described that event in the greatest possible detail and had put the affect into words."

They warned, "Recollection without affect almost invariably produces no result." In other words, there had to be expression of emotion. Words alone—intellectualization—were of no help.

Freud's classic line, "Hysterics suffer mainly from reminiscences," appears in this article. He explained that the reminiscences in question relate to situations where an impulse to act was repressed. The symptoms appear "in place of" the action and represent a "strangulated" emotion. Both the traumatic incident and the emotion are lost to the patient's memory as though they had never happened. But the symptoms persist.

Hysterical symptoms arise when the emotion involved in a mental process is prevented from being worked over consciously in the normal way and is diverted into "a wrong path," such as conversion into physical illness, as in the case of Breuer's young patient. Because her emotional reaction to an event that was traumatic in her life had been repressed, the emotion remained attached to the memory, hidden in the unconscious.

The authors explained that an injury that has been repaid, even if only in words, is recollected quite differently from one that has had to be accepted without an emotional outlet. The injured person's reaction to the trauma only has a completely "cathartic" effect if it is an adequate reaction, "as, for instance, revenge," if there has been hurt.

Language may serve as a substitute for action, they maintained. With the help of language, an emotion can be discharged almost as effectively as if it had been expressed at the time it was felt. Speaking itself is an adequate reaction when, for instance, "it is a lamentation or giving utterance to a tormenting secret, e.g., a confession." If there is no such reaction, in deeds or words, "or in the mildest cases in tears," any recollection of the event retains its emotional tone.

But if the original experience, along with the emotions it produced, can be brought into consciousness, the "imprisoned" emotion is discharged, the force that maintains the symptom ceases to operate, and the symptom disappears. This treatment the authors call "the cathartic method."

Freud then persuaded Breuer to join him in the writing of a book, *Studies on Hysteria,* published in 1895 in Leipzig and Vienna. It is the world's first book on psychoanalysis. It contains a fuller account of the treatment of Breuer's young patient, the study of whose "remarkable case" led to the "Preliminary Communication," according to the authors.

The basic concepts of psychoanalysis appear in the book, including repression, psychic determinism, unconscious mental activity, overdetermination, defenses, resistance, the sexual cause of neurosis, psychic trauma, conflict, conversion, transference, and ambivalence. Another of Freud's classic lines is found here: "Much is won if we succeed in transforming hysterical misery into common unhappiness."

And here, for the first time, Breuer's young patient is given a name—a pseudonym, for it was medical custom to bestow a false name on a patient to protect the identity both of the patient and his family. Breuer's patient was called Anna O.

He admitted he had "suppressed a large number of quite interesting details" in the study. But in comparison with the medical cases of that era, it was an "extensive" case history.

He ended his description of her treatment by saying: "After this she left Vienna and traveled for a while, but it was a considerable time before she regained her mental balance entirely. Since then she has enjoyed complete health."

Though in his chapter on her treatment Breuer notes "a complete lack of sexuality" in Anna O., saying she never spoke of love, in his chapter on theory he maintains, "The sexual instinct is undoubtedly the most powerful source of persisting increases of excitation (and consequently of neurosis)." Traumatic experiences produce quantities of excitation, or energy charge, to the nerves, too large to be dealt with in the normal way and thus create neuroses.

While hysteria is usually caused by a sexual problem, the case of Anna O. "proves that a fairly severe case of hysteria can develop, flourish, and be resolved without having a sexual basis," Breuer wrote in a letter to the psychiatrist Auguste Forel on November 21st, 1907, twelve years after *Studies on Hysteria* appeared. Breuer added, "I confess that plunging into sexuality in theory and practice is not to my taste. But what have my taste and my feeling about what is seemly and what is unseemly to do with the question of what is true?"

Freud made his only trip to the United States in September, 1909, on the invitation of Clark University in Worcester, Massachusetts, to give five lectures at their Twentieth Anniversary celebration. In his first lecture, he said, "We must grant that it is a merit to have created psychoanalysis, but it is not my merit. I was a student, busy with the passing of my last examinations, when another physician of Vienna, Dr. Josef Breuer, made the first application of this method to the case of a hysterical girl (1880-1882)."

Devoting this lecture to the case of Anna O, Freud

described how for years physicians had not understood hysteria and were reluctant to treat it, being unsympathetic toward it and often "punishing" the patient by withdrawing interest. He added:

"Now Dr. Breuer did not deserve this reproach in this case; he gave his patient sympathy and interest, although at first he did not understand how to help her. Probably this was easier for him on account of those superior qualities of the patient's mind and character to which he bears witness in his account of the case . . . . His sympathetic observation soon found the means which made the first help possible."

It was especially to be noted, Freud pointed out, that Anna O., in almost all traumatic situations, "had to suppress a strong excitement, instead of giving vent to it by appropriate words and deeds . . . . While she was seated by her father's sickbed, she was careful to betray nothing of her anxiety and her painful depression to the patient. When, later, she reproduced the same scene before the physician, the emotion which she had suppressed on the occurrence of the scene burst out with especial strength, as though it had been pent up all along."

Ending this lecture, Freud told the audience, "You have probably also felt, and rightly, that Breuer's investigations gave you only a very incomplete theory and insufficient explanation of the phenomena which we have observed. But complete theories do not fall from Heaven . . . ."

Freud was the one who worked over the years to develop the "complete theory," the theory that started with the case of Anna O. He explored the secrets of the mind, extending the range of psychological observations made by Breuer and himself to include not only his patients but himself. He could accept the advice, "Physician, heal thyself." His own analysis opened the gates to regions of understanding, as he applied to himself the words of Terence: "Nothing that is human is alien to me."

Freud would let nothing deter him in his search for the truth, and Breuer sensed this. Freud wrote to his fiancée on February 2nd, 1886, seven months before they were married:

"Do you know what Breuer said to me one evening? That he had discovered what an infinitely bold and fearless person I concealed behind my mask of shyness. I have always believed that of myself, but never dared to say it to anyone. I have often felt as if I had inherited all the passion of our ancestors when they defended their Temple, as if I could joyfully cast away my life in a great cause. And with all that I was always so powerless and could not express the flowing passions even by a word or a poem. So I have always suppressed myself, and I believe people must notice that in me."

Anna O. had suppressed herself too, but encouraged by Breuer she had finally expressed some of her hidden emotions. This young woman, who had been helped by a devoted young physician without whose dedication she might have killed herself or spent the rest of her days in the jungle of madness, was the one whose treatment Freud described as the starting point of psychoanalysis.

Up to then, mental illness was believed to have an organic cause. It was treated mainly by physical therapy such as mild electrical shocks, drugs, change of diet, and rest cures. Anna O. proved this theory false. Her case showed that the causes of mental aberrations lay within the mind itself.

2

The Revelation

For more than half a century the identity of Anna O. remained a mystery, her secret guarded, her family protected. It looked as though the world would never know the real name of the brilliant, gifted young woman who was the first lady of psychoanalysis.

Then in 1953 Ernest Jones revealed her identity in *The Life and Work of Sigmund Freud.*

Anna O. was Bertha Pappenheim.

Freud had told him this, Jones reported, as had a cousin of Bertha Pappenheim's, Mrs. Ena Lewisohn. In making this revelation about Anna O., Jones wrote, "Since she was the real discoverer of the cathartic method, her name, which was actually Bertha Pappenheim, deserves to be commemorated."

Jones also cleared up another mystery. It was one that had remained hidden, possibly from everyone except Breuer, Freud, and Bertha Pappenheim. Why had Breuer delayed so long in telling the world of the very important "talking cure"?

According to Jones there were "peculiar circumstances surrounding the end of the treatment" and Freud had given him a fuller account than had appeared in Freud's own writings.

Breuer had furnished a faint clue to the "peculiar circumstances" when he wrote in *Studies on Hysteria* that he had "suppressed a large number of quite interesting details." From the very first Freud sensed that Breuer was reluctant to talk

195

about the case, contrary to his usual willingness to discuss all medical details. Freud wondered too why Breuer had suddenly stopped treating hysterical women.

The first reference by Freud to Bertha Pappenheim appears in a letter to Martha Bernays written on July 13th, 1883, at two in the morning. Freud tells his fiancée that he had visited Breuer that evening and Breuer mentioned "your friend Bertha Pappenheim." Both young women were members of the small German-Jewish community in Vienna, where Martha Bernays had arrived from Hamburg in 1869 at the age of thirteen, and knew each other fairly well. They may even have been distantly related, for Martha Bernays' grandfather, Isaac Bernays, chief Rabbi of Hamburg, was related to Heinrich Heine, as was Bertha Pappenheim through her mother.

About a year after Martha Bernays' marriage on September 30th, 1886, she wrote her mother that Bertha Pappenheim had come to see her "more than once," at the Freuds' apartment in the *Suehnhaus*. In this letter, written in 1887, Martha said Bertha Pappenheim seemed pretty well in the daytime but still suffered hallucinatory states as evening approached. Her letter appears never to have been published. Either Freud told Jones about it or Jones was permitted to see it by a member of the Freud family.

At the time that Freud first wrote his fiancée about Bertha Pappenheim, he was on the most intimate terms with Breuer. He referred to him as "the ever-loyal Breuer." Freud also had a "special admiration," Jones says, for Breuer's wife, Mathilde Altmann Breuer, "a beautiful, charming woman." Freud named his youngest daughter Anna, after Anna Hammerschlag, a sister of Breuer's son-in-law. Anna Hammerschlag was also a daughter of one of Freud's old teachers, Samuel Hammerschlag, and one of Freud's favorite patients, Jones adds.

Freud started the letter describing his evening's visit to Breuer remarking to his fiancée that the day was the hottest, "most excruciating," of the whole season and he was "really almost crazy" with exhaustion. Feeling need of refreshment, he went to Breuer's home. Freud found Breuer had a headache, "the poor man" was taking salicyl. The first thing Breuer did was "chase" him into the bathtub, which he left "rejuvenated." Then they had supper upstairs in their shirtsleeves. There followed "a lengthy medical conversation on moral insanity and nervous diseases and strange case histories—your friend Bertha Pappenheim also cropped up—and then we became rather personal and intimate and he told me a number of things about his wife and children and asked me to repeat what he had said only 'after you are married to Martha.' "

The mention of "a lengthy medical conversation on moral insanity and nervous diseases and strange case histories," followed by "your friend Bertha Pappenheim," then becoming "rather personal and intimate," seemed to hint of something "personal and intimate" during Bertha Pappenheim's treatment.

It is possible, incidentally, that Bertha Pappenheim either saw this letter or was told about it by Martha. For, in explaining why she established the Home at Isenburg, the Home that became almost her whole life, Bertha Pappenheim said she conceived of it to help young girls "who obviously tend toward what we call 'moral insanity.' " The use of this phrase seems more than just coincidence. "Moral insanity" was not a term to be used idly by laymen or psychiatrists in the early twentieth century. It would have to possess very special meaning to the one who used it. Whether she was aware of it or not, Bertha Pappenheim may have been saying that she dedicated her life to saving girls like herself, victims of "moral insanity."

The next clue to the "peculiar circumstances" surrounding the end of treatment was furnished in 1914 with the publication of Freud's *History of the Psychoanalytic Movement*. He described the process of "transference" which takes place during psychoanalysis. Each patient "transfers" to the psychoanalyst the pent-up emotions of childhood, the love, hate, trust, distrust, and fear he originally felt for his mother and father. Freud spoke also of the process known as "counter-transference," in which the psychoanalyst "transfers" to the patient some of his childhood feelings. If the psychoanalyst is aware of these feelings and in control of them, he can cope with the patient's emotional outbursts, no matter how intense, and help the patient. But if the psychoanalyst has not resolved these feelings, he is apt to be alarmed by excessive show of love or hate or dependence by the patient and will be of little help.

Freud then said, speaking of Anna O.:

"In his treatment of her case, Breuer could make use of a very intense suggestible *rapport* on the part of the patient, which may serve us as a prototype of what we call 'transference' today. Now I have strong reasons for surmising that after all her symptoms had been relieved Breuer must have discovered from further indications the sexual motivation of this transference, but that the universal nature of this unexpected phenomenon escaped him, with the result that, as though confronted by an 'untoward event,' he broke off all further investigation. He never told me this in so many words, but he gave me at various times indications enough to justify this reconstruction of what happened."

Freud did not go into detail about the "untoward event" or "the sexual motivation" of Anna O.'s transference. But he mentioned transference again in his obituary for Breuer, who died in Vienna on June 20, 1925, at the age of eighty-four. Referring to Breuer's reluctance to treat any more hysterical patients, he said, "I found reason later to suppose that a purely emotional factor, too, had given him an aversion to further work on the elucidation of the neuroses. He had come up against something that is never absent—his patient's transference on to her physician—and he had not grasped the impersonal nature of the process."

That same year, in *An Autobiographical Study*, discussing his break with Breuer over the major part played by sexuality in causing neurosis, a theory that was at first rejected by the medical profession, Freud said:

"Breuer did what he could for some time longer to throw the great weight of his personal influence onto the scales in my favor, but he effected nothing and it was easy to see that he too shrank from recognizing the sexual aetiology [cause] of neuroses. He might have crushed me, or at least disconcerted me, by pointing to his own first patient, in whose case sexual factors had ostensibly played no part whatever. But he never did so, and I could not understand why this was until I came to interpret the case correctly and to reconstruct, from some remarks which he had made, the conclusion of his treatment of it."

Freud then explained: "After the work of catharsis had

seemed to be completed, the girl had suddenly developed a condition of 'transference love;' he had not connected this with her illness, and had therefore retired in dismay. It was obviously painful to him to be reminded of this apparent *contretemps*."

What was the nature of this "transference love?" What had taken place between Bertha Pappenheim and Josef Breuer that had so deeply affected Breuer that he would treat no more hysterical women after having been so profoundly interested in their cure?

What did happen, as revealed by Jones, proved as dramatic as the seemingly magical disappearance of Bertha Pappenheim's physical symptoms.

According to Jones, Breuer was so "engrossed" with his young patient that he talked of her "incessantly" at home. At first his wife "became bored at listening to no other topic." Then, before long, she turned "jealous."

She did not openly show her jealousy but instead, was "unhappy and morose," so that "it was a long time before Breuer, his thoughts elsewhere, divined the meaning of her state of mind." When he did, "it provoked a violent reaction in him, perhaps compounded of love and guilt, and he decided to bring the treatment to an end," Jones said.

The evening after he had concluded the treatment, according to Jones, Breuer was "fetched back" to her home. He discovered his young patient in a "greatly excited state." Jones describes the scene:

"The patient, who, according to him, had appeared to be an asexual being and had never made any allusion to such a forbidden topic throughout the treatment, was now in the throes of an hysterical childbirth (pseudocyesis), the logical termination of a phantom pregnancy that had been invisibly developing in response to Breuer's ministrations."

Though "profoundly shocked," Breuer managed to calm her by hypnotizing her. Then he "fled the house in a cold sweat."

The next day, he and his wife departed for Venice for "a second honeymoon," according to Jones. This resulted "in the conception of a daughter," and "the girl born in these curious circumstances was nearly sixty years later to commit suicide in

New York."

Confirmation of this traumatic end to the treatment, Jones maintained, could be found in a letter Freud wrote his fiancée at the time (also never published) which contains substantially the same story. Martha Bernays, after reading the letter, "at once identified herself with Breuer's wife and said she hoped the same thing would not ever happen to her," Jones says. Whereupon Freud commented, "For that to happen one has to be a Breuer."

There is also confirmation, that Jones did not cite, in a letter written by Freud on June 2, 1932, to Stefan Zweig, a relative of the widow who married Wilhelm Pappenheim, Bertha Pappenheim's brother. Freud wrote to Zweig at Hohe Warte, Vienna, to correct an error Zweig had made in describing the case of Anna O. in his book *Mental Healers*:

"What really happened with Breuer's patient I was able to guess later on, long after the break in our relations, when I suddenly remembered something Breuer had once told me in another context before we had begun to collaborate and which he never repeated. On the evening of the day when all her symptoms had been disposed of, he was summoned to the patient again, found her confused and writhing in abdominal cramps. Asked what was wrong with her, she replied: 'Now Dr. B.'s child is coming!' "

Freud added: "At this moment he held in his hand the key that would have opened the 'doors to the Mothers' [a reference from *Faust* to exploration of the depths] but he let it drop. With all his great intellectual gifts, there was nothing Faustian in his nature. Seized by conventional horror he took flight and abandoned the patient to a colleague. For months afterwards she struggled to regain her health in a sanitarium.

"I was so convinced of this reconstruction of mine that I published it somewhere. Breuer's youngest daughter (born shortly after the above-mentioned treatment, not without significance for the deeper connections) read my account and asked her father about it (shortly before his death). He confirmed my version, and she informed me about it later."

After her break with Breuer, Bertha Pappenheim, "the poor patient," according to Jones "did not fare so well as one might gather from Breuer's published account." She had a

relapse, then was taken to a private sanitarium in Gross Enzer-
dorf where she "inflamed the heart of the psychiatrist in
charge."

At this point, her mother, whom Jones described as
"somewhat of a dragon," rushed to Vienna from Frankfurt,
where she had gone to live, and "took her daughter back to
Frankfurt for good, at the end of the eighties."

One year after he ended treatment, Breuer heard Bertha
Pappenheim had become a morphine addict. He confided to
Freud that she was "quite unhinged and he wished she would
die and so be released from her suffering," Jones reported. But
she evidently gave up the addiction and returned for a while to
her hallucinatory states in the evening, according to the letter
Martha Freud wrote her mother in 1887.

Bertha Pappenheim's case sparked the idea that "hysterics
suffer from reminiscences," that a memory was repressed because of the powerful emotions it evoked that were believed
dangerous to the person's image of himself. Her case also
proved that the conscious was only one part of the human
mind, that there was also an unconscious which could control
conscious acts. Some of her unconscious wishes had been un-
covered under hypnosis when she was able to recall events of
the past, urged to do so by Breuer, sometimes, as he says,
"made" to do so.

As Freud understood the unconscious meaning of a symptom, he could then go on to the understanding of a dream,
which he called "the royal road" to the unconscious. In the
words of Dr. Walter A. Stewart, American psychoanalyst, "The
symptom became the Rosetta Stone that enabled him to interpret a dream."

In all Freud's monumental discoveries, Bertha Pappenheim may claim a share. Breuer made it seem truly a part-
nership between his young patient and himself, as though he
wanted her to share in the startling new psychic discovery, for
he used "we" in writing up The Case of Anna O. He said, "We
evolved the following procedure," speaking of the decision to
hypnotize her twice a day. And again: "We often noticed that
her dread of a memory . . . inhibited its emergence, which
had to be brought about forcibly by the patient or physician."

Freud never altered his belief that Breuer made two fundamental discoveries out of which psychoanalysis developed: a neurotic symptom results from emotions deprived of their normal outlet, and the symptom disappears when its unconscious causes are made conscious.

It is a long way from these two simple but basic discoveries to the complicated theories of psychoanalysis. The disappearance of Anna O.'s symptoms would today be only the start of her psychoanalysis, for much about the nature of emotional illness, with its roots in the sexual and aggressive conflicts of childhood, was discovered by Freud years after Breuer concluded Anna O.'s treatment. These earlier conflicts were never recognized by Breuer.

In a sense Bertha Pappenheim filled a need in Freud's life; perhaps she was the only woman he ever really needed in his work. She was the match that flamed the fire of his mind.

She was never his patient, but he knew her better than anyone else did, even Breuer. For Breuer did not possess Freud's special gifts—an intellectual curiosity that knew no bounds and an imagination that was vivid yet controlled. Breuer became too frightened of his own feelings, whereas Freud, as he demonstrated with his own patients, could stand apart from the anguish, the love, the passion, the hate, the dependency, and the deep yearnings in Bertha Pappenheim and apply his great insights to the understanding of the human mind.

In a letter dated July 8, 1915, written to Dr. James J. Putnam, professor of neurology at Harvard University, Freud wrote:

" . . . I never saw his [Breuer's] famous first case and only learned of it years later from Breuer's report." (Freud may have used "saw" in a professional, rather than a personal, sense.)

On his trip to America to speak at Clark University in 1909, Freud visited the slums of the lower east side of Manhattan. This was the same year Bertha Pappenheim made her only trip to the United States, and she too mentioned visiting those slums, the Henry Street Settlement House in particular.

If Freud ever did meet Bertha Pappenheim, he guarded her secret well.

3

The Lost Years

In 1895 Bertha Pappenheim was appointed director of the Girls Orphanage in Frankfurt. This was the same year *Studies on Hysteria* was published in Leipzig and Vienna. Did she ever read the book that established her as the heroine of psychoanalysis?

Dora Edinger, her relative by marriage and her biographer, believes Bertha Pappenheim did read *Studies on Hysteria*. She says, "Bertha Pappenheim was not the kind of person to avoid reading it. She had great moral courage. I am sure she read everything Freud ever wrote."

Bertha Pappenheim gives several clues which indicate she may have read about herself as Anna O. In a letter to Gertrud Ehrenwerth from the Jewish hospital in Munich after surgery, she writes that she cannot say when she will return to Isenburg "because who says A. has also to say B." Though this was a colloquialism, it might still be construed, taking into account the symbolic language of the unconscious, as "who says A. (Anna) has also to say B. (Bertha)." And also taking into account the possibility that surgery would symbolize castration in her unconscious, representing a cutting off of part of her, it might bring to memory a prior feeling of castration, her phantom pregnancy with Breuer. The birth of a baby, even a fantasied baby, may be felt as loss of part of the body.

She also writes in this letter, " . . . there are possibilities in human beings which grow only if given a chance. This does not mean that one need not talk over things which are not going well or that in constant cooperation nobody can be hurt by sharing something." This could refer to her treatment with Breuer.

Then, in the only letter ever found of her extensive correspondence with Hannah Karminski, she writes:

"Books can actually disturb me if I feel I am forced to read one." Was she by any chance alluding to the "one" book that could "actually disturb" her if she was "forced" to read it? Or re-read it?

She may also be giving a clue to the past in a speech at an educational conference held by the Federation in 1929 when she describes the girls at Isenburg as "homeless and without ties," living an uprooted and empty life. She suggests that the doors of the Home remain closed "to all sources of excitement which might weaken the body and paralyze all forces of resistance, until the patient has learned to apply her own limits."

The use of the word "patient" in this connotation is inaccurate, the girls at the Home were not called "patients." Perhaps, for a moment, she permitted her unconscious to present herself, Breuer's "patient," who had learned so well "to apply her own limits" to keep out "all sources of excitement which might weaken the body and paralyze all forces of resistance."

Her letter to Felix Warburg possibly holds another clue. She tells him she is writing about her trip through a part of French-occupied Germany at the suggestion of their mutual cousin, Louise, whose home is her "sanitarium." This may be subtle reference to the sanitarium where she was reported by Jones to have been sent after the treatment by Breuer. She may be saying she now uses Louise's home as a refuge, a place to rest. She always felt close to Louise; she moved near her older, married cousin when her mother died, and seemed to depend on Louise for comfort as well as for financial contribution to the Home.

Bertha Pappenheim remarked, in answer to the questionnaire about her organizing ability published in the Blatter, that "in human relations and in struggle the courage of free expression is absolutely necessary, but it may also cause even greater difficulties." On a deeper level this might be description of her experience with Breuer, where she was able to indulge in "the courage of free expression" only to find it caused "even greater difficulties" because of her unconscious wish to have his baby.

She told the audience at the 25th anniversary of the Girls' Club, "As you grow older and have your memory firmly under control, you will remember only the things you want to remember and will forget those you don't."

This is apt description of the psychic process of repression, one of the chief concepts to which her experience with Breuer led Freud.

Some of her relatives knew she was Anna O., that in her early twenties she had suffered a "serious breakdown." Dr. Ludwig Edinger, whose wife was Bertha Pappenheim's second cousin, revealed this to his daughter-in-law, Dora Edinger.

Dora Edinger then asked her aunt by marriage, Mrs. Louise Goldschmidt, "Is it true Bertha Pappenheim is the Anna O. mentioned in Freud's book, *Studies on Hysteria?*"

Her aunt replied casually, "Yes."

Dora Edinger says, "Bertha Pappenheim knew I had been told she was Anna O. But showing me the family chart was as far as she would go." She explained that the day Bertha Pappenheim first brought out the family chart, she saw some names underlined in one color, some in another. Bertha Pappenheim explained, pointing to the first color, that these relatives had "the social bacillus," among them the Warburgs and others with a strong social conscience. Then pointing to names underlined in the second color, she said, "and this is the other bacillus," alluding to some who had mental breakdowns. Dora Edinger noted that a few names were underlined in both colors.

Bertha Pappenheim never spoke of her breakdown to her co-workers, probably not even to Hannah Karminski, though no one knows this for certain. Dr. Edinger comments, "This complete silence about the earlier years was surprising, since she liked to talk about herself, her parents, and her education. I think her complete hiding of her analytic experience came from a fear that people would misunderstand and think she was crazy. She had to protect herself. It was a different era."

Some persons outside her family undoubtedly knew Bertha Pappenheim was Anna O., according to Ellen M. Jensen in her article, "Anna O—A Study of Her Later Life," appearing in the *Psychoanalytic Quarterly,* 1970. Miss Jensen, a librarian in the State Hospital in Risskov, Denmark, says:

"Although it is always stated that Anna O's identity was unknown, it seems probable to me that a number of her contemporaries knew that Bertha Pappenheim was Anna O . . . . It is almost unthinkable that people who read the book *Studies on Hysteria,* published by Breuer and Freud and reviewed in a Vienna newspaper, and who remembered that for a long period this same Breuer, a well-known physician, visited the Pappenheim family every day, should not have guessed the connection between these visits and the case history, 'Anna O.' "

There are some skeptics who doubt Bertha Pappenheim was Anna O., but Miss Jensen is convinced, citing Breuer's description of Anna O. as "markedly intelligent, with an astonishingly quick grasp of things and penetrating intuition . . . a powerful intellect . . . great poetic and imaginative gifts, which were under the control of a sharp and critical common sense . . . she was only influenced by arguments, never by mere assertions . . . her willpower was energetic, tenacious, and persistent . . . one of her essential character traits was sympathetic kindness. . . . Even during her illness she herself was greatly assisted by being able to look after a number of poor, sick people, for she was thus able to satisfy a powerful instinct."

Miss Jensen asks:

"Is it possible to read this description of Anna O. and compare it with the character of Bertha Pappenheim and not conclude that they were the same person?"

Dr. Henri Ellenberger, psychiatrist and author of *Discovery of the Unconscious,* is engaged in research into the life of Bertha Pappenheim. He believes that she is Anna O., but he does question several of the facts as stated by Ernest Jones, calling Jones' version of the case "fraught with impossibilities." He adds, "The veil of legend surrounding this story has only partially been lifted by objective research."

Ellenberger, professor of social psychology at the University of Montreal in Canada, discovered that there was no sanitarium in Gross Enzersdorf, the place Jones says Bertha Pappenheim was sent after Bruer's treatment. Ellenberger writes in *Discovery of the Unconscious,* "Mr. Schramm, who wrote a history of the locality [Gross Enzersdorf], told the author that it must have been confused with Inzersdorf, where there was a fashionable sanitarium. Upon inquiry, the author learned that it had been closed, whereupon its medical archives were transferred to the Vienna Psychiatric Hospital. No case history, however, of Bertha Pappenheim could be found there. Jones' version, published more than seventeen years after the event, is based on hearsay, and should be considered with caution."

He also maintains, "Breuer's case history is obviously a reconstruction from memory, written thirteen or fourteen years later, as he himself says, 'from incomplete notes,' and published half-heartedly, to please Freud."

True, there may have been inconsistencies, omissions, and perhaps even a few errors in Breuer's recollection from notes, but the essence of the treatment and the discoveries to which it led are the important issues.

Dr. George H. Pollock, director of the Institute for Psychoanalysis in Chicago, who has also done research on the case of Anna O., discovered Jones erred in stating a daughter was conceived after Breuer precipitously ended the treatment and took his wife on a "second honeymoon" to Venice. Dr. Pollock obtained evidence from members of the Breuer family and from the city records of Vienna showing that this daughter Dora, the Breuers' youngest child, was born March 11, 1882, whereas Bertha Pappenheim's treatment did not end until June 7th; thus the daughter had been conceived the year before.

Dr. Pollock also discovered that this daughter did not later commit suicide in the United States, as reported by Jones, but killed herself in Vienna when the Nazis knocked at her door to take her to a concentration camp. This fact was confirmed in a special interview for the present book with her niece, one of Breuer's granddaughters, now living in the United States.

In continuing the research that Hannah Karminski had started for a biography of Bertha Pappenheim, Dora Edinger could find no record of her existence between June 7, 1882, her last session with Breuer, and her appearance in Frankfurt six years later.

All letters or papers pertaining to those six years were probably destroyed either by Bertha Pappenheim or her mother, Dr. Edinger believes, because "it was obviously painful to think about them." She suggests, "Perhaps when Bertha Pappenheim visited Vienna in 1935 to bring her laces to the Museum, she destroyed all documents referring to her early breakdown and asked for a pledge of complete secrecy from her brother and his wife." Her biography, privately published by Congregation Solel in Highland Park, Illinois, was called *Bertha Pappenheim: Freud's Anna O.* Eric M. Warburg wrote from Hamburg on March 19, 1969, praising the book, saying, "Bertha Pappenheim has meant a very great deal to the older generation of the Warburg family, and my grandmother, Charlotte Warburg, my father Max M. Warburg and my uncle Felix M. Warburg, were under the spell of her personality and her work."

This "spell" was due to "a strange mixture in Bertha Pappenheim," according to Dr. Edinger. The mixture was comprised of "a charming front which hid her real convictions and the dark secrets you also felt existed behind that charm." Dr. Edinger points out that the sensed mystery in the life of Bertha Pappenheim appears in the eloquent memorial tributes of Cora Berliner and Margarethe Susman, who hint at unfathomable depths never explored by others or explained by her.

A charcoal sketch by Joseph Oppenheimer of Bertha Pappenheim when she was seventy-five appears in Dr. Edinger's book. Her face, remarkably youthful, shows a strange combination of strength and delicacy. The blue eyes are wide, the nose patrician, the mouth generous and curved slightly, but very slightly, in quizzical smile. Her white hair is combed loosely behind her ears. She holds the long, graceful fingers of her left hand against her firm chin. She looks directly at the viewer; as the drawing is studied the face almost seems to come alive.

Dr. Edinger gives an illuminating word-picture of Bertha Pappenheim:

"She was slightly built, petite and slim, but with steel springs. Her very delicate features made her appear quite beautiful. Her hair was completely white, prematurely white.

Her eyes were blue, sometimes icy blue. There was nothing particularly unusual about her voice. It was more her words. She spoke like a prophet, according to members of her board. She could be extremely emotional. If she felt deeply, she sounded like a visionary.

"Nothing could be more characteristic of her than the confession in the last months of her life of her error about the Nazis to Mrs. Schoenewald, or the ironic comment she made about the yellow roses matching her sallow complexion, so as not to appear too sentimental. She had an unquenchable spirit which showed itself even as she lay dying.

"I admired her intelligence; she did not suffer fools at all, much less gladly. She was a fascinating, highly sensitive, but extremely complicated person, with an overwhelming, powerful, and persuasive personality.

"She was absolutely bewitching in a group of men. I have seen her twist men around her fingers. She had many admirers. She must have received proposals. Even as an old woman, she could be very seductive with men. She treated some women gently, some with irony, knowing which ones could withstand the irony.

"I would not call her lovable. She did not show warmth except with babies, toward whom she could be very motherly. She unbent most with children when she felt no adult watching.

"She basked in fine, costly things. She felt a kind of intoxication when surrounded by the beauty of lovely objects. Her house was full of treasures, exquisite Viennese china, old glass, antique furniture, and the laces. Everything had to be in good taste. She also had superb manners; they showed in the way she walked or sat—with grace and elegance. The style of old Vienna.

"She was a woman who was very lonely, but a woman who knew herself well. She often walked in the woods near the Home, especially after a difficult day. It was as though she had to return to the beauty of nature, her own element, as Ondine had to return to water. She would walk alone, she did not want company. Much of the time she was friendly, I believe it was a conscious, intellectual effort, not a spontaneous impulse.

"She was utterly independent. You can see this spirit of independence in the charcoal drawing by Joseph Oppenheimer made when she was in her seventies. At first glance the portrait has in it something of a witch, and there was something witch-like about her. She could be very dictatorial at times, for she was accustomed to getting her own way. Interference to her was like criticism to an artist; the criticism may be legitimate, but the artist doesn't want to hear it."

Dr. Edinger recalls that one day in 1928 when she was lecturing in Frieberg, in southwest Germany, an old, frail woman came up to the platform and introduced herself as Selma Fliess. She said that she was the companion who took care of Bertha Pappenheim's mother before she died and that she was now living in Frieberg. She wrote Dr. Edinger in June, 1936, a month after Bertha Pappenheim died:

"The death of Miss Pappenheim touched me deeply. I knew her for almost forty years, and I watched her develop from a beautiful, spoiled daughter, completely wrapped up in the rich Frankfurt family, into a social worker. I also knew her wonderful mother, whom I admired very much and from whom she inherited much."

In the biography by Dr. Edinger, Bertha Pappenheim's life reflects far more facets than one would ever suspect after reading Jones' brief revelation, though in all probability no one will ever know the story of the lost six years. They may have been quiet years, ones in which she recuperated from the shock of the loss of her father and the breaking off with Breuer. Or they may have been stormy years in which the phantoms of the past again tormented her. The secret of those years remains hers alone, as she seems to have wished.

4

𝒯𝒉𝑒 𝒲𝒶𝓈𝓉𝑒𝒹 𝐿𝑜𝓋𝑒

Perhaps the greatest mystery of all in the story of Anna O. is how the hysterical young woman Breuer thought better off dead and out of her misery could turn into a charming, powerful personality whose achievements were respected throughout Europe.

To try to solve this mystery, several important questions must be asked. We must attempt to put together some of the psychic pieces in the puzzle of the life of Bertha Pappenheim, knowing that many important pieces are missing, knowing too that much is mere speculation, but hoping some of it may strike near the truth.

Why did she fall ill in the first place?

Why was she the one, among all others, to lead the way to psychoanalysis, to so haunt Freud that he finally understood the shattering significance of what she had shown?

What was there in Breuer that enabled her to recall repressed memories and emotions—why was he, of all the physicians in the world, the one to share this creative contribution to the understanding of the mind?

If she was "cured," why did she never marry and raise her own family?

If she was not "cured," how could she have led such an apparently rational life?

It in no way detracts from the great achievements of Bertha Pappenheim as a humanist and leader in volunteer social work and the feminist movement, or in her contribution to psychoanalysis, to try to understand some of the conflicts of her inner life. After all, her ability to give partial revelation led to psychoanalysis.

She was a woman of unusual courage marked by a "passionate spirit," as Martin Buber put it, not only in what she championed but the way she championed it.

She had a supreme courage that enabled her, a Jewish woman, at the age of seventy-seven and dying of terminal cancer, to stand up to the Nazis. She cavilled before no critic when it came to her convictions; but she also knew when the time was wrong for attack. She wrote Felix Warburg that when a hostile crowd taunted a Jewish merchant, she asked herself, "Did I remain silent out of cowardice when I twice experienced such vulgar talk [about the Jews]? But there was no hope to convince anyone in so short a time. One has to look for better chances."

She respected the rights of every man, woman, and child, especially child, the always vulnerable child. When a small girl was treated cruelly in a foster home, Bertha Pappenheim battled hunger and cold to rescue her. And when, on this trip through Germany devastated by war, a family offered her soup containing pieces of meat, she saved the meat so they could make another meal of it.

She never flaunted her wealth. As she said, "If one is not sure, then one should always decide to be modest, quiet, and simple in appearance and in the way one lives."

She had unflagging energy, as the artist Samson Schames, who painted her portrait, said. In Dr. Edinger's words, she was made of "steel springs." When she went to Cracow in the fall of 1935, the last trip she was to take, a board member of Beth-Jakob Seminary recalled, as he wrote Dr. Edinger, "I could not keep up with her."

Bertha Pappenheim was propelled in her relentless and unrelenting drive, in large part, by tormenting phantoms, phantoms she spoke of in the treatment with Breuer that she later managed to keep under control but that never really let her be. The same phantoms haunting her at her father's bedside haunted her as a child and were to haunt her the rest of her life.

She wrote, "The less I have to do, the more I have to be." She had to "do" so she could escape having "to be," which would mean being controlled by urges she could not cope with.

Perhaps we cannot expect those who are happy and content to take the giant strides needed to reform the world. For the most part only those whose lives hold deep anguish will, in an effort to escape the anguish, devote a dauntless energy to making the earth a less desperate place. But if a man acts as savior out of his own needs, it does not mean his contribution to a chaotic world is any less worthy of honor.

The more we are able to understand the inner secrets of Bertha Pappenheim's life, the more we may understand the inner secrets of our own. No matter the century, no matter where we live, we all struggle to conquer the same primitive impulses, suffer many of the same tormenting fantasies. It is a great challenge, and holds much reward, to try to make sense out of the non-sense in our own lives, and studying the extreme, a life such as Bertha Pappenheim's, may help clarify the less dramatic life.

Freud discovered that our sexual and aggressive drives are the two most powerful urges we possess. They are closely related and may even be substituted for one another. We may use sex to express repressed aggression—or use aggression to express a repressed sexual wish.

These drives, around which most of our fantasies are built, are subject to what Freud called "vicissitudes." These vicissitudes, and how we face them, differ according to the experiences in our lives. Psychoanalysts have discovered that if a mother and father give a child the sense of feeling loved and wanted, the child as an adult will face life's harsh realities with thoughtfulness and good cheer. But if a parent is either consciously or unconsciously cruel or unable to give the child love or the feeling he is wanted, the child as an adult will have difficulty accepting reality and, psychically crippled, may retreat far into his fantasy world.

What were some of the vicissitudes in the life of Bertha Pappenheim which she had trouble facing, vicissitudes which caused such torment that she had to retreat into fantasy?

In the light of Freud's discoveries, we may speculate about

some of the unconscious conflicts in which Bertha Pappenheim was caught and perhaps come to understand how they led to both her "talking cure" and her later achievements, remembering always that she possessed the same powerful natural desires common to us all. These desires are often deemed ignoble, but their denial may cause deep suffering. It was the partial relief given those dammed-up desires that helped Bertha Pappenheim recover, possibly saved her life, both psychic and physical, since she threatened suicide a number of times when Breuer first saw her.

There are many important things in her life of which we know nothing, including her experiences as a baby and as a child, her early relationship to her mother, her father, her brother, the sister who died at the age of eighteen when Bertha Pappenheim was eight, her grandparents, and her governesses.

But we are fortunate to have so many of Bertha Pappenheim's own words to tell us about her experiences, her thoughts, her feelings. For in every life, but particularly in the life of the emotionally troubled, there exists what Freud called "the repetition compulsion." This is the need to repeat over and over as an adult those experiences from childhood whose emotional impact we have been unable to master. Thus, if we examine some of Bertha Pappenheim's experiences as an adult, her thoughts about them, and the emotions they provoked, we may conjecture about some of her earlier experiences and feelings.

The words we choose often tell something about us. Her writings show her as compassionate, reflective, and philosophic, but they also contain irony and bitterness. In the spoken word she was honest to a fault, so that at times she antagonized others. She even quarreled with her close friend and relative, Louise, and they never patched up the argument, "something about a gift Louise made," says Dr. Edinger.

She was imaginative in her writing and imaginative also about practical things, making up recipes, creating a vest out of old newspapers to protect against the cold, using worn-out elastic to tie up bundles of house linens.

She wore masks, as we all do. Her delicate charm concealed cleverness, intelligence, and deeper conflicts, according to Dr. Edinger. But to the world she presented the facade of a petite, elegant, sophisticated Viennese lady who carried herself like a queen.

Whatever she did, she did on a grand scale. Her achievements were grand, her defiance of the Nazis was grand, her choice of words had grandeur, even her hallucination about Breuer was grand, for what in a woman's life has more grandeur than having a baby? The very expression of her torment was grand.

She was full of contradictions. She was both Spartan and sybarite. She was austere in her living, in her eating, in her loving. No one ever saw her kiss a man, woman, or child, though she did kiss babies. She did not even allow Hannah to use the intimate German "du." Yet she was sybaritic when it came to furniture, laces, jewelry, and meals for the Tuesday guests at her home who enjoyed "Lucullan" feasts, in the words of Sara Eisenstadt, one of the regulars, a paid worker for Care by Women.

There is paradox upon paradox in Bertha Pappenheim's life, but one fact seems clear and inescapable. She was one of the loneliest women in the world. Though she was always active, either at the Home where she put in a full day and often a full night of work, or attending conferences of national and international groups, or traveling, she was always alone, close to no one.

She had to keep running, she could not, as Miss Eisenstadt noted in her memorial tribute, just "while away" time, for she did not dare to "be." Leisure to her was psychic anathema and to be avoided. She called herself a "nomad" as she traveled the earth, always the on-looker, whether in a brothel or a palace.

Dr. Rahel Straus, the Federation board member who spoke in favor of abortion, described the birthday party when the board presented Bertha Pappenheim with gifts for the Home piled high on a table; for a moment she was unable to speak, then she said, tears in her eyes, "Excuse me, please. I'm so little used to love that I am quite overwhelmed."

She told of her loneliness in a prayer written the last months of her life:

"Therefore I lament that I still live:
That I have squandered strength,
That I have wasted love—
Not only this year, but
For many years. . . ."

The saddest of all her words appear in the letter from Warsaw written in 1912:

"I am necessary for nothing and to no one."

She adds, "This is not an accusation—probably it is all my
own fault—only a fact," and thus takes responsibility for her
loneliness, confessing she has arranged her life to be a lonely
one.

Celebrating Chanukah at the end of World War I all by
herself, she writes, as she looks around the room at the
cherished possessions from her old home in Vienna, "What
longing one can have for dead things. Maybe because my life
has left me lonely."

She concludes the letter to Felix Warburg by saying that
when she finally reached her bed she could not get warm or
fall asleep until she had "a good cry." Then asks rhetorically,
"But why need I, an old, lonely woman, wake up in the morning?"

She felt truly alone, as can only a woman feel who, as a
baby, as a child, as a girl, has known excruciating loneliness.

5

The Strange Drama of Healing

In a sense, she had been waiting for Breuer and Breuer had been waiting for her. It was a fortunate meeting of minds and a filling of certain mutual needs. Breuer fit into her "private theatre" of daydreams and unconscious fantasy, and she fit into his scientific work and unconscious fantasy.

He was ready for her revelations at that point in his life, and she was ready to make them at that point in hers. She had the courage to trust him as she had no man before, or ever would after. He had the courage to delve into psychic territory no man had yet explored, territory that held its own particular dangers.

She was willing to reveal her mind's painful secrets, and he was able to listen, the first physician to do so. He listened rather than judged, willing to wait for the true healing to take place rather than make pointless "suggestions" to her hypnotized mind as had been the practice of other doctors up to that time. That was an expedient he sensed would be doomed to failure as soon as he stopped treating her. What he was doing placed great strain on his emotional life, for he established a deep, continual relationship, unaware of its impact on himself or his young patient.

He admired this poetic, imaginative young woman who had a strong mind of her own, eager to take on the world (as she later did) before her fantasies at her father's bedside felled her. Her creative powers and her ability to articulate

stimulated Breuer's interest, and his interest, in turn, stimulated her to further explore the conflicts that were tearing at her
sanity.

Perhaps one reason she was able to speak so freely
stemmed from her education at a Catholic school. There she
had probably heard from classmates of the confessional. In her
essay "The Jewish Woman," she says, "Is it not a goal for a Jew
and a Jewish woman to be an upright, confessing Jew . . . ."
The adjective "confessing" is an odd one applied to a Jew, except in reference to the Day of Atonement. Because of her
Catholic schooling she may have found it easier to "confess"
to Breuer thoughts about her mother, her father, her brother,
her governess, and what Breuer called "the products of her
imagination," rather than being repelled by the idea of such
intimate revelation, as other women in the nineteenth century
would have been.

We cannot underestimate either her charm, which was
mentioned by everyone, including Ernest Jones, or Breuer's
charm, which all who knew him agreed he possessed.

"For that to happen, one has to be a Breuer," commented
Freud after he told his fiancée about Bertha Pappenheim's fantasy of pregnancy.

Breuer was described as "almost Christlike in character
and charity, wise, restrained, lofty in spirit, with that rare balance between the inquiring, intuitive mind and thorough, objective appraisal and research." This description came from
H. K. Becker, quoting her father, Dr. Carl Koller.

"Breuer's patients said he had only to enter the room and
they felt better," recalls one of Breuer's granddaughters now
living in the United States. "They had absolute confidence in
him as a doctor, both in his gentle, quiet, reassuring personality and his diagnostic skill."

She says of her grandfather, "He was the most modest,
least conceited person you could imagine. Once I went downstairs and heard him explaining one of Shakespeare's plays to
the parlor maid. He would talk to a chambermaid the same
way he would to an emperor."

He was an extremely compassionate man. When he retired from regular practice he continued to treat those patients
who could not afford to pay. He was modest in the way he

lived, even renting a carriage rather than owning one. He was never wealthy, though he could afford summer vacations for his family. He did not care much about food, not even in Vienna, known worldwide for its schnitzels and exotic pastries.

"He was not a tall man and looked even shorter because his back was bent over even before he became really old," said his granddaughter. She never saw him sad or melancholy except during the war.

"One day when I was about fifteen years old, I swallowed the stone of a plum," she recalls. "My father was very worried. He rushed downstairs—at that time we lived in an apartment above my grandfather—and said, 'Gretel has swallowed the stone of a plum. What shall she do?'

"My grandfather smiled and said, 'She should swallow another one so it doesn't feel lonely.' "

She remembers he liked literature and music. He was called in as a consultant during the last days of Brahms' life. The night Brahms died, Breuer's son, Robert, then a young doctor and a musician, remained the night by Brahms' bedside.

Breuer liked to walk, not as a tourist hiking up mountains as Freud did, but along country roads. His granddaughter remembers he took off his hat in a gesture of honor every time he passed a foxglove plant, the source of digitalis, mainstay in the treatment of many heart conditions.

Once, when the family was on vacation, Louise, a nurse and general helper who had a heart condition, was given a cup of tea by a neighbor, who said it would be good for her heart. The tea obviously contained digitalis from the native foxglove plant. With Breuer's approval, Louise drank the tea and felt very much better. Breuer, curious, took a sample to a laboratory in Vienna. After being informed of its ingredients, he remarked, "I would never have given that much digitalis to her."

This granddaughter was the one who corroborated the findings of Dr. Pollock that her aunt, Dora, the Breuers' youngest child, did not die in the United States as Jones reported.

"Dora, who never married, stayed in Vienna after Hitler came to power, and when the Gestapo arrived to deport her to a concentration camp, she committed suicide," she said.

Another of Breuer's relatives, a nephew by marriage, Dr.

Ernst Hammerschlag, a psychoanalyst, lives in New York City. In his boyhood Breuer was "like a great-uncle" to him; he often played with Breuer's grandchildren. He also knew Freud's children, "Freud swept past us in the room at times," he recalls, adding thoughtfully, "When you saw Freud, you felt in awe. When you saw Breuer, you felt warm and confident."

Dr. Hammerschlag believes Bertha Pappenheim found in Breuer "a combination of warmth, care, and deep understanding." He adds, "She got better because she sensed his deep interest and the fact he cared so much, cared in the right way, not infantilizing her but helping her grow stronger emotionally.

"He broke away because he knew he had unleashed something he could not control. At first he was overwhelmed. Then he understood that he had come somewhere near the truth. And the truth may be dangerous."

Though Breuer was an excellent scientist, well-versed in physiology, he was at heart a practitioner, the prototype of the family doctor, and according to Dr. Hammerschlag he did not want to give up practice to take on psychological probing. This was not true of Freud, more interested in abstract psychology, always asking "Why?" in his courageous search for truth.

Dr. Hammerschlag recalls Mrs. Breuer as "a very nice woman, very 'comme il faut,' though not as charming as her husband." He says, "Breuer, who was a family man, didn't seem to be a man who was talkative about professional matters. He didn't give the impression he would come home and unburden himself to his wife." Dr. Hammerschlag was referring to Ernest Jones' statement that Breuer had talked so incessantly about his young patient that his wife became jealous.

Dr. Hammerschlag furnished another important clue in the case of Anna O. Wilhelm Pappenheim, whom he knew slightly, had red hair. If Wilhelm had red hair, it was possible his father did too. Thus two of the most important men in Bertha Pappenheim's life, her brother and her father, both had red hair. This might well be one of the reasons she so easily transferred her feelings for her father onto Breuer, since he had reddish-blond hair. And, though Breuer was eighteen years younger than her father, at the time he first saw her he also had four children.

Breuer may have been unconsciously quite seductive with his patients in the traditional "bedside" manner, not to be undervalued as a factor in healing. After Freud had persuaded him to resume treatment of hysterical women, one day he called on Freud to consult with him about a patient, describing her symptoms. Freud remarked they were typical of a fantasy of pregnancy. Whereupon, without saying a word, Breuer "took up his hat and stick" and hurriedly left the house, according to Ernest Jones. Jones comments, "The recurrence of the old situation was too much for Breuer."

As Freud noted, Breuer was able to "make use of a very intense suggestible *rapport* on the part of the patient." It was not long before Bertha Pappenheim had blocked out everyone else in her world, even her mother. Breuer alone became her reason for living; all her passionate spirit centered on his reddish blond head.

Without such transference in analysis, there is no cure. But because of it, there may be hazards. And Breuer, not knowing the nature of transference, suffered and caused his young patient to suffer. He helped her immeasurably, but he also hurt her as he came up against one of the most powerful psychic forces in the treatment that is psychoanalysis.

Breuer did not realize that it was Bertha Pappenheim's dependence on him that created the wild swings in her mood. When he came to see her, she was ecstatically happy. But when he failed to show up, no matter what the reason, she sank into a depressed mood or flailed about in fury.

Just after treatment started, she became "completely dumb" for two weeks. In spite of making sincere efforts, she could not speak a syllable. Breuer commented, "And now for the first time the psychical mechanism of the disorder became clear. As I knew, she had felt very much offended over something and had determined not to speak about it. When I guessed this and obliged her to talk about it, the inhibition, which had made any other kind of utterance impossible as well, disappeared."

He never revealed what "offended" her but it may have been his failure to appear. Each time this occurred she reacted in the same way, so that when he knew he would be absent for a few days, or on vacation, he tried to find a substitute.

He was not aware of it, and believed he was simply being kind, but his taking her for a ride in the *Prater*, particularly in the company of his daughter, increased the sense of intimacy between them. Unconsciously he made her one of the family as he sat with his two "Berthas" (three Berthas, if we include his probable memory of the young mother who died when he was between three and four; her name was also Bertha). Bertha Pappenheim may have had the fantasy that she was his wife as they rode along—something that day so deeply disturbed her that she could hardly see.

The fact she spoke only English when upset may also have been connected with her feelings for him, since only they two spoke English there, which made it their secret language. English to her must have held a strong connection to childhood, for at her moment of greatest horror, when she thought she saw the snake crawl out of the wall, she tried to find words of prayer but could remember only a children's verse in English. This would seem to show that, as a little girl, she had been read verses in English by someone close to her, perhaps her mother, or the older sister who died, or a governess. In times of crises she regressed to the earlier scene when she had felt safe and comforted. The use of English was an unconscious plea to return to a time of less terror.

On every occasion Breuer reported her as depressed or angry, or refusing to eat or talk, he had not seen her for a few days, with one exception—when she sank into depression after her father died. That she was able to give up some of her excessive grief so quickly, that she did not kill herself as she threatened, feeling her whole world destroyed and perhaps unconsciously wishing to join her father, was no doubt due to Breuer's presence.

Shortly after her father's death, when Breuer had to leave Vienna for a few days, she would not accept the consultant he brought to her side. That scene was both comic and tragic. She ignored the strange doctor as though saying, "You don't exist. There is no one in my life but Dr. Breuer," and in his anger the substitute doctor blew smoke in her face. On Breuer's return, he found her in a "wretched state," hallucinating death heads, as she had done by her dying father's side.

When she learned she was to be moved to the country, she reacted "with horror," undoubtedly knowing she would see less of Breuer, that it would be more difficult for him to visit because of the distance. In her rage she smashed windows, repeated her threats to kill herself, and would not eat or sleep for three days until Breuer was once again at her side.

When he later went on vacation, she did accept another doctor, a friend of Breuer's, but she would not honor this doctor with her "talking cure." And when Breuer returned, he found her plunged into such depression that he suggested she be taken back to Vienna for a week so he could see her daily and she could "talk out" her stories at the rate of three a day. He attributed her rage and depression to the lack of outlet for the storytelling. But, on a deeper level, it was probably caused by her fantasy that he, the only person in her life who she felt cared for her, had deserted her.

During that first summer, when she did not see him for two or three days at a time, she regressed almost to infancy. When he appeared she had to "feel" his hands, touch him to make sure it was he, as a baby recognizes its mother. She would allow only him to feed her.

When she sank into a profound stupor after her father's death, she said she did not recognize anyone except Breuer, referred to everyone else as a "wax figure." A corpse in a coffin resembles a wax figure, and it was as though she felt herself a corpse in a world that was unreal, feeling like a wax figure, depersonalized and catatonic, incapable of emotion.

In the unconscious, no parent ever dies, it is there our childhood memories live on forever, and Bertha Pappenheim may have expressed the wish to keep her father alive by her psychic return to the previous year. In recreating that year, she did not have to face the agony of his death as she unconsciously denied he was dead. She started this double life on the first anniversary of her falling ill.

When she complained there was something wrong with her eyes because she knew she was wearing a brown dress but saw it as blue, she was telling Breuer indirectly that she was recreating the events of the year before to keep her father's image alive. He learned from her mother's diary that on that very day the year before she had been making a dressing gown for her father out of the same kind of material as her present dress, but of the color blue. The unconscious part of her mind, in which her father was still alive, had taken control of the conscious, her defenses shattered by his death.

She was able to trust Breuer; it was possibly the first time in her life she could trust anyone. The growth of her trust may be measured by the ever-deepening implications of her words.

At first she spoke only the gibberish he could not understand. Then she started to utter words that made sense. Then she told him about the hallucinations that "tormented" her. She went on to invent fairy tales, most of them obviously derived from her own experiences with her sick father. Then she started to talk of some of her own feelings, including anger at her mother and governess.

After six months of treatment she cleared up a symptom by reliving her emotions at the time the traumatic event—the sight of the "disgusting dog" drinking out of a glass—occurred. Sensing the importance of this session and encouraged by his patient's progress, Breuer then persuaded her to recall when other symptoms first appeared and her emotions at the time.

Freud was later to discover that every symptom was symbolic of a wish believed evil and repressed, and it also represented punishment for that wish, usually a wish from childhood. Breuer was not aware that a childhood wish lay behind a symptom. But it seemed enough for the moment that the emotions Bertha Pappenheim held back at the time of her wishes found release.

Breuer was able to help Bertha Pappenheim increase her self-esteem; he helped her become able to deflect some of her narcissistic love to the world outside. In this way, she could more successfully fight the fantasies she experienced as her father lay dying, so that when her mother died, she was able to continue living in the world of reality, though she did become very depressed for a while. She moved closer to her cousin Louise whose home, she said, became her "sanitarium," but this time she did not have to flee to an actual sanitarium.

She wrote in April, 1928:

> "It looks like strength
> Yet is weakness.
> And when weakness wins
> Let it yet have been strong."

At least now she could fight; she was no longer the little girl who, upon losing her father, screamed hysterically to the world that somebody had to take care of her, that she could not face life alone. Even though she felt her strength came out of weakness, it was a weakness strong enough to win certain battles of life.

She also prayed, "Only not to get blind—not with the soul!" Blindness had been one of her physical symptoms. She had difficulty seeing with her "soul," until Breuer helped clear up her vision. He accepted her, without moral judgment, for he wanted to heal her agonized mind, not preach puritanical platitudes.

But he was not prepared for a show of love; the dramatic acting-out of her secret sexual wish frightened him. The empathy that stemmed in part from his own unconscious conflicts made Breuer a sensitive and willing collaborator in this momentous first step toward psychoanalysis. But these same unconscious conflicts blocked his ability to further help Bertha Pappenheim.

Breuer's fear was understandable; he was the most moral of men, raised on the Talmud by his father. Yet to attribute his anxiety about sexuality and Bertha Pappenheim's hysterical pregnancy to "conventionality," as Freud does in the letter to Stefan Zweig, "is insufficient," according to Dr. George H. Pollock, in his article, "The Possible Significance of Childhood Object Loss in the Josef Breuer-Bertha Pappenheim (Anna O.)-Sigmund Freud Relationship," which appeared in the *Journal of the American Psychoanalytic Association,* October, 1968, Volume 16.

How can one explain Breuer's oscillations about the role of sexuality in neuroses, and his need to withdraw and avoid the obvious diagnosis of hysterical pregnancy symptoms? Pollock asks.

He cites as one clue Breuer's own words in a report of his

life prepared for the *Akademie der Wissenschaften,* published
in Vienna in 1925. Breuer reveals that his father, appointed by
the official Jewish community in Vienna to teach religion, in
1840 "married a pretty young girl, my mother, whom I do not
remember, as she died at the birth of her second boy, my
brother, 'in the blossom of her youth and beauty,' as the inscription on her tombstone reads. After a little while her
mother, a very wise and witty woman, came to live with us and
assumed the command of the household and the role of
mother to the motherless boys."

Breuer does not mention how old he was when his
mother, Bertha Semler Breuer, died. But Pollock, who in this
article reveals unpublished facts obtained from members of
the Breuer family and the *Israelititische Kultusgemeinde* of
Vienna, learned that Breuer was between three and four years
of age when his mother died. His brother, Adolf, always in
poor health, died at twenty of tuberculosis. His father, who
never remarried but devoted himself to his two sons, died
when Breuer was thirty.

Thus like his famous patient, Breuer was no stranger to
death in the family. His mother's death was to him "a disastrous loss," says Pollock, just as the death of her father was to
Bertha Pappenheim. Bertha Pappenheim lost two sisters and a
father, Breuer lost his mother, father and only brother. Both
physician and patient were deeply involved, consciously and
unconsciously, in mourning deaths in the family.

One reason Breuer may have become frightened by
Bertha Pappenheim's pregnancy fantasy might be that in his
mind the birth of a child—even a phantom one—especially if
the woman was named Bertha, symbolized the death of the
mother, since his own mother died in childbirth. Freud, on the
other hand, saw his mother live through almost continuous
pregnancies, for, during the eight years after his birth she was
pregnant six times. She lost only one child, a son eight months
old, who died when Freud was nineteen months, which meant
Freud, too, was involved at an early age in mourning a death in
the family—the impact of this event can be seen in his analysis
of his dreams as an adult.

Breuer was spared further mourning, Pollock points out,
since he died before his wife, children, and grandchildren.
Breuer ends the short report of his life:

"An old Spanish story tells of a king searching in vain for the luck-bringing shirt of a fortunate man. When at long last a man is found who considers himself fortunate, it turns out that he is a beggar who does not own a shirt.

"If to the story of my life, which has been briefly sketched here, I add that I have been, and am, completely happy in my home, that my beloved wife has given me five sturdy, fine children, that I have lost none of them, and that none has ever caused me serious errors—then I may well consider myself a fortunate man—and one who even owns a shirt! If anything is capable of averting the jealousy of the gods, it is my profound conviction that I have been fortunate beyond my deserts."

This short report, consisting of less than twenty brief pages, was published in Vienna in 1925. It contained one paragraph about Anna O.:

"In 1880 I had observed a patient suffering from a severe hysteria, who in the course of her illness displayed such peculiar symptoms as to convince me that here a glimpse was being offered into deeper layers of psychopathological processes. The insights then gained were presented by S. Freud and myself, first in a short preliminary study and later in the *Studies on Hysteria* by Breuer and Freud. This book, which was rather unfavourably received at first, went into its fourth edition last year. It is the seed from which psychoanalysis was developed by Freud."

Why was not Breuer the one to sow the seed? Pollock offers an answer: Breuer became too frightened of the emotions aroused in him by the hysterical pregnancies of Bertha Pappenheim and another later patient, emotions which "related to his own oedipal fixation resulting from his mother's death in childbirth when he was at the peak of the oedipal phase," and he could go no further in exploring the unconscious. This limited his capacity to understand.

"To discover more of psychoanalysis would have led to exposure and confrontation of his infantile neurosis, and this Breuer could not do," says Pollock. "He withdrew from his patient, from other similar clinical situations, from Freud's theories which threatened him, and finally from Freud himself. Breuer could observe and inquire of the outside, but he could not inquire of the 'inside.' "

It is worth noting that the night Freud wrote the letter to

his fiancée mentioning that Breuer brought up the name of "your friend Bertha Pappenheim," was July 13, 1883. This was one year and one month after her treatment had been broken off, and it seemed as though Breuer had to speak of Bertha Pappenheim in a sort of anniversary remembrance, the end of a year's mourning for him. Breuer also had a headache, "the poor man" was taking salicyl, Freud commented, and Breuer may have been thinking, either consciously or unconsciously, of the traumatic conclusion of the treatment—traumatic for him as well as Bertha Pappenheim.

Pollock points out that Breuer had "an apparent fascination with the mourning and grief reactions" of Bertha Pappenheim, in that he made "an over-abundance of careful observations" of her mourning reactions, " . . . Anna O. seemed to be identified with her dead father and in her treatment heavy emphasis on death was manifest."

"On one level Breuer's involvement and fascination with Anna O. seemed to reflect his own curiosity, his secret 'study' and perhaps his oedipal wishes toward her in a mother transference. In addition, there seemed to be an identification with her as the mourning oedipal child. Anna O. was mourning not only for her dead father during her treatment with Breuer, but also for the oedipal father who gave the baby to another. Her knowledge of Breuer's wife's pregnancy may have revived this earlier unresolved conflict from childhood."

It is also a matter of interest, since very little is accident where emotional drama holds sway, as to which one, Freud or Breuer, or perhaps both, chose the pseudonym "Anna" for their famous case. One wonders whether consciously or unconsciously they were alluding to Freud's sister, who was two and a half years younger than Freud, as was Bertha Pappenheim. Or perhaps they took the letter in the alphabet before "B" for Bertha, and selected a similar sounding name, "Anna," and then selected the letter before "P" for Pappenheim, "O.", for her last name.

One reason Bertha Pappenheim may have appealed to Breuer is that she revived in him, because of her attractive appearance and her intelligence, childhood memories of the "pretty" young mother who died when he was four. Though he goes into no further details about his mother, he does describe her mother, who upon the death of her daughter assumed the role of mother to her two grandsons, as "a very wise and witty woman," which could also apply to Bertha Pappenheim.

Bertha Pappenheim in her early twenties may also have awakened childhood memories in Freud of his mother, who was twenty-one when he was born. Though Freud may never have seen Bertha Pappenheim, a description given him by his wife or Breuer may have reminded him of his mother, a charming, clever, witty woman, and capable, as he once wrote, of "passionate emotions."

Pollock also infers Breuer related to Bertha Pappenheim as King Lear did to his daughter Cordelia, who when asked to reveal publicly her love for her father, defiantly refused, and was murdered. The inference is made, Pollock explains, because of the reference to Cordelia in the letter Freud wrote his fiancée on July 13, 1883.

Freud wrote his fiancée that both he and Breuer refer to the woman they love, Breuer, his wife, and Freud, his fiancée, as "Cordelia," though in a different way. Freud tells Breuer his fiancée "is in reality a sweet Cordelia, and we are already on terms of the closest intimacy and can say anything to each other." Breuer tells Freud "he too always calls his wife by that name because she is incapable of displaying affection to others, even including her own father."

Freud later commented in a letter to James S. H. Bransom in 1934 that the last small section of King Lear "discloses the secret meaning of the tragedy, the repressed incestuous claims on the daughter's love . . . Cordelia still clings to him, her love for him is her holy secret . . . ." He says it is curious that in the play there is no mention whatever of the mother, that there must have been a mother, but the play deals primarily with the father's relation to his three daughters. Pollock mentions this letter, then adds parenthetically that Breuer had three daughters, his last child, the daughter, born while he was treating Bertha Pappenheim.

Bertha Pappenheim was also the youngest of three daughters and, since Breuer's oldest daughter, ten years old at the time, was named Bertha, his unconscious emotional involvement with Bertha Pappenheim may have reflected some of his feelings for that daughter, as well as the woman she was named after, his mother.

It is interesting that in the discussion about Cordelia, Breuer said of his wife to Freud, "She is incapable of displaying affection to others, even her own father."

In his short autobiography Breuer praises economist Lorenz von Stein, professor at the University of Vienna, a teacher who "always aimed at showing that what appeared to us as being static things were processes." Breuer applied this theory in his treatment of Bertha Pappenheim. He saw her illness not as "a static thing" but as a "process." In describing how her "talking cure" started, he wrote, "It happened then— to begin with accidentally but later intentionally—that someone near her repeated one of these phrases of hers while she was complaining about the 'tormenting.'"

He tried to understand the "processes" that governed her thoughts, though his first interest was relief of her suffering. While he did not fully realize the revolutionary step he took toward the understanding of the mind, he must have sensed its importance, for he did tell Freud about Bertha Pappenheim five months after her treatment ended, in spite of his horror over her fantasy. He need never have mentioned the case at all.

Because of his dedication Breuer became the first scientist to observe and partially understand how the unconscious works both to save and to destroy man. That Bertha Pappenheim once again felt deserted when he fled her fantasy pregnancy was not his fault. She had grown deeply involved with him; he had become the target of her earlier sexual and aggressive fantasies. This was later understood as part of the transference that occurs in every psychoanalysis.

Bertha Pappenheim has been described by some who knew her as "almost saintlike," as Breuer was called "Christ-like." It was the strange drama of healing played by these two over a period of eighteen months that led the way to psychic salvation for man.

6

The Volcano

Bertha Pappenheim felt deserted by Breuer and thereafter appears to have trusted no man. Her passion went into "things." She collected laces, china figurines, and beads as her father had collected the antique silver and gold goblets that had once graced the black Biedermeier cabinet. She now had the cabinet; her brother Willie had kept the goblets.

And yet, as she wrote in a letter to Sophie Mamelok when she resigned as director of the Girls Orphanage, "Come whatever will come, it is good-bye, and all the old furniture and laces will not help." She was saying that cold, inanimate objects can never take the place of the warmth of a human caress or the sound of a loved one's voice.

Who *are* the lonely people? They are the angry people, the people filled with such repressed rage that it stifles their ability to love.

"I have often thought that if one has nothing to love, to hate something is a good substitute," Bertha Pappenheim wrote in a letter from Warsaw in 1912.

Underneath her charm and graciousness, there simmered a hatred, one she used in good stead. As Margarethe Susman said in her memorial tribute, "This delicate woman took on a world."

Bertha Pappenheim fought on many fronts. She fought for Jewry even as she fought against the exploitation of women by Orthodox civil law. She fought for the right of the persecuted

east European Jew to find a haven in Germany. She fought for
the volunteer worker against the professional. She fought
against the stigma attached to the unwed mother and illegitimate child. And she fought with all those who differed with
her in philosophy.

The astute Cora Berliner, in her memorial tribute, noted,
"She enjoyed a fight. She provoked a fight. . . . She had an essential desire to fight." And: "A volcano lived in this woman,
that erupted when somebody angered her."

Bertha Pappenheim herself said, "I think contact with ad-
versaries gives more strength and energy than contact with
congenial people." Contact with an adversary is less complicated, just as hate is less complicated than love.

She fought consistently and persistently for the rights of
women. There are differences in the ways women fight for
their rights. There are some who fight in a thoughtful way, out
of a quiet conviction that women should have economical, political, and social equality with men. Others fight in an angry
way because they have not come to terms with their unconscious hatred and envy of men.

To Bertha Pappenheim man was the enemy. The enemy
who imposed laws that exploited women. The enemy who
would not help rescue innocent girls from white slavery. The
enemy who did not understand the dedicated woman volunteer worker but championed the selfish professional social
worker. She did not want to work with men, she had no man
on the board of the Home. And when, after the first World
War, men took over the Central Welfare Office which had
been her idea in the first place, she became even more bitter.

Most of all, she hated the wealthy Jewish merchants of
Turkey, who put up the money to purchase the young girls
sold to South American brothels. As Cora Berliner said, "The
misuse of women as sex objects was a pain she experienced almost physically. And the indifference of people toward this
problem was felt by her as a shame which she could never
overcome . . . ."

Bertha Pappenheim's three-act play, *Women's Rights,*
shows her feelings about men. The two men in it are pictured
as villains, seducers, and rapists. The husband proves to be the
poor, dying woman's former lover, who deserted her when

she became pregnant, just as Bertha Pappenheim had provoked Breuer to do as a result of her pregnancy fantasy. Breuer fell into this fantasy; he did not create it. He was used as a target of transference, like a figure in a dream, reflecting her earlier fantasies—about her father.

Tragedy upon tragedy, soap-opera style, makes its appearance in this play. Fiction, particularly, reveals an author's unconscious conflicts, disguised though they may be—and the theme of the play is that a woman's lot is a sorry one from every single aspect.

The wife, shocked at her husband's cruel behavior toward the poor woman he once seduced and made pregnant, tells him that because of their children she will stay with him but from now on she will refuse marital relations as her "woman's right." This may reveal one of Bertha Pappenheim's sexual fantasies, that a deceived wife may refuse to have sex as her "woman's right." In Bertha Pappenheim's fight against the white slave traders, she upholds woman's right to withhold sex from a man—many men—perhaps unconsciously wishing to check her own wild sexual impulses, or, stemming from childhood, wishing to prevent her mother from having sex with her father.

She wrote after her lonely Chanukah celebration in 1919 that she admired Mary Wollstonecraft, who wanted woman to be man's equal and companion, not his plaything. (Her youngest daughter, Mary, who married Shelley, in writing *Frankenstein* concocted a plot in which a man created a plaything—a robot without a heart—that destroyed him.) Looking at a painting she owned of this early feminist, Bertha Pappenheim said, "I'm suddenly glad that I translated her 'Defense of Human Rights' [the correct title is *A Vindication of the Rights of Women*]. I had quite forgotten that I once did. . . ."

She adds that she wishes women might have both the quality of "iron" and yet be "exquisite," characteristics "usually deemed opposite, yet united in a woman like Mary Wollstonecraft." In other words, she wishes a woman could be both masculine (iron) and feminine (exquisite).

Bertha Pappenheim bitterly resented the tradition that the aim of a Jewish girl's life was to be marriage, that a girl was thought to be an uneducable, stupid creature doomed to housework and babies. "My education was so poor," she would lament. She had desperately wanted an education as good as a man's.

Money had been lavished on the education of her brother, a not particularly brilliant student, but she, a highly intelligent, imaginative girl, was forced to stay home, do household chores, embroider, play the piano. In talking of the ancient Jews who "turned against" and enslaved women, denying them education and other rights, she wrote, "This official attitude brought on a serious revenge."

In later life she revenged herself against those who, she felt, "turned against" her, though it was ultimately revenge on herself. Her best revenge would not have been "living well," as the old adage goes, for she had always lived well, but "loving well." This however she could not do, for she was emotionally unable to. But she managed to siphon off anger unremittingly against the wicked Turkish "merchants," white slave traders, rabbis, Zionists, and the occasional women on her boards whom she thought weak, lazy, and procrastinating.

Through her books, her plays, her essays, her letters, her memoranda, her "Prayers," she expressed anger even as she revealed some of the reasons for her repressed rage. One of her prayers was a plea to "bring me mildness," as though fearful her hidden wrath would explode and expose itself. She justified mildness in a memorandum: "When aging, it is better to be considered too mild and too forgiving in social work than to have grown hard and unforgiving."

She asks, in her essay, "The Jewish Woman," speaking of the Jews under Hitler, "How will we survive? How will we bear hatred and misery? By the suicide of individuals? By the suicide of the community? Shall we forget the past? Shall we lament and deny?" She had threatened suicide in her treatment with Breuer. She had to forget the past, for it was too painful. And she could not afford to lament, so great her anguish. So she denied.

As Martin Buber recognized, she had a "passionate spirit," one that was capable of great bitterness. Writing from Lodz in 1912 she says, "How happy are present-day girls! I remember how difficult people made it for me at this age trying to keep me from the way that was right for me. Forget it!" She thus confesses she had a very difficult time as a girl, that people wanted to keep her "from the way that was right for me." Another time she speaks of her "hate" for the "coarse fingers that destroy beautiful patterned structures and tear and disturb the threads," perhaps unconsciously alluding to the pattern of her own life.

Bertha Pappenheim was opinionated, strong-willed, and stubborn, and it is probable that her mother and father were too. In one of her prayers she says, "Thou art a demanding God to me . . . ." reflecting the way she may have felt that her mother and father, her childhood gods, acted. We don't know too much about her father except that he was very religious and "scoffed" at her dreams.

In her letter to the young prostitute convicted of murder, she says, "No science can predict whether bad parents may not have good children." She may have been unconsciously referring to her parents, for she tried hard to be a "good child," do "good works," atone for what she felt "evil" in herself.

Her physical symptoms as she grew old may have been part of the repressed rage, as the earlier ones with Breuer had been—the rheumatism, where once again her limbs became rigid, the intestinal pains that reflected early eating conflicts, the imagined weak heart, and perhaps even the final cancer of the liver.

Why was she so furious? For many reasons—some realistic, some unrealistic. For one, her parents appear not to have let her forget that they had wanted a son. Three daughters came first, and with each girl the wish for a boy probably grew more intense. Her mother stopped having children once she finally produced her son.

One letter shows how Bertha Pappenheim may have thought her mother felt about girls. From Lemberg on June 8, 1912, after meeting the head of the art gallery, "Miss D., painter, a feminist, friend of the late poetess Konognitzka," Bertha Pappenheim wrote:

"Funny, I think I disappointed her—she had expected a big, strong, black person, and met a slim, small, white one."

It was as though she were saying, speaking of her own appearance in the world, that her mother had expected a boy, a "big, strong, black person" but instead got a girl, "slim, small, white," and: "I think I disappointed her."

Bertha Pappenheim's wish to be a man seems evident in her writings. They show her envy of men, her anger at them, her identification with them, and her imitation of them as, at the same time, she ardently defends woman. Her words, "If there will be justice in the world to come, women will be law-givers, and men will have babies," is a dead giveaway. She asks for a reversal of roles, saying there is no justice under the present natural order.

Her choice of a pen name for her first books tells of her wish to be a man—she chooses the masculine version of her first name as the last name and the name "Paul" as first name. It is interesting that she went from the pen name "Paul Berth-old," definitely masculine, in 1895, to "P. Berthold," half mas-culine, in 1899, and then to her own, feminine, name in 1900, keeping that thereafter.

The word "tragedy" played its part in her life; one of the things she undoubtedly felt as tragedy was that she had been born a girl. In the Rummage Store tells of tragedies in the lives of the former owners of objects in the store. In her trilogy, "Tragic Incidents," she quotes a young Jew as saying he feels bound to the culture he has inherited through centuries in Western Europe, that he needs the books, the paintings, the stage, the newspapers, the struggle between opinions and in-terests and urban industry with its technical facilities. He says, "I cannot play the role of a peasant . . . I cannot, Father." Perhaps to her, "peasant" meant the inferior "woman," and she was saying, "I cannot play the role of a woman . . . I can-not, Father."

In the title she gives her book of travel letters, Sisyphus Work, she identifies with a man who works, but who works in vain. The cruel King of Corinth, doomed forever to rolling a large stone up a mountain, probably is a revealing image of herself. She writes in the preface that she felt what she origi-nally set out to do in her travels had been tried in vain—to arouse women in many nations to form a league to protect in-nocent girls from being seduced into white slavery.

Outwardly she was feminine; she loved elegance in clothes, jewelry, and furniture. But many of the characteristics for which people praised her were masculine—her leadership, her organizing ability, her powerful personality, her determination.

It was not men in general she envied but, as it always is, specific men, the men in her early life—her father and brother. She was jealous of their masculinity.

She wrote in 1929: "Because of the nature of things, the girls are the ones who get hurt, the boys are the ones who derive the pleasure." This indicates how she felt about the difference between her brother and herself, she was the one to get hurt, he the one to derive pleasure.

In her letter to Hannah Karminski, discussing the book-burnings in Germany and the value of books, she says, "I do not believe that people who own many books and have read many books are smarter than others, nor that they are better." Her brother, a leader of the Jewish community in Vienna, owned one of the most complete social science libraries in Central Europe, and she may well have been referring to him, for in the sentence that follows, in parentheses, as though to emphasize it, she says, "I wonder whether a lifetime is long enough to read all the books a well-to-do boy gets for his bar mitzvah?" And the very next sentence may have a double meaning: "Not all bibliophiles [her brother had inherited the family library] are spiritual princes [Wilhelm was probably treated as a little prince]—just as not all kleptomaniacs [sisters] are thieves [want to steal the penis of their brother], they are only driven to it [by envy]."

Both Dr. Edinger and Mrs. Jenny Wolf recall that Bertha Pappenheim and her brother did not get along very well. Dr. Edinger says they quarreled at times. Mrs. Wolf remarks they could not have been very close as he visited his sister only once in the last fourteen years of Bertha Pappenheim's life. Mrs. Leo Goldschmidt, the former Alice Bock, who married Bertha Pappenheim's first cousin (Leo's father, Seligmann Goldschmidt, was Recha Goldschmidt's brother), said she thought Bertha Pappenheim and her brother "were proud of each other, but they couldn't get along. They were maybe too similar. They were very outstanding personalities."

Mrs. Goldschmidt, who now lives in New York City, worked as secretary for Care by Women for several years after her marriage. She often invited Bertha Pappenheim to her home for dinner and describes her as "a very self-contained person. I don't think she was happy, except in her work. She wasn't happy in her life."

Mrs. Goldschmidt and Wilhelm became quite close, after she met him on one of his visits to Frankfurt to see his sister. She says, "I liked him, though he was not a friendly man; he had a very biting tongue. But somehow he took a liking to me. He had a round face, a stubby beard, and slight baldness."

Bertha Pappenheim told Breuer she had lost her voice when her brother shook her "angrily" as she listened outside the door of the sickroom (listening for what?). When she had the breakdown, he was in law school and probably living at home, one of the "close relatives" she fantasied as a wax figure after her father died.

She may also have had the fantasy that to be a girl meant to die, as her two sisters had died, and that the only way to survive was to be a boy. Her dream of the two jackals, the second of the only two dreams she left to posterity, possibly tells of this fantasy, among others. A dream reveals wishes inadmissable to the conscious mind, stemming from childhood, which are pictured in the dream as fulfilled.

The "jackals" dream occurs while she is afloat on the Mediterranean. The sea is a symbol of birth, and the ship, "she," symbolizes woman. The night before the dream Bertha Pappenheim had an argument at the Captain's table about the feminist movement with a "playboy" who is furious at Helene Lange, the German woman feminist leader. Another man, the inspector of lighthouses, knowing she is interested in investigating white slavery, asks her to get off the ship with him at Beirut, saying, "I could show you depravity." He also asks if she is married and, when she says no, urges her to dye her white hair to look younger. Thus as she fell asleep, she might have been thinking about a "change" in bodily appearance after much talk all night about "men" and "women."

In her dream she tells her mother she tamed two small jackals. Her mother will not believe her. She brings the two jackals to her mother. Though previously she was quite sure they were jackals, she now sees two cats on a leash. She feels angry. She pulls the leash. The two cats then change into two men, whereupon her mother "graciously" asks them to sit down in the dining room at their apartment on *Leerbach-strasse*.

When she woke, her stateroom "actually smelled of real jackals," she says. The word "jackal" comes from the Turkish "chagal," a yellowish-gray, meat-eating, wild dog of Asia and northern Africa. The size of a police dog, it runs in packs and hunts its prey at night, often stealing into villages to raid the garbage.

She is the "jackal" in her dream, the hungry little child of infancy, who was "tamed"—toilet-trained at the anal stage—and castrated in fantasy at the later phallic stage, turned into a cat—a woman—which makes her "angry." She pulls the leash, a reference to masturbation with a penis, since a leash is a long, thin object, and the cats change into men. This pleases her mother, who "graciously" asks the men to dine. The actual words of the inspector of the lighthouse, "I could show you depravity," may have stimulated in her unconscious, images of masturbation, the first sexual "depravity" a child knows.

The implication is that her mother will feed men but starve to death a woman. One of the hidden wishes from childhood she fulfills in her dream may be that she, the cat, the woman, turns into a man and thus pleases her mother, who prefers boys. Thus she, the little girl, will get fed and not die like her two sisters. If she can "pull" a leash, she has a penis like a man, that makes her a man.

Because of Bertha Pappenheim's unconscious wish to be a man, stemming from her belief that the role of a man in the world is far more pleasurable than that of a woman, she could never enjoy her "right" to be a woman, no matter how many "equal rights" would have been granted her.

7

The Fantasy Whore

Many women gave money to help the delinquent girl and unwed mother but Bertha Pappenheim not only gave money, she became emotionally involved with the girls and their babies. She built an institution where she could take care of the "unfortunate" girls and "retrain them morally."

Her conscious motives were noble. But what of the unconscious motives? Why did she arrange her life so she was always around the deserted, unwed, pregnant girl? Until the day she died, she watched the never-ending procession of young, unwed, pregnant girls, victims of man's sexual desires and their own uncontrollable sexual urge. But as a result of these actions, a baby was born who Bertha Pappenheim could cuddle and kiss as though, for a moment, it were her own.

She carved out a career which successfully hid her deeper wishes from most people. But her very pursuits revealed her hidden conflicts, the ones reflected in her pregnancy fantasy with Breuer. The girls acted out the fantasy she had spun about Breuer.

Bertha Pappenheim spent her life rescuing women who did what she dared not do—who became whores, flaunted their sexual desires, got pregnant. A woman with less moral upbringing, given the strength of Bertha Pappenheim's fantasies may have plunged into prostitution. Instead, her severe conscience, prodded by her intelligence and compassion, drove her at times into almost foolhardy courage.

241

It was dangerous for a woman to travel alone to slums and brothels, to become involved in investigating the white slave "racket," threatening huge underworld financial interests. But she did not care, she *had* to search and find out the facts. She traveled to Turkey, Egypt, Jerusalem, Russia, to view the "shame" of Jewish prostitutes, unconsciously reliving her "shame" with Breuer, her own wild fantasies denied.

To her own life she applied harsh discipline and self-denial. It was a life devoid of sex. It is possible she never even kissed a man in passion, for she wrote, after the inspector of lighthouses had seemed interested in her, "Well, I think, if I were not so utterly without practice and experience and had not insisted on my birth certificate my trip might have had a sudden, romantic ending." Here she says she was *utterly without practice and experience* in the art of love.

Then she confesses:

> "I have wasted love—
> Not only this year, but
> For many years . . . ."

For all the years of her life. Instead of giving herself sexually to a man, she saved wayward girls, as perhaps she wished her mother might have saved her from being consumed by the illicit sexual desire shown in the acting-out with Breuer. She wonders what kind of mother the beautiful prostitute Jolanthe has, a mother who did not save her daughter from a life of vice. "Mother, save me, save me, from my savage sexual hunger," seemed to be one cry of Bertha Pappenheim's life, even as she tried to save others.

She told Breuer, "I have two selves. A real one and an evil one that forces me to behave badly." When we say "evil," we are often alluding to sexual desires.

Her wish to be a prostitute is shown in her letter from Soloniki. Who to her is the most beautiful woman she has ever met? A prostitute named Jolanthe. She thinks, after meeting Jolanthe, "Maybe I'll dream of beautiful Jolanthe," as though wistfully hoping she will have a dream about someone she admires and envies.

When she describes the prostitutes in Alexandria, she

mentions they wore "strands of beads and coins on strings around their necks," and it was shortly after this she started to make her own necklaces, strands of tiny beads on strings to be worn around the neck.

For a woman to travel long distances just to walk into brothels and speak to prostitutes, even though motivated by a desire to help, seems strange. It makes sense only if we realize that in Bertha Pappenheim's unconscious, as she identified with prostitutes, she sought over and over to master one of her deepest conflicts—the wish to sexually possess her father. This wish, opposed by the Jewish Orthodox "conscience" that forbids the very thought of incest, was later transferred to Breuer. To Bertha Pappenheim, part of her "evil" self may have been the little girl who wanted her father sexually, a fantasy that may have found expression during masturbation, unless she was even too inhibited for that release, natural at a certain age.

The wish to be a whore is a universal fantasy; the little girl wants to take her father from her mother. A prostitute may act out this fantasy with many men, most of whom are married, but though there may be many men, there is only one man in her fantasy, her father.

Breuer believed Bertha Pappenheim had never "been in love," and that the "element of sexuality was astonishingly undeveloped in her," because none of her hallucinations were of a sexual nature (except the final one!) and she never spoke of love. He did not realize she was unable to fall in love with a suitable man because the great love of her life was her father. Breuer wrote she was "passionately fond" of her "adored" father. But a young woman of twenty-one should be "passionately fond" of a man outside her family, especially in that era when women married at an early age. Bertha Pappenheim's own mother had married at eighteen. Bertha Pappenheim had not been able to transfer her passion until she met Breuer.

"Breuer's conviction that, because his patient showed no overt interest in sex, hysteria has no sexual etiology [cause] was disproved when Bertha Pappenheim, in her middle age, made the fight against illegitimate sexuality the main concern of her life," Dr. Richard Karpe points out in his article, "The Rescue Complex in Anna O.'s Final Identity," published in the *Psychoanalytic Quarterly,* 1961.

Dr. Karpe, a psychoanalyst in Hartford, Connecticut, who has studied the life of Bertha Pappenheim, says that "during her father's illness her own phallic wishes and her aggressions against the male conflicted with her maternal identifications and her wishes to take care of the helpless. After her recovery she could sublimate both in her fight against white slavery."

He believes it significant that her father and Freud had the same first name. "She had escaped from nursing her father, Siegmund Pappenheim, by herself becoming sick," he explains. "She then suffered a disappointment in transference with her psychotherapist, Breuer. After these experiences she was not ready to accept the implications of another Sigmund (Freud) that she had a sexual conflict. Such an assumption may have seemed to her a manifestation of masculine designs on pure and innocent girls. She did not attack Freud in her published work, but displaced her accusations from Freud onto the 'traders' of girls."

It does not matter whether or not she read Freud, for in her mind her accusations were actually levelled against her father, the seducer. He, like Breuer, may have been quite a seductive man underneath his strict Orthodox mien, and if he was, this would be another reason why Bertha Pappenheim could relate so easily to Breuer, love him with the same passion she did her father, hate him with the same passion when she believed he abandoned her.

Since Bertha Pappenheim seemed to hate so intensely the men who exploited young girls, we might speculate that she felt sexually exploited by a seductive father, a man who might not have been openly affectionate but who seethed with suppressed sexuality, as she did. She probably had the same seductive, charming, vivacious qualities as a little girl that she possessed as an adult. Breuer found her very attractive, and she "inflamed the heart" of the psychiatrist at the sanitarium, according to Jones. Dr. Edinger described her as "very seductive" with men, saying she could "twist a man around her fingers if she wanted to."

When a father has been very seductive to a little girl—partially seducing her, then not following through sexually, she will unconsciously hate him because her frustration is so intense. Though a daughter knows consciously that the sexual act of incest is taboo, her unconscious has no conscience. Because of her hate, as well as her love, Bertha Pappenheim would feel guilty and turn her murderous impulses on herself, as she did during her breakdown, crippling herself physically and psychically.

Writing of white slavery, she said, "In the 'traffic in girls,' merchants [and her father was a wealthy merchant] as well as merchandise [the young girls] are mostly Jewish. We know that family life today is not what it used to be, that the men, both fathers and son, do not protect themselves and their homes from being soiled and that the dirt cannot be washed away by the tears of deceived and damaged women."

In her fantasy she may have thought of herself as "a deceived and damaged woman," both because she was not born a boy and because her father led her to believe she was the love of his life but then rejected her sexually.

All the qualities Breuer admired—her intelligence, her wit, her strong will, her creative imagination—may be related to an early sexual precocity, the stimulation of her sensual feelings when she was a little girl, arousing vivid sexual fantasies which then had to be repressed.

It did not occur to Bertha Pappenheim that a prostitute may have sought the life she led, just as it did not occur to her that she sought the life she led. She mistakenly thought "education" would save girls at the Home and the women of the world, just as she may have thought "education" would have saved her from sexual fantasies. Her refusal to accept the newly developed psychoanalytic insights, her lack of awareness that every unwed mother and delinquent girl is emotionally disturbed and needs psychological help far more than education, meant she never found the answers to her deepest questions. At the age of seventy, she was still searching for answers in the Greek philosophers.

For Bertha Pappenheim there was no sex; there was no baby, nor was there ever to be except in fantasy. In answering the questionnaires about her ability to organize, she said she thought important the "observation of all details, collection of all experiences which may accomplish the purpose, uncompromising determination not to lose sight of the moral background, and most of all: a blessed fantasy—which will keep the creation (you call it organization) alive in outlook. I go so far as to say that it is impossible to organize without fantasy."

In an unconscious literal sense she might be speaking of her phantom pregnancy with Breuer, and the earlier fantasy of pregnancy by her father, as she speaks of a "creation" being kept "alive" in outlook by "a blessed fantasy." For "organize" we could substitute the words "give birth," so her sentence reads: "I go so far as to say that it is impossible to give birth without fantasy." But all she ever experienced was the fantasy of birth.

It was all of a piece—her earlier life, her eighteen months with Breuer, her later sublimation. She wanted only one man, her father, and she would have no other.

In spite of the daring she showed in many respects, sexually Bertha Pappenheim was an extremely inhibited woman. The prudish times in which she lived cannot be blamed, because it did not keep most women from marrying and bearing children.

In her memorial tribute Margarethe Susman said of Bertha Pappenheim, "She mistrusted love for a single person . . . she felt love for a single person veiled love for mankind." But this is a rhetorical rationalization. She could not love because she was too afraid of a man.

Yet fearful as she was of sex, Bertha Pappenheim accepted the sexual indiscretions of others. She judged moralistically, but she also understood how women might become the victims both of their own sexual desire and of men.

In all probability she did not get her knowledge about sex from her parents but from the stablehands, the rough men who saddled the horses she rode in Vienna and Frankfurt. Dr. Edinger recalls that several of the women who went riding with Bertha Pappenheim in Frankfurt, including Dr. Edinger's mother-in-law, mentioned how openly the stablehands talked of sex. The riding itself must have excited her sexually; horseback riding is a sensual activity.

The constant "fighting" in her later life was an outlet for both her sexual and aggressive emotions. This may be one of the reasons she never had another breakdown. Her adult life appears to show a monumental sublimation of her sexual instincts; but she used anger to further the welfare of mankind rather than trying to destroy it, as did many of her fellow-countrymen in the two world wars they started.

We may gauge the intensity of her repressed emotions, and of her stifled sexual and aggressive urges, by the intensity of her need for a "conscience" to control the wild desires in her slim body. Her basic prayer, according to Margarethe Susman, who knew her well the last ten years of her life, was: "Strength, strength, do not forsake me so that I can discover accurately right and wrong." This prayer "dominated all her work and returned in always-changing form," says Miss Susman. The emphasis she placed on discipline was almost pathological.

Bertha Pappenheim wrote, "How good it is to have a conscience!" Miss Susman points out that many people live in torture under the "iron law" of an almost unbearable conscience, but Bertha Pappenheim considered hers "not as coercion but as a blessing." As well she might, for without it her fantasies possibly would have destroyed her psychically had she continued to act them out as she did with Breuer. Instead, she let others act out. In addition to the sexual "acting out" in reality done by the girls before coming to the Home, there were the plays she wrote to be acted out and the stories she read for the children to pantomime in shadow plays.

She was able to harness her fantasies, both sexual and aggressive, and to use her mind constructively. "My disastrous brain always has to breed plans," she said. Why does she describe as "disastrous" her very able brain? She is speaking perhaps not of its ability to think but of the fantasies reeling within it that she had to hold in tight harness—fantasies of being a delinquent girl who might go sexually astray any moment, a whore, and an unwed mother.

The savior is always suspect. What he so fanatically "saves" may reveal his deepest wish.

8

The Waif

The life of Bertha Pappenheim is a psychic tale of two cities—
Vienna, where she spent her youth, and Frankfurt, where she
lived as a woman. Her mother's return to Frankfurt was a royal
homecoming; she had left there as a girl of eighteen, partner
to an "arranged" marriage. There was something special about
belonging to one of the oldest Jewish families in a city like
Frankfurt, especially when that family was involved in international banking.

In Vienna, Bertha Pappenheim had been a nobody, just a
"girl," not allowed to go to a university, unable to be like her
friend, Martha Bernays, and most other young women and fall
in love and marry. But in Frankfurt she became a "somebody,"
her name was known not only there but throughout much of
Europe, and though she never married and had children, it did
not matter; she had her substitute "daughters." As she wrote,
women who miss the happiness of "real personal motherhood" may have the chance of "spiritual motherhood" by caring for those whose parents failed.

When her own mother died, this left her an orphan in a
sense, and soon after she resigned as director of the Orphanage to help unwed mothers, now apparently identifying more
closely with the mother.

There is a daguerreotype of her mother showing Mrs. Pappenheim as a young woman. Her face is Modigliani-like, a
strange, sad cast to it. Her dark hair, parted in the middle, is

drawn severely behind her ears.

Bertha Pappenheim's description of her mother does not sound as though the lady were a "dragon," as Jones called her. She says in a prayer written July, 1933, "Mother, I remember your kindness, your wisdom without harshness, your industry, your ability, your tact, your modesty."

Dr. Edinger suggests Jones may have received the description of Mrs. Pappenheim from Martha Freud, because the word "dragon" does not seem to fit either Freud's or Breuer's vocabulary.

Mrs. Alice Goldschmidt recalls Mrs. Pappenheim as "a very modest, kind person, soft of voice and manner." But she also remembers, "Once Mrs. Pappenheim sent a sample of her writing to a handwriting expert. He wrote, 'The battling rooster looks out from all corners.' We laughed at his analysis."

The late Dr. Paul P. Homburger, whose grandmother was Mrs. Pappenheim's sister Bella and who knew Mrs. Pappenheim as a boy, told Dr. Edinger, "No one found Aunt Recha anything but gentle and very retiring. How could anyone say she was a dragon?"

But some outwardly gentle, obsequious women may at moments display an almost matriarchal madness. It is difficult to be certain what takes place between mother and child, especially in the early years of the child's life. Bertha Pappenheim's feelings about her mother, as well as her father, were ambivalent—a mixture of love and hate. This mixture always exists between mother and child as the child's struggle to achieve his own identity comes into conflict with his long and deep dependence on his mother. This dependence is what Freud called "the human condition."

On the one hand Bertha Pappenheim would not forsake Germany because it was her mother's homeland; it symbolized her mother. She said in her essay, "The Jewish Woman," that "we who owe so incredibly much to the German civilization . . . we cannot forsake it; it would be stupid and ungrateful." Mrs. Jenny Wolf says Bertha Pappenheim tried to convince German Jews not to leave the country, saying, "Don't go. From what I know of history, it can't last." When people did leave, she would say, "Only rats desert a sinking ship."

But in indirect expression, she seemed very critical of her

mother at times. The "Study Plan" for Jewish children, no longer allowed to attend German schools when Hitler came to power, was the last thing she wrote for publication. It held her philosophy about training girls to undertake tasks in their homes, which she believed necessary. She said:

"It is wrong if a mother says, 'I can do it better and faster myself.' It is the duty of mothers to teach what they know (and truly, they know very little) even if things run badly and unpleasantly for a while."

In a sense she may be saying of her own mother that "truly she knows very little," a mother who may have told her daughter, "I can do it better and faster myself."

Bertha Pappenheim wrote further, "It is their own pampering which makes mothers unable in many cases to bring up their daughters," in all likelihood a reference to her own pampered mother, the daughter of wealthy parents.

She also says in this essay, "Most mothers have so little sense that they do not understand the consequences of their own actions and omissions." And closes with the words, "These suggestions are for the few who have sense." She may have felt her mother did not.

Her unconscious hatred of her mother is also seen in her fights with women board members who were "weak" or "procrastinating," adjectives that may also have been applied to her mother, who did not seem to impress those who knew her as particularly decisive or dynamic.

Bertha Pappenheim would describe how her parents were married in a small border town between Austria and Hungary, possibly Pressburg, where her father was born and many of his relatives still lived. It was an outdoor ceremony, with ducks and geese squawking around the lawn. As a rule, the wedding ceremony was performed in the bride's home town, but 1848 was a time of revolution and street fighting in both Frankfurt and Vienna.

Inasmuch as the marriage was "arranged," it may have proved a rather loveless one. But whether Mrs. Pappenheim was happy or not, she would have remained in the marriage. Bertha Pappenheim was "very pessimistic" about marriage, says Dr. Edinger. "She didn't think of marriage as the happy ending. She was realistic."

From Bertha Pappenheim's own words, she appears to have been emotionally as well as academically starved. Perhaps she was even undernourished physically at times as an infant. When she became angry and depressed during her treatment with Breuer, she refused to eat, as though saying to her mother, you once starved me, you wanted me to die, so now I will starve myself and die.

It is significant that Bertha Pappenheim liked and often repeated the story told by Gluckel of the parent-bird who dropped the first two little birds in the raging river because he believed they lied to him when they said they would take care of him in his old age, but saved the third little bird, who did not lie but said he could only promise to care for *his* little ones. Bertha Pappenheim, the third little sister, had been saved, and she kept her promise, she did take care of her "little ones."

The birth of another baby one year after her daughter would not have seemed strange to Mrs. Pappenheim, who was only seven months old when her mother conceived her next baby. But Bertha Pappenheim probably did not get too much of her mother's attention when she was again pregnant, and, when Bertha Pappenheim was one year old and a little boy was born, she may have received even less, her needs subservient to those of the new creature with the prized phallus.

"Leave me now gloriously alone. This crawling and cringing and shrieking shall not touch me, shall not move me. I search for words to answer....." she wrote as one of her prayers. These might have been her thoughts as she looked at the new baby crawling around the floor, shrieking for food, cringing when she tried to touch him. And her life was, in a way, a "search for words to answer." To answer what? The questions a child asks: Where did this new baby come from? How did he get inside my mother? Why is he here taking away her love? Why doesn't he go away and never come back?

She wrote in a letter from Moscow in 1912, "If I have to wait—I always have to ...." and this might echo her cry from earliest days when she needed food, attention, or the warmth of a caress.

Bertha Pappenheim had her mother all to herself for only one year as a baby. Perhaps her reaction at the end of one year with Breuer was a repetition of how she felt at the end of one year with her mother when a new baby came on the scene. She sank back psychically into the year before, what she may have done as a bereft little baby, furious at her mother for having given birth to a rival with whom she could not as yet cope, furious too at the newcomer who was both an enemy and a boy.

Feeling her mother failed her, she may have later turned to her father in her hunger for warmth, caresses, and attention. But behind her intense attachment to him would always lie the earlier equally strong and passionate attachment to her mother. She clung to her father as substitute, identified with him in many aspects—her wish to be a man, to "save" Jewry, to be a "good mother" to the world, just as she felt he had been her substitute "good mother."

This overwhelming dependence on her father, reflecting an earlier overwhelming dependence on her mother, would be a further explanation of why Bertha Pappenheim went to pieces as her father lay dying and why she wanted to kill herself after he died, feeling she had no one left. It might also explain why she would wish unconsciously to deny he was dead by returning psychically to the year before in her treatment with Breuer. Whenever an adult suffers a breakdown, the earlier unmet need for emotional nourishment that chains a child to dependence, usually plays a large part.

Perhaps Bertha Pappenheim accepted her mother more after she received a certain amount of mothering from Breuer. Her transference to him was primarily that of a child who hungers for love, rather than a woman who sexually desires a man. This may be one reason Breuer became so alarmed, sensing this. Perhaps part of his "ordeal" was the deep dependency Bertha Pappenheim thrust on him, more than he, or any physician at that time, knew how to handle.

Breuer unknowingly became to Bertha Pappenheim the good mother, not the dragon mother. She allowed only him, during her illness, to feed her, to keep her alive, refusing to take food from her own mother. Breuer soothed her with touch, glance, word, as he looked deep into her eyes every day, sometimes twice a day, to hypnotize her. At first, as some physicians did, he may have placed his hand on her forehead as he hypnotized her.

Her love for Breuer, as for her father was destined to remain unfulfilled, since it was a tabooed love. It was a love that could never be satisfied because it also held so much of the need for a mother's comforting love. Her life, as she later lived it, showed the search for this kind of love rather than the love of a man.

In one way Bertha Pappenheim may have achieved what she wanted unconsciously—her very early wish to be the only one in her mother's life, all rivals disposed of. She lived alone with her mother in Frankfurt for seventeen years, until the day of her mother's death. It was she and her mother against the world, just as it was she and the little orphans against the world, then she and the unwed mothers.

When she and her mother moved to Vienna, in a sense she took her father's place as she went out into the world to work, an unusual act in that era for a wealthy woman. Her work gave her outlet for her "long-repressed vitality," and in her words a "hard-won but happy freedom—the breaking of all links and forms."

First she worked with orphans deserted by their mothers and fathers. Then with unwed mothers, deserted by the man who made them pregnant. Then, to free the *Agunah*, wives deserted by husbands. And also with prostitutes, girls deserted psychologically by their mothers. It seemed as though her life was dedicated to the deserted.

What great conflict drove Bertha Pappenheim to her rescue of the orphan, the unwed mother, the whore, the deserted wife, the illegitimate child? What was the thread that linked all the abandoned in her mind?

9

The Ultimate Desertion

The great conflict in Bertha Pappenheim's life was revealed in the pregnancy fantasy that so frightened Breuer. It was a conflict also depicted in her hallucination of the snake crawling out of the wall to attack her father. It was present too in the various physical symptoms she inflicted on herself.

The conflict was between her desperate wish to have a baby and her desperate fear of having one. The fear is apparent in her inability to marry and give birth. It is also seen in her plea, "If there will be justice in the world to come, women will be lawgivers, and men have to have babies." Let the men suffer for a change, let the men go through the agony of childbirth and face possible death, she is saying. Let them be the victims of sexual exploitation. Let them be deserted. In her own words, "The girls are the ones who get hurt, the boys are the ones who derive pleasure."

The conflict about pregnancy appears clearly in her career. On the one hand, she gives help to unwed mothers and illegitimate children, on the other hand, tries to keep young girls from becoming delinquents and whores, so they will not have babies.

She urged women on her board to have children, wrote poignant letters when they gave birth. She spoke of pregnancy as "the highest happiness" of woman.

Her preoccupation with pregnancy is also shown in her "Prayers," in that many of them hold references to air and breathing, which to the unconscious symbolize birth. In one she mentions the "foul air" that is "hard to breathe," just after speaking of herself as "often seriously harmed and hurt by man."

In the prayer where she says, "The dregs of life's cup are tears," this line follows her description of the ability to "fill life's cup and be allowed to carry it so that its dew and rain overflow as a blessing for many," as a gift from God. In the unconscious, an empty vessel, such as a cup, may represent the vagina, and the "dew and rain" may symbolize the semen which, put into it, "overflow" in the blessing of a child. This "gift from God" was denied her. All she ever had were "tears," the dregs of the cup.

In a third prayer she refers to herself as "childless," then expresses the thought that she wishes for her gravestone small memorial stones with the inscription, "She was very severe," thus connecting childlessness with severity. She had to be severe with herself lest she carry through on her impulse to get pregnant in a primitive way that meant death.

For the wish to be pregnant in Bertha Pappenheim's life was not the simple wish to have her father's baby, a wish normal to every little girl, one she later transfers to a man outside her family. Bertha Pappenheim's wish was complicated because it was overlaid with fantasies about pregnancy from the earliest days of her life, when she could not understand reality. Yet with the birth of her little brother when she was one year old, she somehow had to explain to herself where he came from.

The two strongest instinctual urges in mankind are to survive and to procreate. If the urge to give birth is thwarted or denied, it will somehow find expression. Plagued by earlier fantasies of pregnancy, Bertha Pappenheim managed to express some measure of her desire as she took care of the babies of other women.

Why did she deny herself what she called woman's "highest happiness?" Why was she afraid to have her own baby?

Because of conflicts and fantasies, rooted in infancy, that persisted over the years, stemming from her being "an angrily hungry" baby, says Dr. Walter A. Stewart.

He explains that how angry a baby becomes depends on

two things: the quality of care given by the mother, which is influenced by whether she is fearful, depressed, impatient, or ignorant of the baby's needs, and the capacity of the baby to accept delay, to tolerate frustration. The quality of care and this capacity to delay sets an emotional tone that accompanies all the psychosexual stages—oral, anal, phallic and genital. Whatever that tone, be it tenderness and understanding or anger and anxiety, it will pervade his entire life.

As an infant, Bertha Pappenheim probably had a wet nurse, according to Dr. Edinger, because in that era a woman who wanted to conceive another child did not nurse a baby, believing this would prevent conception. Also, becoming pregnant dries up the milk flow so her mother would have been unable to nurse her little daughter more than a few months.

But whether wet nurse or her own mother, Bertha Pappenheim may have had great difficulty accepting weaning, a separation from the mother. It is felt as the first injury in life, because up until then a baby believes that he and his mother are one, and when weaned, he imagines part of himself has been taken away.

An angry baby will try to regain what he considers part of him, believing in this way he can again control his mother and prevent her leaving him. He imagines that if he bites off her breast, swallows it, gets it inside him, as he does food, she will be his forever. This is what Freud called "incorporation" of the mother by "oral aggression."

This possibly was the fantasy of Bertha Pappenheim when she was weaned. Or when she watched her mother breast-feed her new rival, the little boy, while she, the inferior girl, had been relegated to a wet nurse.

One indication that there may have been deep jealousy and anger appears in her "drinking-glass" symptom, when she could not drink water out of a glass after she saw the "disgusting" little dog do so, encouraged by the governess who owned him. The governess, the woman taking care of her, may have symbolized the mother of her earlier days, and the "disgusting" dog represented her brother, for in the unconscious animals may represent siblings. For Bertha Pappenheim to feel such disgust at the sight of an innocent dog drinking water meant that to her the dog symbolized something other than man's best friend.

Her symptom, not being able to drink water even though she felt parched, represented both her wish, one she felt evil, and punishment for that wish. The wish, as she wistfully watched her tiny brother at her mother's breast, may have been that he be poisoned by the milk from her mother. A happy baby thinks of milk from the breast as "good" if the mother gives it willingly and easily. But if the mother breast-feeds her baby unwillingly or fearfully, the baby thinks of the milk as "bad."

At the wish that her brother be poisoned by the milk, Bertha Pappenheim would feel very guilty, then fear that in retaliation *she* would be poisoned—an eye for an eye, our primitive thinking goes.

This would explain why she was unable to drink the water even though suffering excruciating thirst. She was afraid of being poisoned because of her wish to poison. Thus we punish ourselves for fantasied crimes, for in the unconscious the wish is as powerful as the deed.

It is significant that when Breuer first saw her, when she was refusing food, she would eat only one thing—oranges, round and juicy like the breast of a feeding mother. When her father died, or whenever she felt Breuer deserted her by not seeing her for several days, she starved herself like an angry baby abandoned by his mother expects to starve. To her, Breuer's failure to appear was a threat of death. On his return to Vienna after an absence of several days, following her father's death, he found her hallucinating death's heads, as though telling him she was dying.

The loss of anyone she loved through death also meant abandonment, and when someone close to her died she became furious. She could not mourn the death of a loved one because of a greed she was unable to face—her early hunger for her mother, which meant she had great difficulty in separating from her mother physically and psychologically, thus achieving her own identity. Babies must be able to endure separating from a mother, to give up the illusion they and the mother are one, so they may eventually become independent. Bertha Pappenheim projected this early inability to separate onto her father, then it became almost an obsession in her adult life. She never wanted families to separate, always tried desperately to keep them together.

Because she had been an angry baby, she transferred the tone of anger and the fantasies of that time to her whole psychosexual development. When she became aware of her genitals, she imagined her vagina as a hungry mouth, wanting to devour and swallow the penis in order to get pregnant. In other words, the fantasy of angrily biting her mother's breast to get her mother inside was carried over into her understanding of pregnancy. To get pregnant, she would have to bite off her father's penis, swallow it, and it would grow inside. This is not an unusual fantasy in children, Dr. Stewart said.

The "biting" quality of her life was also seen in her "biting" words and an underlying philosophy of bitterness.

Many of her symptoms were connected to biting or eating. Her muteness was traced back to a fight with her mother that occurred when she left her father's side to go to the kitchen to eat—bite and swallow. Her deafness first struck when her father asked for wine—swallowing. Her cough, Dr. Stewart points out, could be connected to the wish to swallow. She related it to the wish to dance at the party next door, a wish to be held close, to have sexual intercourse—in her fantasy the primitive act of biting off the penis.

As an adult, this fantasy, reflecting her earlier "angry hunger," came into conflict with the taboo on incest, as well as the taboo on cannibalism and murder. She feared death not only as retaliation for her wished-for crime but as a projection of her own feelings onto the baby that would grow inside and wish to eat her up as she had wished to eat up her mother.

When women fear pregnancy, they may regress to the wish to be a man, explains Dr. Stewart. "Penis envy is not a lifelong state to which women are doomed," he says. "It is a regressive fixation in women afraid of their femininity."

The wish to be a man may also be linked to the childhood fantasy that sex is an assault upon a woman. The child does not as yet understand adult sex and interprets what he sees, hears, or fantasizes occurring between his parents in bed, on the level of what he does understand, his own aggressive impulses.

Bertha Pappenheim's hallucination at her father's bedside

makes psychic sense once we grasp its symbolic meaning. Symbolism is part of the language of the unconscious, and Bertha Pappenheim at that moment was controlled by her unconscious. Symbols refer to the primitive, forgotten language of infancy in which the part represents the whole, or two objects similar in one aspect, such as shape and color, are believed identical, or words that sound alike stand for each other or a third word that also sounds the same. Freud discovered, chiefly from studying the dreams of patients, that certain symbols are universal, appearing in folklore, myths, and fairy tales. Long thin objects, such as a snake, a candle, a whip, a knife, or parts of the body such as the nose, arm, or leg, represent the penis. Open receptacles, such as boxes, closets, houses, shoes, or parts of the body such as the mouth, ears, and anus, symbolize the vagina.

The symbols in Bertha Pappenheim's hallucination combined two of her deepest wishes—to become pregnant and to be a man. The fantasies spun around these two wishes were: she would become pregnant by biting off her father's penis and swallowing it, and she would become masculine by swallowing it, absorbing the power of the penis and growing strong as it nourished her like food, the belief of some primitive tribes about their powerful enemies.

These wishes and fantasies are shown symbolically by the hallucination and her symptoms. The hallucination started as a large black snake emerged from the wall behind her father's bed and moved slowly toward him. She may actually have seen a moving shadow which, to her tortured, exhausted mind, took on the shape of a snake. She tried to attack the snake, but frozen with horror, found her right arm paralyzed.

Freud later interpreted this moment: "Anyone who reads the history of Breuer's case now, in the light of the knowledge gained in the last twenty years, will at once perceive the symbolism in it—the snake, the stiffening, the disabling of the arm—and, on taking into account the situation at the bedside of the sick father, will easily guess the real interpretation of her symptom-formation."

At this moment in Bertha Pappenheim's life her sexual desires were probably very intense. A lovely girl of twenty-one, brought up in an authoritarian family, she was suddenly asked to nurse her dying father, the man who meant more to her than anyone else, the love and lust object of her girlhood fantasies. She was forced to take care of his most intimate needs, change his night shirt, help him to the bathroom, perhaps even bring the bedpan to his bed. She must have seen, or at least been very conscious of, his penis, as he lay under the sheets in front of her eyes, hour after hour, night after night, week after week, month after month, for five months. Weary, her defenses weakening, she fell prey to powerful impulses that had to find outlet.

Breuer believed her occasional near-blindness caused by the tears which prevented her from taking a clear look at the watch when her father asked the hour. But that does not seem a powerful enough reason for her to punish herself by losing her eyesight, the self-inflicted punishment of Oedipus when he discovered he had been sexually intimate with his mother.

This wish to become pregnant by her father emerged in the form of a hallucination symbolized by the threatening snake. On an even earlier level in her life, it represented the forbidden breast, the one denied her, the one she wished would poison her brother, for the bite of a snake may be fatal. Our unconscious condenses, and one symbol may stand for several wishes or fantasies.

Why would she want to attack the snake if it represented her wishes? Because she was afraid of incest, pregnancy, murder. She was caught in conflict—the wish opposed by the fear. She wished in fantasy that the snake (herself) would attack her father, but in reality she had to stop herself.

So she paralyzed her right arm, the arm that might have reached out and touched her father's penis. Her stiffened arm, as Freud pointed out, symbolized both the wish to castrate her father and punishment for that wish, as well as punishment for the wish to have a baby by one of the two men forbidden her by the incest taboo.

Then her fingernails turned into death's heads. Death leered at her from her very fingertips as, for the moment, she turned her fingers into little snakes. Fingers also are "evil" if used to touch the forbidden, either on oneself, or one's father. No wonder Bertha Pappenheim hated the painted fingernails of the woman board member who showed up for a day, they probably aroused memory of the nails that once turned into death's heads.

In later years she was always proud of her graceful fingers, insisting they be shown prominently in her portraits, the fingers she kept busy grasping objects more acceptable than penis or breast, as she tatted lace, strung beads, or wrote compulsively. She was almost fanatic in her insistence that women keep their "clever fingers" busy, as she founded a mending school and taught others to "patch" torn household linens, one of the ways she carried out her wish to "touch." She speaks of her father's black Biedermeier cabinet with the sparkling silver and gold goblets as "over-awing" her as a child, and she was probably forbidden to touch the goblets— they too were taboo; they too belonged to her father.

What precipitated the explosion of her monstrous fantasy? Why was it unloosed from the prison of her mind at that particular moment? She gives the answer.

She told Breuer that at any moment she expected the surgeon to arrive and operate on her father—to "cut" him, which was what she unconsciously wanted to do. The surgeon was coming as though to carry out her wish, and if her father died, she would be his murderer.

Perhaps fearing her father would die soon, the hallucination represented a desperate attempt to get pregnant before he deserted her. Certainly this was true with Breuer.

But why?

Each time she felt someone she loved was leaving her forever, Bertha Pappenheim became desperate. This was her torment. The desperation born of fear of separation. She had never been able to accept separation. To her it meant desertion. She would fly into a fury, then imagine unconsciously that she could restore the person she felt she was losing by getting part of him inside her.

The first desertion of her life, the one that set the pattern for all others, was when she felt her mother withdraw from her as a baby and wanted to bite her mother's breast to take her inside, where she could control her. When she thought her father might die with the coming of the surgeon, she was in a later psychosexual stage of development and she wanted his baby inside as a way of preserving him—her concept of pregnancy overlaid with the earlier fantasy of biting as a way of incorporating someone she loved and needed.

Only when Breuer told her he was leaving her did she have the pregnancy fantasy, as though this were her way of keeping him inside. But she had been helped enough by him so that instead of fantasizing a snake to symbolize the sexual act and resultant pregnancy, she acted out her fantasy in direct fashion. She had been able to trust Breuer enough to give up some of the hallucinatory quality of her wishes. It is a measure of her trust that the two doctors of her life both had the same first name, Josef.

Why was Bertha Pappenheim such an angry baby? It is speculation, but we might suspect that, upon discovering she had given birth to a third girl, not a boy, her mother might have been even more depressed than usual. The fact she conceived so soon after seems to show she wished to try again for a boy. And her depression was acutely felt by her newborn little girl, who responded with anger, as one usually does to a mother's depression. Bertha Pappenheim's mother was only ten years old when her mother died, and from all indications, she was probably quite a depressed woman and undoubtedly frightened of pregnancy, at a time when both child and maternal mortality was high.

"Bertha Pappenheim's life is both tragic and inspiring," sums up Dr. Stewart. "It illustrates the remarkable restrictions a neurosis imposes but it also shows the remarkable way emotions can be sublimated and put to good use. She made the best possible use of her illness. The illness gave her life a fanatic quality. She could not have achieved what she did without the illness and the ability to sublimate."

The mothering she received from Breuer was temporary help, but in the long run it is insight that produces the deep changes within, not mothering. The insights could not be given her however because psychoanalysis had not as yet been discovered. Even so, she found a fragile, incomplete, precarious preoccupation with pregnancy that allowed her to live an outwardly effective life.

10

The "Small Fire"

Bertha Pappenheim wanted people to take her seriously. "Usually people don't notice me, but if by chance we begin to talk, very soon they take me seriously," she said. Through her work she *made* people take her seriously. Her words may also allude to the experience with Breuer, for when she did begin to talk he very soon took her seriously.

Her interest in orphans, unwed mothers, delinquents, and prostitutes proved to be both her life and the way she psychically saved her life. A year after her mother's death, she wrote to Sophie Mamelok, "For me, work, and you children are my entire life, a life I had to conquer."

Conquer it she did. Once she regained emotional footing, after Breuer came to her rescue, a sense of duty ingrained in her by her parents helped her defeat any future wish to retreat completely into fantasy.

She had learned from her parents the word "duty," a word she said she liked: "It means a very good and necessary equivalent to my fantasy, which goes on at a galloping pace as if there were no duties." Without a sense of duty as "a very good and necessary equivalent," her fantasy, which ran on at a "galloping pace," would have pulled her into the world of unreality. Therefore, she refused to give in to moods or to allow anyone else to express them, she who once indulged in the wildest of moods.

She wrote, "Everyone—man or woman—should do what

he has to do, out of his strength or his lack of strength." Her life showed both her strength, her many achievements, and her lack of strength, her failure to marry and have children.

When Breuer left her so abruptly, she undoubtedly felt poised on the edge of a psychic precipice, below her the chasm of psychosis, behind her the safety of reality. She wavered, turned for a moment to morphine. But then she decided to take the way of safety. Breuer's help had been just enough so she could make that decision. She would never understand the deeper conflicts of her life, but at least she was saved from suicide, possibly psychosis, for the rest of her life.

She asked that her regards be sent to every member of the staff in the letter she wrote Gertrud Ehrenwerth from Munich after surgery. She added, "Nobody will be forgotten by me."

She may have feared she had long ago been forgotten by those she had loved—her mother, her father, her brother, Breuer.

But she will never be forgotten by the world. She will be remembered as part of the history of Germany, of Vienna, of countries where families now live who are descended from a boy or girl she cared for at the Orphanage or Home, as well as those countries where volunteers trained by her and inspired by her devotion now work to help the oppressed and needy.

Most of all, she will be remembered by every man, woman, and child who has been, or ever will be, helped by psychoanalysis. In the achievement of Freud's monumental discoveries, ones that for the first time in history made possible the understanding of man's irrational behavior—war, murder, suicide, sexual perversions—Bertha Pappenheim was entitled to a share of the honor.

"The very best a woman can do is to mean something to someone, and I am happy if I feel at times that I will not die without having warmed someone at my small fire," she wrote while aboard the Russian ship.

Her "small fire" was to warm many as it helped ignite the blaze lit by Freud that illuminated heaven and hell—the unconscious mind of man.

BIBLIOGRAPHY

Books

Breuer, Josef and Freud, Sigmund. *Studies on Hysteria.* Basic Books, 1957.

Edinger, Dora. *Bertha Pappenheim: Freud's Anna O.* Congregation Solel, 1968.

Ellenberger, Henri F. *Discovery of the Unconscious.* Harper. 1970.

Freud, Sigmund. *An Autobiographical Study.* W. W. Norton & Co. 1952.

————— *Lectures Delivered Before the Department of Psychology, Clark University.* Reprinted from *The American Journal of Psychology,* Vol. XXI, Nos. 2 and 3, 1910. Translated by Harry W. Chase, revised by Sigmund Freud. Printed for Clark University, Worcester, Mass. 1910.

————— *Three Essays on the Theory of Sexuality.* Standard Edition. VII.

————— *On the History of the Psychoanalytic Movement.* Standard Edition. XIV.

————— *The Origins of Psychoanalysis.* Sigmund Freud's Letters to Wilhelm Fliess, Drafts and Notes 1887-1902. Basic Books, 1954.

Jones, Ernest. *The Life and Work of Sigmund Freud.* Three Volumes. Basic Books. 1953-1957.

Stewart, Walter, *Psychoanalysis: The First Ten Years.* Macmillan. 1967.

————— with Lucy Freeman, *The Secret of Dreams,* Macmillan, 1971.

Articles

Bram, Frederick M., "The Gift of Anna O." British Journal of Medical Psychology, 1965.

Cranefield, Paul F. "Joseph Breuer's Evaluation of His Contribution to Psychoanalysis." International Journal of Psychoanalysis, XXXIX. 1958.

Freud, Sigmund. "Psychoanalysis: Exploring the Hidden Recesses of the Mind." Chapter in *These Eventful Years: The Twentieth Century in the Making, as Told by Many of Its Makers.* Translated by A. A. Brill. Encyclopedia Britannica Publishing Company 1924.

———— "Josef Breuer" (Obituary). Standard Edition, XIX.

Jensen, Ellen M. "Anna O—A Study of Her Later Life." *The Psychoanalytic Quarterly.*

Karpe, Richard. "The Rescue Complex in Anna O's Final Identity." *The Psychoanalytic Quarterly.* Vol 30, No. 1, 1961.

Oberndorf, C. P. "Autobiography of Josef Breuer." *International Journal of Psychoanalysis.* Volume 34, 1953.

Pollock, George H. "The Possible Significance of Childhood Object Loss in the Josef Breuer-Bertha Pappenheim (Anna O.)-Sigmund Freud Relationship. *The Journal of the American Psychoanalytic Association,* Volume 16, October, 1968.

———— Gluckel von Hameln: Bertha Pappenheim's Idealized Ancestor. *American Imago,* Volume 28, Fall, 1971.

Schlessinger, N., et. al.; "The Scientific Style of Breuer and Freud in the Origins of Psychoanalysis." *Journal of the American Psychoanalytic Association,* 1967. Volume 15.

———— "Studies on Hysteria: A Methodological Evaluation. *Journal of the American Psychoanalytic Association,* 1959. Volume 12.